Photograph by Zumbrun, Peking, China

International group of Army, Navy and Marine officers in full dress uniform

The nations represented are the United States, Great Britain, France, Belgium, Italy, Japan, Russia, Holland, Austria and Germany

Army and Navy Uniforms and Insignia

How to know Rank, Corps and Service in the Military and Naval Forces of the United States and Foreign Countries

By

Colonel Dion Williams
United States Marine Corps

With Eight Illustrations in Color and One Hundred and Seventeen in Black and White

New York
Frederick A. Stokes Company
Publishers

CONTENTS

ARMY AND NAVY UNIFORMS AND INSIGNIA

CHAPTER I

ORIGIN AND HISTORY OF UNIFORM

In its military sense the word "uniform," as a noun, is specifically used to denote the distinctive style of dress and equipment established by governmental regulation and worn by any naval or military organization in order that all of the individual elements of that organization will present a homogeneous appearance. In general all uniforms are divided into two principal classes, dress uniforms and undress or service uniforms, the modern field uniforms belonging to the latter class. Dress uniforms are for use on occasions of ceremony and, as in the case of civilian attire, they are usually more ornate and gaudy than the working service uniforms.

The use of some form of uniform dress for fighting men both on land and sea is common to all civilized nations and this general custom has resulted from a gradual growth during the whole Christian era. In this growth military necessity, convenience, economical considerations and sentiment have all played a part.

The famed Legions of Cæsar were by imperial order all garbed and armed alike, which is one of the first recorded cases of the use of a uniform for soldiers. Some of the regiments of Hannibal also wore distinctive colors practically amounting to a uniform. The galley slaves of ancient Rome, the "motive power" of the man-of-war of that day, were all garbed in a costume of identical cut and color bearing the number of the galley in which they served, but this should be looked upon more as a badge of servitude than as a naval uniform.

As time went by the leaders in command of the land forces perceived the necessity for some mark or badge to designate the members of their forces and to distinguish them from the foe. This resulted in the use of various distinctive badges, such as plumes of a certain color to be worn upon the helmet, initials, numbers or devices in the nature of a coat of arms to be worn upon the front of the helmet, on the breast plate of armor, on the tops of the shoulders or upon the shield, a custom which still prevails in the armies of to-day.

When Gustavus Adolphus, "the Whirlwind of the North," swept down over Europe with his victorious army of Sweden, he marked the brigades of his army with sashes worn diagonally across the body from one shoulder, a distinctive color for each brigade, and as a result history records the valorous deeds of the "Red Brigade" or the "Green Brigade" of that wonderful army. This species of uniform survives in the General's sash for the dress uniforms of the present time.

Early in the seventeenth century the King of France by royal decree established a uniform dress for his army and regulations were issued prescribing the color and style of the various articles of dress for officers and men and the occasions on which they were to be worn. At that time in England various princes and lords had armed forces of retainers and each such force was dressed and armed according to the individual taste of its overlord.

When the Great Rebellion in England resulted in the establishment of the Commonwealth under Cromwell as Protector in 1653, the New Model army was established as a national force and, while this force was clothed in the style of the day, distinctive colors were ordered so that the whole force was uniform in appearance. The hat of the period was the high crowned, wide brimmed felt "slouch" hat, and in its various shapes this head dress has been retained down to the present. First its brim was pinned up on one side by a rosette of the colors of the government of the date, then to add to its jauntiness it was pinned up in three places resulting in the three-cornered "cocked hat" of the American Revolutionary period, and to-day we see it again almost in its original form in the modern "field hat" of the United States Army and Marine Corps, a head dress which is also worn by the British Colonial troops from Aüstralia, Canada and New Zealand.

The wide brimmed hat was not suitable for wear at sea as it "carried too much sail in a gale," and the naval officers fastened it up against the crown on both sides and crushed the crown together in a "fore and aft" line. In this form the erstwhile "slouch hat" now appears as the chapeau or cocked hat worn with dress uniforms by the officers of all modern navies and by the general officers of the United States Army with full dress uniform.

Cords of various colors were worn around the base of the crown of the "slouch hat" when it was first adopted, and for ornamentation these cords had tassels at the ends, while the different colors of the hat cords indicated the regiment, corps or service of the wearer. These cords in various colors, depending upon the service or corps of the wearer, are now worn on the field hats of officers and men in the United States Army and Marine Corps, as described later in this book, and the tradition of the hat cord tassels is still kept in the cocked hat of the naval officer by the gold bullion tassels at the front and rear peaks. Likewise the influence of the original loop strap and button for fastening up the brim of the original "slouch hat" is seen in the United States naval officer's cocked hat in the shape of the gold lace strap and gilt button on the side of the crown.

When the Restoration in England brought Charles II to the throne in 1660 a royal army was organized in England, this action being due to the fact that the success of the revolutionists under Cromwell had proved the unreliability of the previous system. The standard colors chosen by the king for his soldiers were red and blue, the colors of the royal livery, and these colors survive to-day in the British infantry full dress uniforms of red with blue facings.

As time went by various regiments of foot and horse were raised, the men from any given regiment coming as a rule from one locality or county. The officers of these troops were practically all drawn from the nobility and upper classes, and it became common for the colonelcy to be conferred upon the head of the local noble house. These colonels chose many slight variations in uniform for their men in accordance with their tastes in dress and style, in deference to some local habits of dress or as might be limited by the length of their purse.

These regiments came to be known by the name of the county or city from which they were recruited; a custom which still prevails in the British service, and which to a great extent has been followed in the army of the United States, especially with the volunteers of our former wars.

In England this brought about a condition as to uniform that was apparently directly the opposite of uniform, as each territorial regiment had its own distinctive dress and decorations. Gradually, however, with the consolidation of all of the armed forces of the United Kingdom into one national army, the regulars forming the first line and the militia or "Territorials" forming the second line, or reserve, a universal service uniform was adopted for active service and came to be known as a "field" uniform. The older distinctive colors and styles of regimental uniforms were preserved in the full dress uniforms and reserved for peace time parade.

As a result of the use of heraldic devices for badges of the different regiments and corps under the old territorial system, each regiment has its own coat of arms, and in the later national army of Great Britain these were retained as "regimental badges." These badges bear the coat of arms of some great colonel of the regiment, the name and date of some famous victory in which the regiment won renown, or some distinctive device appropriate to the county or colony from which the men of the regiment are recruited.

Such regimental badges, founded largely upon sentiment but still appealing mightily to the imagination of the young recruit that joins the colors with the high heart of youth, are a great aid to discipline and efficiency, since discipline means the implicit obedience on the part of every one in the service to the orders from higher authority in such a manner as to secure the greatest cohesion and coordination and hence the greatest effect. These little metal badges bearing the symbols and mottoes that bring daily to the minds of their wearers the valorous deeds that their regiment has done in the past arouse the spirit of emulation and competition, the desire to fight as well or better than the old regiment fought on some other bloody field perhaps a century ago, and help to create *esprit de corps* — the soul of an army.

In the United States services there are also distinctive regimental and corps devices which, while indicating the branch and corps to which the wearer belongs, also keep alive the glorious traditions of the past wars.

As France was the first country of modern times to establish by governmental regulation and order a uniform dress for her armed forces on shore, so has she been the most consistent of all countries in dressing all branches of her service on much the same color scheme, though here as in the other countries is sometimes seen the influence of the native dress of the lands into which the French have extended their colonial activities.

Until quite recently the common uniform of the French army consisted of red trousers or breeches, blue coats and red caps. From the Barbary coast of North Africa and especially the French colony of Algeria the French colonial troops derived the style of dress known as "Zouave" uniform, with baggy trousers, short braid decorated jacket and tasselled turban. But even in these uniforms the general color scheme of red trousers and blue coat with red head dress was carried out.

In the United States the influence of the Zouave uniform can be traced to the same style of dress used by certain regiments of our great Civil War of 1860–65. Notable among these regiments were the "Louisiana

Tigers" of the Confederate Army and the "Zouave Division" of the Union Army.

In the uniforms of Germany the influence of the many individual states and principalities which went to form the greater Germany of to-day is seen in the colors and styles of the various regiments. The dress uniforms of the German Army still retain some of the distinctive colors of the original armies of Prussia, Bavaria, Saxony, Wurttemburg and Brandenburg, but for field service in war the whole army has a uniform of dull gray color, the various territorial distinctions being indicated by colored stripes and straps only.

The Italian troops have a number of distinctive uniforms for different corps and services, but the universal full dress coat is of a dark blue shade, the color of the trousers varying with the corps, and the different colors are used as cuffs and facings to distinguish different branches. Their field uniform is almost universally of a gray shade, though the influence of the prevailing background upon the color of uniform is seen in the white uniforms worn by the troops that must fight in the snow covered mountains of the northern frontier, and the use of khaki is becoming more common.

In Austria-Hungary the effect of the many different peoples that go to make up that empire has resulted in a great variety of colors and styles for uniforms, almost every color and shade being shown in the dress uniforms of the different corps. But for the field uniforms necessity has again ruled and dull shades of gray and green predominate.

Up to 1866 the Austrian regiments wore a great deal of white in their uniforms, while the picturesque dress of the Hungarian civil population was reflected in the

Army, and, with the granting of national financial aid to these state troops and the issue to them of government regulation clothing and equipment, all of the armed forces of the country, regular, state and volunteer, gradually came to wear the same uniform, the different kinds of troops being distinguished by the design of the buttons or by letters worn on the collars.

In one feature the United States troops of to-day, both in the Army and the Marine Corps, still retain a relic of the " stock " of former times; this is the close-fitting, standing collar of the coats for both full dress and service uniforms. The original idea of the stock was to make the soldier hold his head up and stand stiffly erect, and it dates from the time when Frederick the Great introduced mathematical precision into every motion of drill and maneuver.

In the early days when the marines wore a leather stock the sailor in his wide collared shirt dubbed the marine a " leatherneck," a term still applied to him in the slang phrase of the service.

Military necessity has often dictated the color of the clothing worn by troops in the field. An early example of this was the adoption in 1755 of a dark green uniform by the British Royal American Regiment while fighting against the French and Indians in the forest covered country in the northwest of the original American colonies. The North American Indian was an adept at " bush-whacking " and concealment in the forest, and to meet him on anything like an equal footing it was necessary for the British and colonial troops to wear a color suited to the prevailing background. In later years this regiment's name was changed to " King's Royal Rifles " and as an heirloom of its first service the rifle regiments of the British Army still wear green coats for their full dress uniform.

In the days when smooth-bore muskets were the arms of infantry, the range of such weapons was very short and the opposing battle lines approached each other so closely that the figures of the men were plainly visible whatever the color of their clothing might be. Histories of the wars of a century ago tell of the colonels' commands to "wait till you see the whites of their eyes before you fire" and "hold your fire until you can count their coat buttons."

Under such circumstances striking and distinctive uniforms of gaudy colors bedecked with gold and silver braid and bright buttons were no detriment, but with the great increase in the range and accuracy of modern rifles it has become necessary to render the men on the battle line as inconspicuous as possible, and, as a result, in all of the great armies of the world dull colored uniforms of neutral shade have replaced the brilliant reds, blues, yellows and greens of former times, and brass buttons have given way to buttons of bronze, leather or iron, the bright hued uniforms with their corresponding brass buttons and braid being kept for full dress and peace time parade.

In the United States Army and Marine Corps the prevalent color for the field service uniforms is some shade of the dull brown commonly known as "khaki," and the bright gilt and silver buttons, corps and regimental devices and numbers and belt buckles have been replaced to a great extent by dull bronze buttons and ornaments, insignia of rank for officers only being still made of silver and gold.

"Khaki" (pronounced *kar-key,* with the accent on

the second syllable) is an East Indian word meaning "dust color" or "earth color." In the dry season in India the fields and vegetation turn brown and the roads are heavy with dust which, carried by the winds, soon covers the foliage of trees and shrubbery, so that the whole landscape presents a somber aspect in one brown, dust-colored hue.

In the earlier days of the British occupation of India the British and loyal Indian troops wore white cotton or duck uniforms in the hot weather of the dry season, but these stood out so plainly against the prevailing dust color of the roads and surrounding country as to make their wearers distinct targets for the bush-whacking snipers of the enemy tribesmen. Learning from bitter experience the necessity for making themselves less conspicuous, the soldiers dipped their uniforms in muddy pools and streams to give them the same color as the background against which they must appear.

This expedient showed good results in reducing the casualty lists, and dust-colored or "khaki" uniforms gradually replaced the white uniforms with bright colored trimmings for summer service, and later for the same reasons the same or a similar color was also adopted for the winter field or "fighting" uniforms of the British Army.

Grim necessity gradually overcame the natural conservatism of the military mind and the sentimental traditions that hung around the colors of the uniforms that the troops had worn in famous campaigns, until all of the great nations have now adopted "khaki" or other dull-colored uniforms for their troops in the field. This has taken away from the battlefield much of its former picturesqueness and pomp; gone from the battlefield is the "thin red line" of English poetry and song, the red and blue of the French infantry, the gray and white of the Austrians, and the blue, white and gold of the German Uhlans, while the "American Boys in Blue" no longer charge with bayonets glittering in the sun beneath the Stars and Stripes. To paraphrase a well-known quotation, "It is not magnificent but it is war."

In the naval services of the world the adoption of a regulation uniform dress for officers and enlisted men came at a much later date than in the armies, although the marines, being essentially "sea soldiers," followed the uniform regulations of the shore forces to a great extent and were put in uniform much earlier than the sailors of the ships' crews.

In the British Navy of Nelson's time the officers wore uniforms following certain prescribed styles, and the rank of the officer was marked by insignia upon the epaulets and by sleeve and cuff decorations as well, but the sailors who set and worked the sails and manned the guns had no prescribed dress. It was the custom of those days for each commodore and captain to prescribe a uniform dress for the crew of his "barge" or "gig" (the "barge" being the special small boat propelled by oars in which the admiral or commodore went from ship to shore and *vice versa,* and the "gig" being the name for a similar boat used especially by the captain of the ship).

These uniforms for the special boats' crews were often fanciful in design and gay in color schemes and served to enliven the landing places at many a busy port.

During the Revolution the ships of the American Navy consisted at first of merchantmen armed with a few guns and manned by the hardy seamen of the merchant marine of the colonies. Later men-of-war were especially built for that service and manned by duly commissioned officers and men enlisted into the government service, but the British Navy was so large that the colonials could make no headway against its strong fleets, and a cruising and raiding warfare was resorted to for the purpose of destroying as much British merchant shipping as possible. This warfare was carried on principally by privateers, merchantmen armed and heavily manned for the purpose and in some cases fast ships especially built for such service. These privateers were officered by the splendid sea captains of that date who were granted "letters of marque" by the Colonial Government to carry the flag and prey upon the commerce of the enemy, dividing the profits derived from the captured cargoes in fixed proportion between the owners and crew of the privateers and the Government.

Under such conditions there was no fixed uniform, and though the officers frequently provided themselves with a dress patterned after that of the French Navy with which they were allied, the men wore any kind of clothing suited to their fancy.

After the Revolution the standing or regular army went out of existence, but it soon became necessary to establish a regular navy which consisted of a few fast, heavily gunned sailing frigates of the type of the *Constitution, Constellation* and *Chesapeake.* When the War of 1812 came on it was this small but remarkably efficient regular navy that alone saved the United States from disaster and dishonor.

By 1812 a regulation uniform had been prescribed for the officers of the Navy, but the men were still allowed to wear any kind of clothing suited to their work. Long cruises in distant seas made it necessary, however, for a supply of clothing for the members of the crew to be carried by the purser (the paymaster of that day), and as a measure of economy and convenience these clothes were all made in the same style, a custom which gradually brought about a certain uniformity in the garb of the enlisted personnel of the Navy.

Thus it came about that the accepted sailor uniform consisted of easy fitting garments suited to the work of hauling on the ropes, working aloft on the rigging, masts and spars of the sailing ships and pulling at the oars of the small boats. From this beginning came the sailor uniform of to-day, the bell-mouthed trousers that could be rolled up quickly and easily when the bare-footed sailors washed down the decks, the easy-fitting, loose-necked shirt or "jumper," the short overcoat or "peacoat" for winter wear, and the loose-topped, brimless cap which to give it a smarter appearance when going ashore "on liberty" (the sailor term for leave of absence) was provided with a light ring or "grommet" to stretch the crown out flat, resulting in the common sailor "flat-hat" of to-day.

This sailor uniform was originally designed for wear aboard ships driven by sail-power, and though it is not especially suited to the great steam-driven dreadnaughts of the modern navy it is still retained, partly on account of sentiment and tradition and partly on account of the fact that the Navy is probably more conservative than any other profession or calling.

The uniforms of both officers and enlisted men in the United States Navy follow rather closely in style, color and cut those worn in the British Navy, and some interesting traditions of the latter service may be seen even in our naval service. For instance, the black neckerchief worn alike by the British and American sailor was made black after Trafalgar as an emblem of mourning for the Great Nelson, and the three white stripes around the edges of the collar were so placed to commemorate Nelson's three great victories, Copenhagen, the Nile and Trafalgar.

In all countries naval uniforms follow much the same patterns and practically all are of the same colors; dark blue, the so-called "navy blue," for winter wear, and white for summer wear.

The need of an inconspicuous uniform for naval officers and men is not so apparent as it is in the case of the land forces, since in the battles of ships at sea it is the ship which is the target and not the personnel as in the battles on land.

Thus we see how tradition, sentiment and military necessity have each played a part in the development of the uniforms worn by the fighting forces of our country on land and sea.

CHAPTER II

SERVICE, CORPS AND RANK

THE armed forces of the United States of America provided by the statute law of the land pursuant to the provisions of the Constitution are embraced within two grand divisions, the land forces and the sea forces, under the supreme command of the President as Commander-in-Chief.

These two grand divisions are subdivided into various services according to the duties required of them and the laws establishing and maintaining them.

The Land Forces.— The land forces of the United States are made up of the regular army or as it is sometimes called the "standing army," the organized land militia when called into the service of the United States which is practically the same as the so-called national guards of the several states, and such volunteers and drafted men as may be authorized by the Congress from time to time as occasion demands.

In times of peace the Army consists of the regular army, but in case of an invasion or threatened invasion of the territory of the United States or of rebellion or threatened war against the constituted government of the nation, this force may be augmented by calling the organized militia into service and further augmented if necessary by the employment of volunteers or drafted men, with the authorization of the Congress.

The land forces, however raised, are also divided into

the Mobile Army and the Coast Artillery. The mobile army is intended for active offensive operations against the enemy and is so called on account of the fact that for its duties it requires the greatest degree of mobility possible, while the coast artillery is intended to man and fight the fixed and movable elements of land and coast fortifications including land mines, submarine mines and torpedo defenses pertaining to the fortifications.

These two groups frequently assist each other, the mobile forces protecting the flanks and approaches to the fixed defenses, and the latter being used as turning points or supporting points to the lines of the mobile forces.

The Army is divided into various arms or corps according to the duties required, as follows: infantry, cavalry, field artillery, coast artillery corps, engineer corps, signal corps including aviation section, quartermaster corps, ordnance corps, judge advocate's corps, inspector general's corps and medical corps. Each of these arms or corps has a distinctive badge to be worn on all uniforms and a distinctive color for the facings and trimmings of dress uniforms, as described and illustrated in Chapter IV.

For purposes of administration and control under war conditions the mobile land forces are organized into Field Armies, the basis of the organization being the Division. The division as prescribed in the United States Army is an organization containing all of the arms and services necessary for independent action.

A field army may be divided into army corps, each such being composed of two or more divisions.

Divisions are subdivided into brigades, which are in turn subdivided into regiments. A regiment of infantry is usually composed of three battalions of four companies each; a regiment of cavalry of three squadrons of four troops each; and a regiment of field artillery of two battalions of three batteries each. Engineers are formed into regiments according to the special requirements of their duties. The Coast Artillery is organized into companies, the number of companies in any one command depending upon the size of the forts to be garrisoned.

Signal Corps troops are organized into companies and larger organizations according to the duties assigned to them.

The Quartermaster Corps is charged with providing the supplies required and with the transportation of both men and supplies.

The Medical Corps has charge of the hospitals and the personnel required by them both at the permanent stations and in the field, and for this purpose the corps is organized into ambulance companies and field hospitals.

Chaplains are assigned to regiments and other organizations as may be required.

Veterinarians, who are commissioned officers, are assigned to the cavalry, field artillery and quartermaster transport trains, and also have charge of such veterinary hospitals as may be required at permanent posts or in the field.

The command of the Army is exercised by the President as Commander-in-Chief through the medium of the Secretary of War and the Chief of Staff, the latter officer having the rank of General and taking the place of the former Commanding General of the Army.

The General Staff Corps of the Army, consisting of commissioned officers detailed from the various branches of the Army for a term of four years' service, is charged with the duties of effecting under the direction of the Chief of Staff the coordination and harmonious cooperation of all branches of the military service, both line and staff, in the execution of the military policies of the Government in peace and war.

The administration of the Army and the War Department is effected under the Secretary of War through the Chief of Staff by various bureaus or offices, as follows: the Coast Artillery under a chief with the rank of Major General; the Adjutant General's Department under an Adjutant General with the rank of Major General, which is the department of records, orders and correspondence of the Army and the Militia; the Judge Advocate General's Department, under a Judge Advocate General with the rank of Major General, which is the legal department of the Army; the Inspector General's Department under an Inspector General with the rank of Major General; the Quartermaster Department, under a Quartermaster General with the rank of Major General, which has charge of supply and transportation; the Medical Department, under a Surgeon General with the rank of Major General; the Corps of Engineers, under a Chief of Engineers with the rank of Major General; the Ordnance Corps, under a Chief of Ordnance with the rank of Major General; and the Signal Corps, under a Chief Signal Officer with the rank of Major General.

The Sea Forces.— The sea forces of the United States consist of the regular Navy, the Marine Corps, the Naval Militia of the several States and territories when mustered into the service of the United States, and the Coast Guard and Lighthouse Service when transferred to the jurisdiction of the Navy Department in time of war or when war is imminent, including in each case both the vessels and the personnel pertaining to them, afloat and ashore. The vessels of the Coast and Geodetic Survey and of the Bureau of Fisheries may also be transferred to the jurisdiction of the Navy in time of war.

The vessels of the Navy are organized into fleets which are divided for purposes of administration and tactics into forces, squadrons, divisions, and sections.

A " Fleet " is an aggregation of vessels of various classes in one organization under one command.

Fleets are subdivided into " Forces," each " Force " being made up of the vessels of a fleet that are of the same class or type that are assigned to perform the same duty.

A " Force " is subdivided into " Squadrons," and in turn, a " Squadron " is subdivided into " Divisions," and a " Division " is subdivided into " Sections."

A " Section " consists of two vessels of the larger classes or three vessels of the smaller classes; a " Division " normally consists of two " Sections," and a " Squadron " usually consists of two " Divisions," although the numbers in each subdivision may be varied to suit special occasions or duties.

A squadron of torpedo vessels is called a " Flotilla," in deference to long established custom.

A completely organized Fleet is composed of a Battleship Force, a Scout Force, a Cruiser Force, a Destroyer Force, a Submarine Force, a Mine Force and a Train Force, the latter consisting of the supply ships and repair vessels and transports and being usually referred to as the " Train."

The Navy is administered ashore by a bureau system, consisting of a number of bureaus and offices having charge of the various activities required for the building and upkeep of the fleets at sea, and all directed by the

Secretary of the Navy through the Office of Naval Operations, the Chief of Naval Operations with the rank of Admiral being the senior or ranking officer of the Navy.

The bureaus are the Bureau of Navigation, whose Chief has the rank of Rear Admiral, and which has charge of the issuing and enforcing of orders to officers and enlisted men and the keeping of the records; the Bureau of Ordnance, whose Chief has the rank of Rear Admiral, and which has charge of the design, manufacture and repair of guns, torpedoes and ammunition; the Bureau of Construction and Repair, whose head is the Chief Constructor of the Navy and has the rank of Rear Admiral, and which has charge of the designing, construction and repair of all of the vessels of the Navy; the Bureau of Steam Engineering, whose head is the Engineer-in-Chief of the Navy, with the rank of Rear Admiral, and which has charge of the designing, construction and repair of the engines and boilers in the ships of the Navy; a Bureau of Supplies and Accounts, whose head is the Paymaster General of the Navy, with the rank of Rear Admiral, and which has charge of the purchase and issue of supplies and provisions for the Navy and the paying of the officers and enlisted men; the Bureau of Medicine and Surgery, whose head is the Surgeon General of the Navy, with the rank of Rear Admiral, and which has charge of the hospitals ashore, the hospital ships, and the health and sanitation of the Navy both afloat and ashore; the Bureau of Yards and Docks, whose Chief has the rank of Rear Admiral, and which has charge of the designing and construction and repair of the buildings and docks at the shore establishments of the Navy; and the Office of the Judge Advocate General, whose head is the Judge Advocate General of the Navy with the rank of Captain, and which has charge of the courts-martial and legal affairs of the Navy.

For purposes of command and organization afloat and ashore the officers of the Navy are divided into the "Line," composed of the officers holding the military command in the various ranks, and of a number of "Staff Corps," composed of officers who have charge of the various coordinate duties.

These "Staff Corps" are the Medical Corps, the Pay Corps, the Chaplains, the Corps of Naval Constructors, the Corps of Civil Engineers and the Professors of Mathematics. Prior to 1899 there was also a separate Corps of Engineers, but in that year this corps was consolidated with the Line and since that time the only officers holding the ranks of Chief Engineer, Passed Assistant Engineer and Assistant Engineer in the Navy are officers of the old Engineer Corps who are now carried on the Retired List of Officers.

The Marine Corps.— The Marine Corps is a distinct military organization normally forming an integral part of the Navy, but when the President so orders any portion of the corps may be detached for service with the Army, and in every war in which the United States has been engaged the marines have fought as a part of the crews of the fighting ships of the Navy, as landing forces and expeditionary forces with the Navy and also on detached service with the Army.

The Marine Corps is commanded by a Major General Commandant whose station is at Headquarters of the Corps in Washington, and who is assisted by a staff consisting of an Adjutant and Inspector's Department, a Quartermaster's Department and a Paymaster's Department, each headed by a Brigadier General.

The officers of the Adjutant and Inspector's Department perform the duties that are performed in the Army by the Departments of the Adjutant General and the Inspector General; the Quartermaster's Department has charge of the supplies, provisions, transportation and the construction and maintenance of barracks and buildings; and the Paymaster's Department has charge of the accounts and pay of the officers and enlisted men of the Corps.

Detachments of the marines are stationed at all of the Navy Yards and Naval Stations of the United States both at home and abroad, and they also serve as Legation Guards for American Legations in countries where such guards are considered necessary, as expeditionary forces with the Fleet and for the protection of Americans and their rights in foreign countries during revolutions and disorders, on detached duty with the Army as circumstances require in time of war, and aboard the battleships and cruisers of the Navy as a part of the crew, their special duties aboard ship being as crews for the Torpedo Defense batteries of guns of intermediate caliber and rapid-fire guns.

The Marines of a Fleet are organized into a regiment for duty as a landing force, the detachment from each ship forming one of the companies, and the Colonel commanding the regiment serves on the Staff of the Admiral in command of the Fleet.

When assigned to shore duty the Marines are organized into permanent companies, these companies being combined into provisional battalions, regiments and brigades according to the service or duty required.

The Marine Detachment or company serving on board a ship of the Navy is paraded as the guard of honor when such a guard is turned out to receive the President, the ruler of any foreign country, or any lesser officer or official entitled to such honors.

The Coast Guard.— The Coast Guard was established by act of Congress in January, 1915, which provided that the then existing Revenue-Cutter Service and Life-Saving Service should be combined into one service to be known as the Coast Guard, which shall constitute a part of the military forces of the United States and which shall operate under the Treasury Department in time of peace and operate as a part of the Navy, subject to the orders of the Navy Department, in time of war, or at other times when the President shall so direct.

In time of peace the Coast Guard is charged with the enforcement of the revenue laws as applying to sea-borne commerce, with giving aid to vessels in distress at sea, with the protection of the seal fisheries, and with maintaining and operating the life-saving stations along the coasts of the United States and its insular possessions. In time of war or when so directed by the President it acts as a part of the Navy, and the ships and personnel of the service become to all intents and purposes a portion of the regular navy.

The Lighthouse Service.— This service is charged with the duties of establishing and maintaining the lighthouses and other aids to navigation, such as buoys and beacons and range marks on shore, that are required for the safe navigation of the waters adjacent to our coasts, the harbors and the channels leading to them, and the inland waterways.

In normal times the Lighthouse Service is operated under the Department of Commerce, but by act of Congress of August, 1916, the President is authorized to transfer the stations, vessels, equipment and personnel of the service, as may be required, to the jurisdiction of the Navy Department or to that of the War Department.

When so transferred to the Navy Department or to the War Department, the Lighthouse Service becomes for the time being a portion of the Navy or of the Army, as the case may be, and its officers and men are subject to the laws and regulations of the service to which it is so transferred.

The Coast and Geodetic Survey.— This branch of the government service is charged with surveying the harbors and waters contiguous to the coasts of the United States and the insular possessions thereof and the lakes and inland waterways contained therein, and with making charts from such surveys for use in navigation.

The service is under the jurisdiction of the Department of Commerce, but in time of war its vessels may be transferred to the Navy Department and their crews taken into the naval service, in which case they become subject to the laws and regulations of the Navy.

Rank, Title and Precedence

Rank in its military sense is the character or quality bestowed upon the men of the military and naval services which carries with it the eligibility to exercise command or authority over other members of the services within the limits prescribed by law and regulation. Rank is divided into many different grades to mark the relative positions of the persons upon whom it is conferred and to limit the extent of the authority carried with it.

In all of the services of the United States, "Commissioned Officers" are those who have received a commission from the President "by and with the advice and consent of the Senate of the United States"; and "Appointed Officers" are those who are appointed by the President or by his order but who are not "commissioned" and confirmed by the Senate.

In the Army the "Appointed Officers" are Aviators, Army Field Clerks, Field Clerks Quartermaster Corps, and Cadets at the Military Academy.

In the Navy the "Appointed Officers" are Warrant Officers and Midshipmen.

In the Marine Corps the "Appointed Officers" are Warrant Officers.

In the Army and Marine Corps "Noncommissioned Officers" are selected enlisted men who are appointed to the various ranks of enlisted authority by orders from their proper military commanders.

"Petty Officers" in the Navy are appointed enlisted men corresponding to noncommissioned officers in the Army and Marine Corps.

The "Title" of an officer is the name of the rank or grade in which he holds a commission, the formal term by which he is officially addressed in communicating with him, although custom sanctions some variations from this general rule.

In the Army and the Marine Corps all commissioned officers, line and staff, have positive rank in the several grades, and it is customary to address them when communicating orally with them by the name of the rank they hold, the variations being that all General Officers (Generals, Lieutenant Generals, Major Generals and Brigadier Generals) are commonly addressed as "General," that Lieutenant Colonels are addressed as "Colonel," and that all subalterns (First Lieutenants and Second Lieutenants) are addressed as either "Lieutenant" or as "Mister."

In the Navy it is customary to address officers of the Line (the command branch of the service) by the name of their rank, and to address officers of the Staff Corps either by the name of their rank or as "Mister," for all except officers of the Medical Corps, who are usually addressed as "Doctor." The exceptions to this rule are that all Flag Officers (Admirals, Vice-Admirals and Rear Admirals) are usually addressed orally as "Admiral," and that Lieutenant Commanders, Lieutenants and Ensigns are often addressed as "Mister."

It is customary to address the Warrant Officers of the Navy and Marine Corps as "Mister."

The precedence of the commissioned officers and other officers of the Army, Navy and Marine Corps is determined first by the grade or rank which the officers hold by virtue of their commissions or appointments, and if of the same grade or rank, then by the date of commission or appointment in the grade. There are certain exceptions to this latter rule in the case of some grades in the Staff Corps of the Navy.

The precedence of the warrant officers, noncommissioned officers and petty officers of all the services is determined upon the same principle, the seniority of the different grades and the relative seniority of the grades in different services being determined by regulations and orders, and the precedence in each grade being determined by the dates of the warrants or appointments.

The accompanying table shows the rank and title of each grade in the Army, Navy, Marine Corps and Coast Guard, all of the grades having the same relative rank being on the same horizontal line.

The personnel of the Army, as provided by statute law, consists of commissioned officers, appointed officers,

TABLE OF RELATIVE RANK OF OFFICERS IN THE NAVAL AND MILITARY SERVICES OF THE UNITED STATES

COMMISSIONED OFFICERS

Army	Navy	Marine Corps	Coast Guard	Public Health Service
None	Admiral of the Navy	None	None	None
General	Admiral	None	None	None
Lieutenant General	Vice Admiral	None	None	None
Major General	Rear Admiral	Major General	None	None
Brigadier General *	Commodore	Brigadier General	None	Surgeon General
Colonel	Captain	Colonel	Captain Commandant	Assistant Surgeon General
Lieutenant Colonel.	Commander	Lieutenant Colonel	Senior Captain	Senior Surgeon
Major	Lieutenant Commander	Major	Captain	Surgeon
Captain	Lieutenant	Captain	First Lieutenant	Passed Assistant Surgeon
First Lieutenant	Lieutenant, Junior Grade	First Lieutenant	Second Lieutenant	Assistant Surgeon
Second Lieutenant	Ensign	Second Lieutenant	Third Lieutenant	None
	Chief Boatswain, Chief Gunner, Chief Machinist, Chief Carpenter, Chief Sailmaker, Chief Pharmacist, Chief Pay Clerk			

APPOINTED OFFICERS

Army	Navy	Marine Corps	Coast Guard	Public Health Service
Aviator, Signal Corps Cadet at the Military Academy, West Point	Midshipman at the Naval Academy, Annapolis, Md.	None	Cadet and Cadet Engineer at the Coast Guard Academy, New London, Conn.	

WARRANT OFFICERS

Army	Navy	Marine Corps	Coast Guard	Public Health Service
Army Field Clerk Field Clerk Quartermaster Corps.	Boatswain, Gunner, Machinist, Carpenter, Sailmaker, Pharmacist, Pay Clerk, Mate	Marine Gunner Quartermaster Clerk	Boatswain, Gunner, Machinist, Carpenter, Keeper, Master's Mate.	Interne Pharmacist Clerk

* In accordance with an Act of Congress of October 6, 1917, Brigadier Generals of the Army and Marine Corps take relative rank with Rear Admirals of the lower half of the grade of Rear Admiral.

noncommissioned officers and privates as follows, according to grade or rank:

Officers

COMMISSIONED OFFICERS

1. General.
2. Lieutenant General.
3. Major General.
4. Brigadier General.
5. Colonel.
6. Lieutenant Colonel.
7. Major.
8. Captain.
9. First Lieutenant.
10. Second Lieutenant.

APPOINTED OFFICERS

11. Aviator, Signal Corps.
12. Cadet.
13. Field Clerk, Field Clerk Quartermaster Corps.

Enlisted Men

NONCOMMISSIONED OFFICERS AND PRIVATES

14. (a) Sergeant major, regimental; sergeant major, senior grade, Coast Artillery Corps; (b) quartermaster sergeant, senior grade, Quartermaster Corps; master hospital sergeant, Medical Department; master engineer, senior grade, Corps of Engineers; master electrician, Coast Artillery Corps; master signal electrician; band leader; (c) hospital sergeant, Medical Department; master engineer, junior grade, Corps of Engineers; engineer, Coast Artillery Corps.

15. Ordnance sergeant; quartermaster sergeant, Quartermaster Corps; supply sergeant, regimental.

16. Sergeant major, squadron and battalion; sergeant major, junior grade, Coast Artillery Corps; supply sergeant, battalion.

17. (a) First sergeant; (b) sergeant, first class, Medical Department; sergeant, first class, Quartermaster Corps; sergeant, first class, Corps of Engineers; sergeant, first class, Signal Corps; electrician sergeant, first class, Coast Artillery Corps; electrician sergeant, Artillery Detachment, United States Military Academy; assistant engineer, Coast Artillery Corps; (c) master gunner, Coast Artillery Corps; master gunner, Artillery Detachment, United States Military Academy; band sergeant and assistant leader, United States Military Academy Band; assistant band leader; sergeant bugler; electrician sergeant, second class, Coast Artillery Corps; electrician sergeant, second class, Artillery Detachment, United States Military Academy; radio sergeant.

18. Color sergeant.

19. Sergeant; supply sergeant, company; mess sergeant; stable sergeant; fireman, Coast Artillery Corps.

20. Corporal.

21. (a) First Class Private; (b) Private.

The personnel of the Navy, pursuant to the provisions of the statute law, consists of commissioned officers, appointed officers, warrant officers, petty officers and seamen, in the various grades as follows:

Officers of the Navy

COMMISSIONED OFFICERS OF THE LINE

1. Admiral of the Navy.

(This rank is now vacant. By special act of

Congress it was conferred upon Admiral George Dewey on March 2, 1899, and held by him until his death on January 16, 1917. The rank is the same as that of Admiral of the Fleet in foreign navies and that of Field Marshal in foreign armies.)

2. Admiral.
3. Vice-Admiral.
4. Rear-Admiral.
5. Commodore.

   (This rank was abolished for the active list by act of Congress on March 3, 1899, and since that date has been held by officers of that rank on the Retired List of the Navy only.)

6. Captain.
7. Commander.
8. Lieutenant Commander.
9. Lieutenant.
10. Lieutenant Junior Grade.
11. Ensign.
12. Chief Boatswain.
    Chief Gunner.
    Chief Machinist.

    (The commissioned officers of these three titles are of the same grade; they rank next after ensigns.)

COMMISSIONED OFFICERS OF THE MEDICAL CORPS

1. Medical Director with the rank of Rear Admiral.
2. Medical Director with the rank of Captain.
3. Medical Inspector with the rank of Commander.
4. Surgeon with the rank of Lieutenant Commander.
5. Passed Assistant Surgeon with the rank of Lieutenant Commander.

6. Passed Assistant Surgeon with the rank of Lieutenant.

7. Assistant Surgeon with the rank of Lieutenant.

8. Assistant Surgeon with the rank of Lieutenant, Junior Grade.

9. Dental Surgeon with the rank of Lieutenant, Junior Grade.

10. Chief Pharmacist.

COMMISSIONED OFFICERS OF THE PAY CORPS

1. Pay Director with the rank of Rear Admiral.

2. Pay Director with the rank of Captain.

3. Pay Inspector with the rank of Commander.

4. Paymaster with the rank of Lieutenant Commander.

5. Passed Assistant Paymaster with the rank of Lieutenant Commander.

6. Passed Assistant Paymaster with the rank of Lieutenant.

7. Passed Assistant Paymaster with the rank of Lieutenant, Junior Grade.

8. Assistant Paymaster with the rank of Lieutenant, Junior Grade.

9. Assistant Paymaster with the rank of Ensign.

10. Chief Pay Clerk.

COMMISSIONED OFFICERS OF THE CORPS OF NAVAL CONSTRUCTORS

1. Naval Constructor with the rank of Rear Admiral.

2. Naval Constructor with the rank of Captain.

3. Naval Constructor with the rank of Commander.

4. Naval Constructor with the rank of Lieutenant Commander.

5. Naval Constructor with the rank of Lieutenant.

6. Assistant Naval Constructor with the rank of Lieutenant.

7. Assistant Naval Constructor with the rank of Lieutenant, Junior Grade.

8. Chief Carpenter.
   Chief Sailmaker.

COMMISSIONED OFFICERS OF THE CORPS OF CIVIL ENGINEERS

1. Civil Engineer with the rank of Rear Admiral.
2. Civil Engineer with the rank of Captain.
3. Civil Engineer with the rank of Commander.
4. Civil Engineer with the rank of Lieutenant Commander.
5. Civil Engineer with the rank of Lieutenant.
6. Assistant Civil Engineer with the rank of Lieutenant.
7. Assistant Civil Engineer with the rank of Lieutenant, Junior Grade.
8. Assistant Civil Engineer with the rank of Ensign.

Chaplains hold the relative rank of Captain, Commander, Lieutenant Commander, Lieutenant or Lieutenant, Junior Grade, according to length of service.

Professors of Mathematics hold the rank of Captain, Commander, Lieutenant Commander or Lieutenant according to length of service. This corps was established to provide especially trained mathematicians for duty as astronomers at the Naval Observatories and as Instructors at the Naval Academy, but pursuant to the act of Congress of August 29, 1916, no further officers are to be commissioned in this corps.

In the days of sailing ships officers having the title of Sailmaker were provided for the then important work of superintending the manufacture of sails, but since the advent of steam and electricity this branch has been discontinued and only a few are still borne on the official register. The commissioned officers of this branch have the title of Chief Sailmaker and relative rank the same as that of Chief Boatswain, Chief Gunners, Chief Machinists, Chief Carpenters, Chief Pay Clerks and Chief Pharmacists, that is, they rank with but next after Ensigns.

MIDSHIPMEN

Midshipmen are appointed officers undergoing the course of instruction at the Naval Academy at Annapolis, Maryland. Each senator, representative and delegate in Congress has the appointment of three midshipmen to be at the Naval Academy at any one time, the President is empowered to appoint two midshipmen and the Secretary of the Navy is empowered to appoint one hundred midshipmen each year to be selected from enlisted men of the Navy and Marine Corps who are not over the age of twenty years.

The Corps of Midshipmen consists of four classes, the First Class corresponding to " seniors " at universities, the Second Class corresponding to " juniors," the Third Class corresponding to " sophomores " and the Fourth Class corresponding to " freshmen."

The regular course of study is four years although the President was authorized by the act of Congress of March 4, 1917, to reduce the course to three years for a period of two years from the passage of the act, owing to the urgent need of more officers in the Navy.

WARRANT OFFICERS

Warrant officers form an intermediate class between the commissioned officers and the enlisted personnel. They receive appointments from the President but are not confirmed by the Senate. They are appointed by selection from the most efficient and deserving enlisted petty officers. After six years' service as warrant officers, if found qualified, they are commissioned by the President, " by and with the advice and consent of the Senate," as Chief Boatswains, Chief Gunners, Chief Machinists, Chief Carpenters, Chief Sailmakers, Chief Pharmacists and Chief Pay Clerks, as the case may be, to take rank with but next after Ensigns.

The Warrant Officers of the Line are as follows:

Boatswain
Gunner
Machinst

The Warrant Officers of the Staff are as follows:

Carpenter
Sailmaker
Pharmacist
Pay Clerk

All warrant officers take rank and precedence next after commissioned officers, their relative rank among themselves being determined by date of appointment.

Warrant officers are eligible to be commissioned as Ensigns after passing the prescribed examination, in which case they are advanced to higher rank in the same manner as other Ensigns commissioned after graduation from the Naval Academy. In this manner a young man who proves himself worthy of the honor may rise from the lowest enlisted grade to be an Admiral.

Enlisted Men of the Navy

The highest grade of enlisted men in the U. S. Navy is that of Mate. Mates are rated by authority of the Secretary of the Navy from seamen of over two years' service. They have no relative rank, but take precedence over all other enlisted men. They wear a uniform like that of warrant officers with a distinctive insignia as later described.

The classes of enlisted men in the Navy corresponding to the "noncommissioned officers" of the Army and Marine Corps are styled "Petty Officers."

All of the enlisted men of the Navy are divided into branches according to their principal duties, the different grades in these several branches being as follows:

CHIEF PETTY OFFICERS

Seaman Branch	Artificer Branch	Special Branch
Chief Master at Arms.	Chief Machinist's Mate.	Chief Yeoman.
Chief Boatswain's Mate.	Chief Electrician.	Hospital Steward.
Chief Gunner's Mate.	Chief Carpenter's Mate.	Bandmaster.
Chief Turret Captain.	Chief Water Tender.	Chief Commissary Steward.
Chief Quartermaster.		

PETTY OFFICERS, FIRST CLASS

Seaman Branch	Artificer Branch	Special Branch
Master at Arms, first class.	Machinist's Mate, first class.	First Musician.
Boatswain's Mate, first class.	Electrician, first class.	Yeoman, first class.
Turret Captain, first class.	Boilermaker.	Commissary Steward.
Gunner's Mate, first class.	Coppersmith.	Ship's Cook, first class.
Gun Captain, first class.	Blacksmith.	Baker, first class.
Quartermaster, first class.	Plumber and Fitter.	
	Sailmaker's Mate.	
	Carpenter's Mate, first class.	
	Water Tender.	
	Ship Fitter, first class.	
	Painter, first class.	

PETTY OFFICERS, SECOND CLASS

Seaman Branch	Artificer Branch	Special Branch
Masters at Arms, second class.	Machinist's Mates, second class.	Yeoman, second class.
Boatswain's Mates, second class.	Electricians, second class.	Ship's Cooks, second class.
Gunner's Mates, second class.	Carpenter's Mates, second class.	
Gun Captains, second class.	Printers.	
Quartermasters, second class.	Oilers.	
	Ship Fitters, second class.	
	Painters, second class.	

PETTY OFFICERS, THIRD CLASS

Seaman Branch	Artificer Branch	Special Branch
Masters at Arms, third class. Coxswains Gunner's Mates, third class. Quartermasters, third class.	Electricians, third class Carpenter's Mates, third class. Painters, third class.	Yeoman, third class. Hospital Apprentices, first class.

SEAMEN, FIRST CLASS

Seaman Branch	Artificer Branch	Special Branch
Seaman Gunners. Seamen.	Firemen, first class.	Musicians, first class. Ship's Cooks, third class. Bakers, second class.

SEAMEN, SECOND CLASS

Seaman Branch	Artificer Branch	Special Branch
Ordinary Seamen.	Firemen, second class. Shipwrights.	Musicians, second class. Buglers. Hospital Apprentices. Ship's Cooks, fourth class.

SEAMEN, THIRD CLASS

Seaman Branch	Artificer Branch	Special Branch
Apprentice Seamen.	Coal Passers. Landsmen.	Landsmen.

MESSMAN BRANCH

Stewards to Commanders in Chief.	Wardroom Cooks.
Cooks to Commanders in Chief.	Steerage Stewards
Stewards to Commandants.	Steerage Cooks.
Cooks to Commandants.	Warrant Officers' Stewards.
Cabin Stewards.	Warrant Officers' Cooks.
Cabin Cooks.	Mess Attendants, first class.
Wardroom Stewards.	Mess Attendants, second class.
	Mess Attendants, third class.

The personnel of the Marine Corps, in accordance with the provisions of the statute law, consists of commissioned officers, warrant officers, noncommissioned officers and privates, in the various grades as follows:

Officers of the Marine Corps

COMMISSIONED OFFICERS OF THE LINE AND STAFF

1. Major General Commandant.
2. Brigadier General.
3. Colonel.
4. Lieutenant Colonel.
5. Major.
6. Captain.
7. First Lieutenant.
8. Second Lieutenant.

WARRANT OFFICERS

Marine Gunner.
Quartermaster Clerk.

Enlisted Men of the Marine Corps

1. Sergeant Major.
   Quartermaster Sergeant.
2. First Sergeant.
   Gunnery Sergeant.
3. Drum Major.
4. Leader of Band.
5. Second Leader of Band.
6. Sergeant.
7. Corporal.
8. Principal Musician.
9. Musician first class.
10. Musician second class.
11. Musician third class.
12. Drummer.
    Trumpeter.
    Private.

The personnel of the Coast Guard, in accordance with the statute law, consists of commissioned officers, appointed officers, warrant officers, petty officers and seamen as follows:

Officers of the Coast Guard

COMMISSIONED OFFICERS OF THE LINE

1. Captain Commandant.
2. Senior Captain.
3. Captain.
4. First Lieutenant.

5. Second Lieutenant.
6. Third Lieutenant.

COMMISSIONED OFFICERS OF ENGINEERS

1. Engineer in Chief.
2. Captain of Engineers.
3. First Lieutenant of Engineers.
4. Second Lieutenant of Engineers.
5. Third Lieutenant of Engineers.

COMMISSIONED OFFICERS OF CONSTRUCTION BRANCH

1. Constructor (with rank of first lieutenant).

APPOINTED OFFICERS

Cadet
Undergoing three years course of instruction at the Coast Guard Academy at New London, Connecticut.
Cadet Engineer.

WARRANT OFFICERS

Master's Mate.
Keeper. (In charge of Life-Saving Station).
Boatswain.
Gunner.
Machinist.
Carpenter.
Sailmaker.

Enlisted Men of the Coast Guard

The enlisted men of the Coast Guard have ratings, or grades, similar to those of the Navy, as follows:

SEAMAN BRANCH	ARTIFICER BRANCH	SPECIAL BRANCH
Master at Arms.	Electrician.	Yeoman.
No. 1 Surfman.	Electrician, first class.	Ship's Writer.
Signal Quartermaster.	Machinist, first class.	Bayman (nurse).
Wheelman.	Carpenter, first class.	Cabin Steward.
Assistant Master at Arms.	Sailmaker, first class.	Wardroom Steward.
Quartermaster.	Oiler, first class.	Cook.
Coxswain.	Blacksmith, first class.	Cadet's Cook.
Seaman.	Plumber, first class.	Steerage Cook.
Surfman.	Painter, first class.	Bugler.
Ordinary Seaman.	Electrician, second class.	Boy, first class.
	Carpenter, second class.	Boy, second class.
	Oiler, second class.	
	Electrician, third class.	
	Fireman.	
	Coal Heaver.	

The personnel of the Lighthouse Service pursuant to statute law consists of the officers and enlisted men in the following grades:

FOR SERVICE AFLOAT IN LIGHTSHIPS AND TENDERS

Captain
Master
Master and Pilot
First Officer
Second Officer
Third Officer
Cadet Officer
Mate
Second Mate
Mate and Carpenter
Quartermaster
Mess attendant
Chief Engineer
Engineer
Assistant Engineer
First Assistant Engineer
Second Assistant Engineer
Cadet Engineer
Wireless Operator
Machinist
Oiler

Seaman
Deck hand
Shipkeeper
Steward
Cook
Fireman, first class
Fireman, second class

FOR SERVICE ASHORE AT LIGHTHOUSES

Keeper
Laborer
Assistant Keeper
Assistant Laborer

Command

Since rank and grade carry with them the corresponding responsibilities and duties appropriate to the office it is necessary to know the commands to which the various grades are ordinarily assigned in order to properly understand the meaning of rank and grade.

In the Army the commands considered appropriate for the officers of the various grades are as follows:

COMMISSIONED OFFICERS

General .... Two or more Field Armies operating together.
Lieutenant General ...... A Field Army.
Major General .... A Corps or a Division.
Brigadier General ...... A Brigade.
Colonel .... A Regiment.
Lieutenant Colonel ...... Second in Command of a Regiment.
Major .... A Battalion of Infantry or Artillery or a Squadron of Cavalry.
Captain .... A Company of Infantry, a Battery of Artillery or a Troop of Cavalry.

First Lieutenant Second Lieutenant	Junior Officers of a Company, Battery or Troop.

NONCOMMISSIONED OFFICERS

Sergeant Major, Regimental	The senior or highest noncommissioned officer of a regiment.
Sergeant Major, Battalion or Squadron	The senior noncommissioned officer of a battalion of infantry or artillery or of a squadron of cavalry.
First Sergeant	The senior noncommissioned officer of a company, battery or troop.
Color Sergeant	The noncommissioned officer who carries the national flag, or colors, of a regiment.
Sergeant	The noncommissioned officer who acts as the right and left guide of a company, battery or troop, or of a subdivision of such a unit.
Corporal	The noncommissioned officer who acts as a squad leader.

The duties of the corresponding grades of noncommissioned officers as given in the list on pages 30 and 31 are explained to a great extent by their titles.

The Privates are the enlisted men of the rank and file who form the great body of the fighting force of the Army in all of its arms and branches.

In the Navy the commands usually assigned to the Line officers of the various grades are as follows:

COMMISSIONED OFFICERS

Admiral	Command of a Fleet.
Vice Admiral	Second in command of a Fleet.
Rear Admiral	Command of a Force or a Division.
Captain	Command of a First Class ship.
Commander	Command of a Second Class ship or Second in command of a First Class ship.
Lieutenant Commander	Command of a large Destroyer or a Gunboat, second in command of a Second Class ship, or head of a Department in a First Class ship.
Lieutenant	Command of a small Destroyer or a river Gunboat, second in command of a large Destroyer or a Gunboat, or Division Officer of a First or Second Class ship.

Lieutenant, Junior Grade	Command of a Torpedo Boat or Submarine, or Division Officer of a First or Second Class ship.
Ensign	Command of a small submarine, Division Officer of a First or Second Class ship or Destroyer, or Junior Officer on a Ship.

WARRANT OFFICERS

The duties assigned to the Commissioned Warrant Officers and Warrant Officers aboard ship are as follows:

The Chief Boatswain or Boatswain attached to a ship has general charge of all of the rigging, anchors, chains, hawsers, boat gear and tackles of the ship and is responsible for the condition of such stores.

The Chief Gunner or Gunner attached to a ship is assigned to ordnance duty under the Gunnery Officer and has charge of the ordnance stores and ammunition and the repairs to guns and their gear.

The Gunner assigned to Electrical duty has general charge of the electrical plants and wiring of the ship and the stores pertaining thereto.

The Chief Carpenter or Carpenter attached to a ship has charge of the repairs to the structure of the ship which are made by the ship's force and the stores for this purpose, including paint.

The Chief Sailmaker or Sailmaker has charge of the sails and awnings and the repairs to them.

The Chief Pay Clerk or Pay Clerk is the assistant

to the Paymaster in the Commissary and Supply Department of the ship.

The Chief Pharmacist or Pharmacist is attached to the Medical Department of a ship and has charge of the medical stores and their issue under the orders of the Surgeon.

PETTY OFFICERS

Petty Officers in the Navy correspond to the noncommissioned officers of the Army, and they are divided into three general Branches, the Seaman Branch consisting of the deck force which mans the guns of the battery and performs the strictly "sailor" duties; the Artificer Branch composed of the engineering force, the electricians, the carpenters and the painters; and the Special Branch made up of yeomen, or clerical force, the commissary stewards, cooks and bakers, the hospital nurses and the bandsmen.

As a rule the special duties of each of the Petty Officers are indicated by their titles, or "ratings," as it is styled in the Navy, as given in the list on pages 37–40, but a few words of explanation may not be amiss.

Masters-at-Arms are the policemen of the ship; boatswain's mates are the petty officers who assist the boatswain and see that the orders of the officer of the deck are carried out in the different parts of the ship; turret captains are the petty officers who have charge of the turret guns crews under the Division Officer; gunner's mates are the petty officers who assist the gunner and see to the repairs of the guns of the battery and have charge of the issue of powder and shell from the magazines to the guns; gun captains are the petty officers in charge of the individual gun crews; quartermasters are the petty officers who stand the watch at the wheel and steer the ship under the orders of the Officer of the Deck; machinist's mates are the petty officers on duty at the engines and machinery; water tenders see that the proper amount of water is kept in the boilers, and the duties of the other petty officers are as indicated by their "ratings."

The ordinary enlisted men are apportioned to the three branches in the same manner as the petty officers, the Seaman Branch having seamen gunners especially trained for duty at the guns, seamen, ordinary seamen and apprentice seamen under training; the Artificer Branch having firemen who tend the fires under the boilers, coal passers who transfer the coal from the bunkers to the firerooms and landsmen or untrained men; and the Special Branch having the musicians of the band and buglers, and the lower ratings of cooks, bakers and hospital men.

In the Marine Corps the commands considered appropriate for the officers of the different grades are as follows:

COMMISSIONED OFFICERS

Major General Commandant .... In command of the Marine Corps, at Headquarters, Washington, D. C.

Brigadier General .... A Brigade.

Colonel .... A Regiment of Infantry or Artillery, or as Fleet Marine Officer of a Fleet. (In command of the Fleet Regiment of Marines when it is landed for service on shore).

Lieutenant Colonel ...... Second in Command of a Regiment of Infantry or Artillery, or as Fleet Marine Officer.

Major .... A Battalion of Infantry or Artillery.

Captain .... A Company of Infantry or a Battery of Artillery, or in command of a Marine Detachment of a First Class ship.

First Lieutenant .... Junior Officer of a Company or Battery, or in command of a Marine Detachment of a Second Class ship.

Second Lieutenant ...... Junior Officer of a Company or Battery or of a Marine Detachment of a First Class ship.

WARRANT OFFICERS

Marine Gunners perform duty in the Marine Corps analogous to that performed by Gunners in the Navy.

Quartermaster Clerks perform duties as assistants to the officers of the Paymaster and Quartermaster Departments of the Marine Corps corresponding to the duties of Pay Clerks in the Navy.

NONCOMMISSIONED OFFICERS

The noncommissioned officers of the Marine Corps perform duties ashore similar to those performed by noncommissioned officers of infantry and artillery in the Army and also perform duties aboard ship similar to those performed by certain of the petty officers of the Navy.

The Marine Detachments assigned to some of the smaller ships of the Navy are commanded by First Sergeants.

Gunnery Sergeants are assigned duties afloat similar to those performed by Gunner's Mates in the Navy, while on shore their duties are normally in connection with the care and repair of the guns of the artillery, both heavy and light.

In the Coast Guard in times of peace when the service is operating under the Treasury Department the duties of the various grades of officers are as follows:

COMMISSIONED OFFICERS

Captain Commandant	In charge of the service at the Headquarters in Washington, D. C.
Senior Captain	In charge of a Division of the Service.
Captain	Command of a Cruising Cutter.
First Lieutenant	Command of a Harbor Cutter or Executive Officer of a Cruising Cutter.
Second Lieutenant Third Lieutenant	Watch Officer on a Cruising Cutter.

Engineer Captains and Lieutenants perform engineering duty on the cruising and harbor cutters in accordance with their rank.

WARRANT OFFICERS

Keepers are in charge of the Life-Saving stations all along the coast of the United States, while the other warrant officers, Boatswains, Gunners, Machinists and Carpenters, perform duties of the same nature as the corresponding ranks in the Navy.

The petty officers and seamen perform the duties as indicated by their "ratings," similar to those performed by men of like "ratings" in the Navy.

In the Lighthouse Service the appropriate commands and duties performed by the officers and men in the various ranks and ratings are as indicated by their titles and ratings, these duties in general being similar to those performed by the officers and men of various grades in the other Sea Services in so far as these duties apply to the peculiar needs of the Lighthouse Service afloat and ashore.

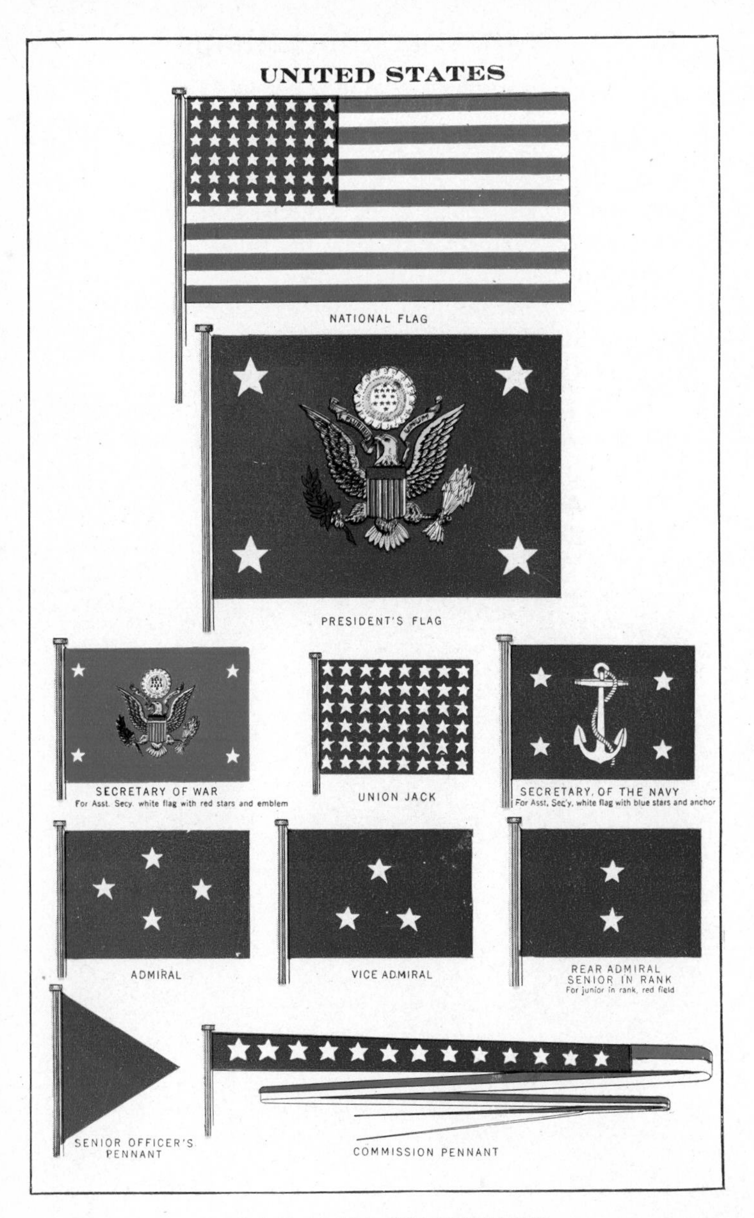

ENSIGNS, FLAGS AND PENNANTS.

CHAPTER III

ENSIGNS, FLAGS AND PENNANTS

THE National Flag of a country is the flag which bears the device of the nation, the emblem by which the nationality of the state is shown.

An Ensign is the flag or insignia used to show the nationality of the armed forces of a nation; more properly speaking, it is the colors displayed by a ship of war or carried by a regiment of soldiers.

In some countries flags of different designs from those of their national flags are prescribed to be carried by the troops of the armies or displayed as "colors" by the ships of war, but in the United States of America the National Flag, the "Stars and Stripes," is carried by the Army and displayed as the colors by all ships of the Navy.

The flag of the United States was authorized by a resolution of Congress of June 14, 1777, reading as follows:

> *Resolved,* That the flag of the thirteen United States be thirteen stripes, alternate red and white; that the union be thirteen stars, white in a blue field, representing a new constellation.

For the design of the flag made in accordance with this resolution it was decided to make the stripes of equal width and the stars five-pointed.

Vermont was admitted as a State in 1791 and Kentucky was admitted in 1792, and as a result an act of Congress approved on January 13, 1794, provided:

That from and after the first day of May, Anno Domini one thousand seven hundred and ninety-five, the flag of the United States be fifteen stripes, alternate red and white. That the union be fifteen stars, white in a blue field.

The rapid increase in the number of States in the succeeding years caused much confusion regarding the exact design of the flag and there came to be a great diversity as to the numbers of stars and stripes. In order to clear up all doubt the Fifteenth Congress passed an act, which was approved by the President on April 4, 1818, entitled,

AN ACT TO ESTABLISH THE FLAG OF THE UNITED STATES

Be it enacted by the Senate and House of Representatives of the United States of America in congress assembled, That from and after the fourth day of July next, the flag of the United States be thirteen horizontal stripes, alternate red and white; that the union be twenty stars, white in a blue field.

SECTION 2. *And be it further enacted,* That on the admission of every new state into the Union, one star be added to the union of the flag; and that such addition shall take effect on the fourth day of July then next succeeding such admission.

In accordance with this law there are at present forty-eight stars in the union of the flag. The proportions of the national flag as prescribed by the Presidential Executive Order No. 1637, dated October 29, 1912, are as follows:

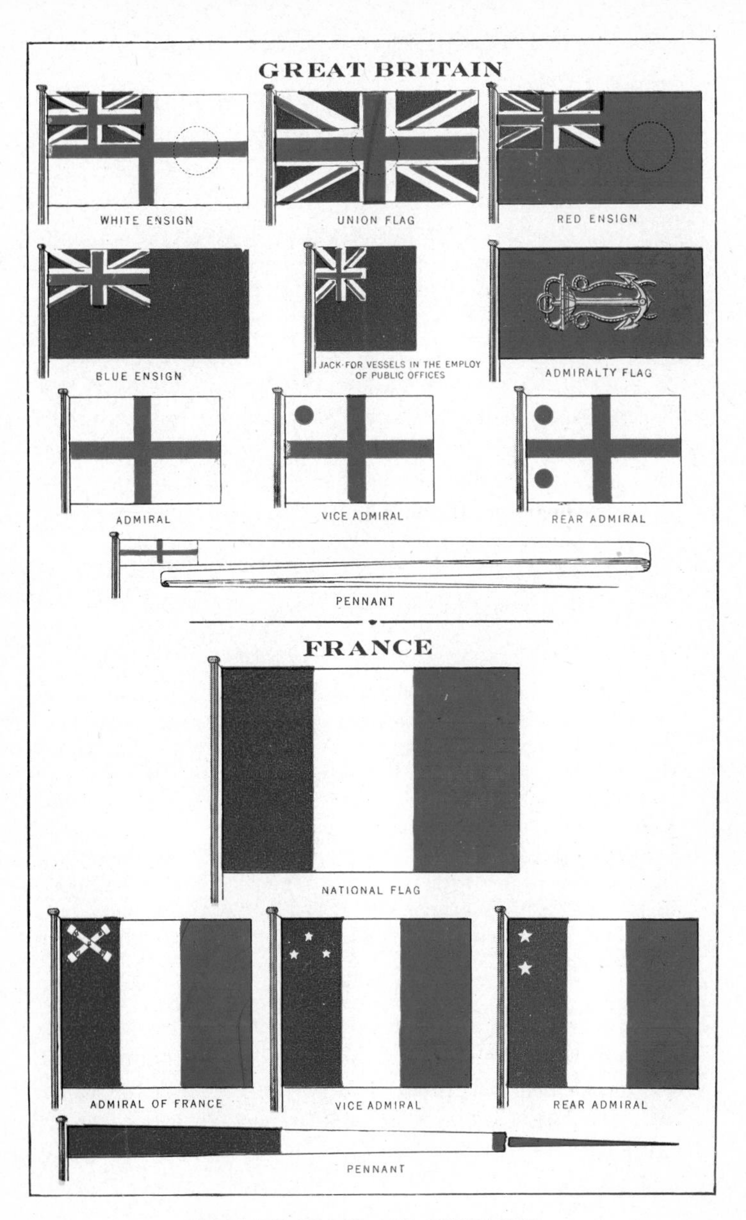

ENSIGNS, FLAGS AND PENNANTS.

Hoist (or width) of flag	1
Fly (or length) of flag	1.9
Hoist (or width) of union	7/13
Fly (or length) of union	.76
Width of each stripe	1/13

There is an exception made in these proportions in the case of the flags carried by the troops, in which case the sizes are established by special orders for the Army and Navy.

For the small flags flown by the small boats and launches of the ships of war and other government ships the executive order places the number of stars in the union at thirteen on account of the fact that the identity of the several stars would be lost if the whole number of forty-eight were used.

The Union Jack is a flag consisting of the union of the national flag, and it is flown at the jackstaff in the bow of ships of war. Its size should be the same as that of the union of the flag with which it is flown.

A pennant is triangular shaped, in some cases having a V-shaped notch cut in the outer end of the fly.

The "commission pennant" is long and narrow, the portion next the hoist, or mast, having a blue field with thirteen white stars and the remainder being divided longitudinally into two parts, red and white. It is flown at the mainmast head of all ships in commission which have no officer on board above the rank of Captain in the Navy, and indicates that the ship carrying it is "in commission," or on active service.

On ships of war carrying an officer senior in rank to a Captain the prescribed distinctive flag for such officer is flown at the mainmast head in place of the commission pennant, and the ship is known as a "Flagship."

Naval officers above the rank of Captain in the Navy are called " Flag Officers."

These distinctive flags of higher command are shown in the illustrations. When two or more flag officers of the same grade are in the same fleet the senior one flies the blue flag of his grade and all the others fly the red flag of the grade.

On any one ship of war only the distinctive flag of the senior officer of flag or higher rank is flown; thus, if the President is aboard an Admiral's flagship the flag of the President is flown but not that of the Admiral.

In former times the flag was carried into the front line of battle by the troops who used it as their rallying point, but in the battles of to-day, where every attempt is made to disguise and screen the lines of troops from the enemy, the flags and standards of the brigades and regiments would serve to mark the exact position of the lines and thus convey valuable information to the enemy and enable him to concentrate the fire of artillery and machine guns upon them. Therefore the flags are kept far in the rear to be carried in parades and ceremonies only or when the victorious troops march in triumph through the streets of cities captured from the enemy.

In the accompanying illustrations the ensigns, flags and pennants of the principal maritime nations are shown, the national flag and the ensigns carried by the land troops being indicated in each case.

In addition to the flags of the United States shown in the illustrations special flags are provided as distinguishing insignia for the Naval Reserve, the Naval Militia of the several States and territories, and for the merchant ships operated under the United States Shipping Board.

The Naval Reserve Flag.— This flag is a " swallow-

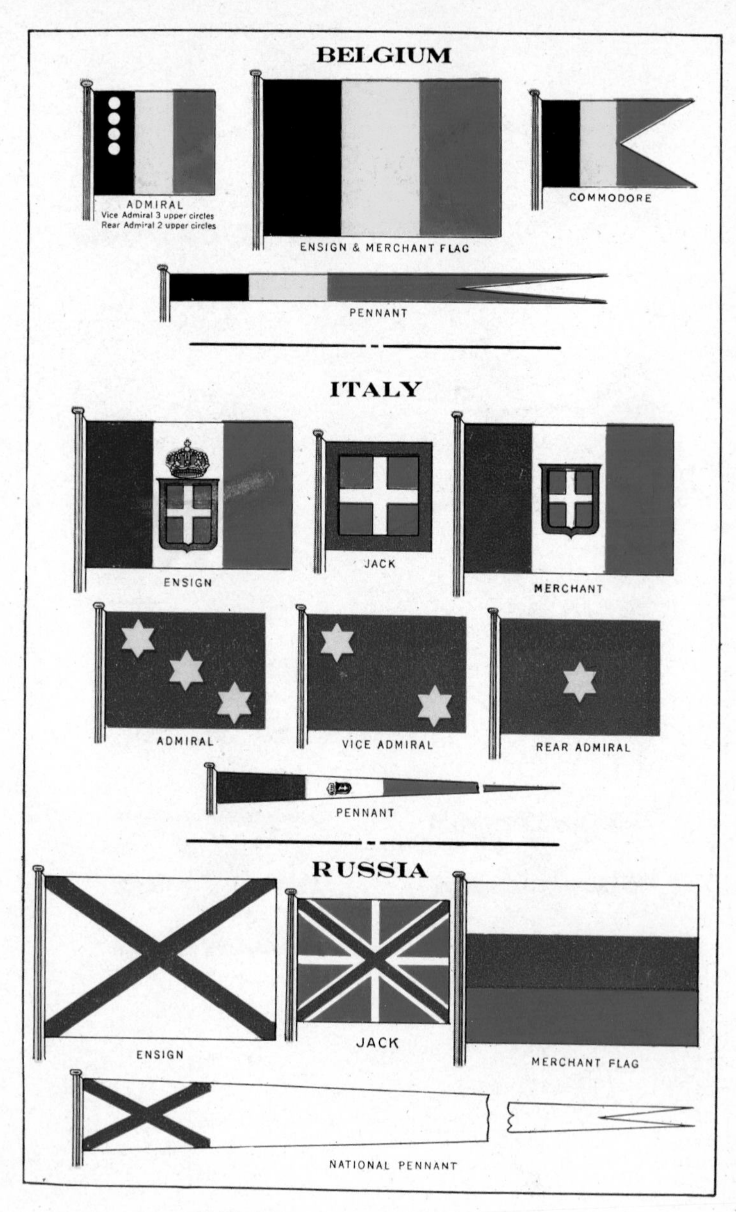

ENSIGNS, FLAGS AND PENNANTS.

ENSIGNS, FLAGS AND PENNANTS.

tailed" pennant of blue bunting bearing a design in the center consisting of two crossed anchors surcharged by a shield of the United States and surmounted by a spread eagle, the design being in white, the thirteen stars on the shield being blue and the bars on the shield being alternate white and red. This flag may be flown as an insignia on private vessels or vessels of the merchant service commanded by officers of the Naval Reserve Force, but shall not be flown in lieu of the national ensign.

The Naval Militia Flag.— This flag is flown as a distinguishing flag by ships of the Naval Militia of the several States and territories when not in the service of the United States. It has a blue field with a yellow diamond in the center and a blue vertical foul anchor in the center of the diamond. These ships of the Naval Militia also fly a pennant at the mainmast, the part next the mast being white with the yellow diamond and blue foul anchor design upon it and the remainder of the pennant is divided longitudinally into two equal stripes of blue and yellow.

The Shipping Board Flag.— This flag is flown as a distinguishing flag, or "house flag," by the merchant ships operated under the United States Shipping Board, and consists of a white flag bearing a shield of the United States in the center supported by a blue anchor with the letters "U. S. A." above the design and the letters "S. B." below it. The shield has a blue field with thirteen white stars and the thirteen stripes are alternate white and red.

The National Ensign carried by each regiment of United States troops is 4 feet 4 inches in height and 5 feet 6 inches long, on a pike or staff 9 feet long, with the edges trimmed with knotted yellow silk fringe 2½ inches wide and a cord and two tassels of red, white and blue silk strands.

In addition to the National Ensign each regiment carries a Regimental Standard of the same dimensions as the National Flag, this standard being of the distinctive color for the arm of the service to which the regiment belongs, and bearing the corps insignia and the number of the regiment.

In the Army the Regimental Standards are as follows:

Regiments of Engineers, of scarlet silk having embroidered upon it in proper colors the Coat of Arms of the United States, with below it the insignia of the Corps of Engineers and a scroll bearing the inscription "5 U. S. ENGINEERS" (the number being that of the regiment) embroidered in white silk, trimmed around the edges with white silk fringe and having a cord and tassels of white and scarlet silk strands.

Coast Artillery Corps, of scarlet silk having embroidered upon it in proper colors the Coat of Arms of the United States, with below it two cannons crossed embroidered in yellow silk and a scroll bearing the inscription "U. S. COAST ARTILLERY CORPS" embroidered in red silk, trimmed around the edges with yellow silk fringe and having a cord and tassels of red and yellow silk strands.

Infantry Regiments, of blue silk having embroidered upon it in proper colors the Coat of Arms of the United States, with below it a scroll bearing the inscription "24 U. S. INFANTRY" (the number being that of the regiment) embroidered in white silk, trimmed around the edges with yellow silk fringe and having a cord and tassels of blue and white silk strands.

Cavalry Regiments, of yellow silk having embroidered

upon it in proper colors the Coat of Arms of the United States, with below it a scroll bearing the inscription "7 U. S. CAVALRY" (the number being that of the regiment) embroidered in yellow silk, trimmed around the edges with yellow silk fringe.

Field Artillery Regiments, of scarlet silk having embroidered upon it in proper colors the Coat of Arms of the United States, with below it a scroll bearing the inscription "8 U. S. FIELD ARTILLERY" (the number being that of the regiment) embroidered in red silk, trimmed around the edges with yellow silk fringe.

Signal Corps Battalions, of orange silk having embroidered upon it in proper colors the Coat of Arms of the United States, with below it the insignia of the Signal Corps and a scroll bearing the inscription "4 BATTALION SIGNAL CORPS" (the number being that of the Battalion) embroidered in white silk, trimmed around the edges with white silk fringe.

The United States Navy Regimental Standard, carried by infantry regiments of sailors when landed for shore operations, is of blue silk with a white diamond in the center and a vertical blue anchor upon the white diamond.

The United States Navy Regimental Standard, carried by artillery regiments of sailors when landed for shore operations, is of red silk with a white diamond in the center and a vertical red anchor upon the white diamond.

The United States Naval Militia Regimental Standards are of the same design as those for the regular Navy except that the diamond in the center is yellow.

The United States Marine Corps Regimental Standard is of blue silk having embroidered upon it in the center the Marine Corps insignia in shades of white, gold and gray silk to represent silver and gold, with above it a scroll in red silk bearing the designation of the regiment in white silk embroidery, and below it a scroll of red silk bearing the inscription "U. S. MARINE CORPS," trimmed around the edges with yellow silk fringe and having a cord and tassels of yellow and red silk strands.

Each regimental National Ensign and Regimental Standard has upon the staff beneath the flag a silver plate for each battle in which the regiment has been engaged, the name and date of the battle being engraved thereon.

Flags are provided for the use of general officers of the United States Army to be flown from a staff in the bow of a boat when making official trips by water, or from a staff at the front of an automobile; these flags being of red bunting bearing four white stars for a general, three white stars for a lieutenant general, two white stars for a major general and one white star for a brigadier general.

The flag for the Chief of Staff of the United States Army is of scarlet and white silk, divided diagonally from the lower left hand corner to the upper right hand corner, bearing in the center a large five pointed star embroidered in white silk surcharged with the coat of arms of the United States embroidered in proper colors. In the upper left hand corner on the scarlet silk is a large five pointed star embroidered in white and in the lower right hand corner a large five pointed star embroidered in red.

For a coast defense district commander a red flag bearing two cannon, crossed, in yellow, is authorized, and for a post commander a pennant, the third next the

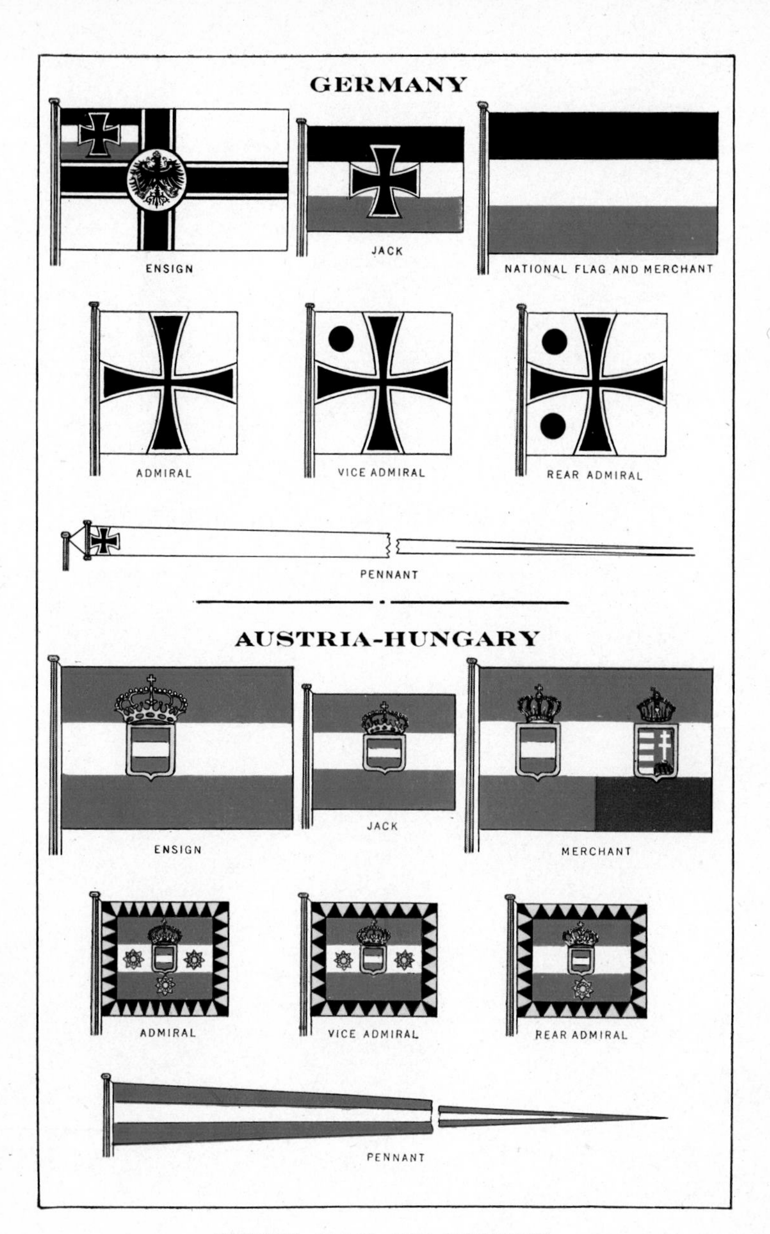

ENSIGNS, FLAGS AND PENNANTS.

staff being blue bunting with thirteen white stars and the remainder being of red bunting.

For the general officers and post commanders of the United States Marine Corps flags and pennants of similar design, but with the addition of the Marine Corps insignia in white added, are provided.

A Guidon is a small flag or pennant carried by each troop of cavalry, company of mounted engineers, battery of field artillery, mounted company of the signal corps, field hospital, ambulance company and motor truck company, to designate the unit which carries it.

The cavalry guidon is made up of two horizontal stripes, the upper one red and the lower one white, the outer end being notched or cut "swallow-tailed," with the number of the regiment in white on the upper stripe and the letter of the troop in red on the lower stripe.

The field artillery guidon is of the same shape and colors as the cavalry guidon with the addition of two cannons crossed in the center, the cannons and the regimental number and battery letter being in yellow.

The guidon for a company of mounted engineers is of the same shape as the cavalry guidon, of scarlet with the corps insignia of the engineers in the center, the word "MOUNTED" above it and the number of the company below it, the insignia, letters and numbers being in silver embroidery.

The guidon for a mounted company of the signal corps is of the same shape as the cavalry guidon, of orange with two flags crossed of white with red centers in the center and the letter of the company in white above them.

Each aero squadron carries a guidon of orange silk with the insignia of the signal corps in white and red in the center, the number of the squadron above the insignia in white and a white eagle with wings spread below the insignia.

Each telegraph company carries a guidon similar to the one for the aero squadron except that in place of the eagle there is a design representing forked lightning.

The guidon for each field hospital organization and ambulance company is of the same shape as the cavalry guidon, of maroon color, having in the center the insignia of the hospital corps, a caduceus, in white, with the number of the organization above the insignia and the initials " F. H." for field hospital or " A. C." for ambulance company in white below the insignia.

The guidon for a motor truck company is a pennant, triangular in shape, of red, white and blue, the white portion being diamond shaped with one of the horizontal points at the staff and the other at the outer end of the pennant, the triangular portion above the white diamond next to the staff being red and the corresponding triangular portion below the white diamond being blue, with the quartermaster corps insignia in blue at the center of the white diamond.

The flag of the Geneva Convention, to be used in connection with the national flag in time of war with a country which was a signatory of that convention, is a white flag having a red Greek cross in the center. It is used to mark hospitals, hospital ships, field hospitals, ambulances and ambulance vessels and boats. The size prescribed to mark general hospitals in the United States Army is 5 feet hoist (high) by 9 feet fly (wide) with the red cross 4 feet high and 4 feet wide and the arms of the cross 16 inches wide. The smaller Geneva Convention flags are of the same general proportions.

An interesting development of warfare resulting from

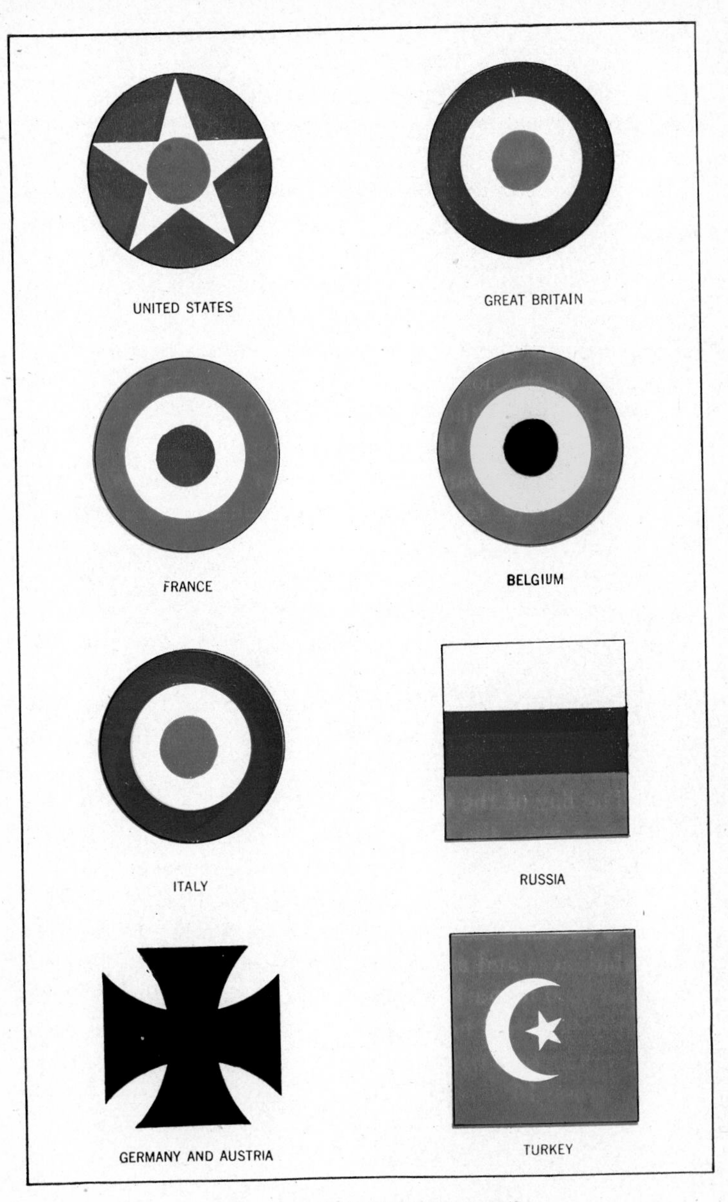

AIRCRAFT DISTINGUISHING MARKS

the increasing use of aircraft in war is the use of distinguishing marks for the aircraft of the different nations. At first the national flags were used for this purpose, but it was found that they would not serve to identify the nationality of the aeroplane or dirigible airship when viewed from all directions and another system of distinguishing marks has been adopted.

These aircraft distinguishing marks for the aircraft of the principal nations are shown in the accompanying illustration. In order that the aircraft carrying them may be distinguished both from above and below these marks are painted on the upper side of each upper wing and on the lower side of each lower wing of aeroplanes and on both the upper and lower sides of the gas bags of dirigible airships and balloons. The marks are also carried on the sides of the fusilage near the bow and on the sides of the vertical rudders of aeroplanes in many cases.

These distinguishing marks are necessary for the aircraft employed in war in order that friend may be distinguished from foe by the airmen and by the gunners and riflemen afloat and ashore.

SEAL OF THE U. S. WAR DEPARTMENT

CHAPTER IV

UNIFORMS AND INSIGNIA OF THE UNITED STATES ARMY

The uniforms for the officers and enlisted men of the United States Army are made of blue cloth for wear on dress occasions and of olive-drab colored material for wear on general service and field service occasions, and in addition the officers have uniforms of white linen or cotton duck for wear as a dress uniform in the tropics or during hot weather.

The service uniforms of the olive drab color are made of woolen cloth or serge for cold weather and of cotton duck for hot weather, the latter being usually known as "khaki" uniforms, though the regulation color is of a somewhat darker shade than that universally known as "khaki."

Copyright by Underwood & Underwood

General Tasker H. Bliss, Chief of Staff, U. S. Army, and Major General Hugh L. Scott, U. S. Army

It is a general rule that the officers serving with the troops in garrison or in the field must appear in the same style of uniform as that prescribed for the enlisted men.

During peace times officers serving on detached duty or in the offices of the Departments where there are no enlisted men on duty ordinarily wear civilian clothes, but in time of war all officers and enlisted men are required to wear the olive drab service uniform at all times except when the full dress and dress uniforms are prescribed for some appropriate special occasion. Officers ordered on active field service are required to carry with them only the service uniforms.

UNITED STATES ARMY OFFICERS' UNIFORMS

Commissioned officers of the Army are required to have complete outfits of service uniform (woolen olive-drab for temperate and cold weather and cotton olive-drab or "khaki" for the tropics and hot weather), dress uniform, full dress uniform, white uniform and special evening dress uniform, and for wear on certain occasions in the evening a mess dress uniform of blue and one of white is optional.

The occasions upon which these uniforms are usually worn are given in the regulations as follows:

TABLE OF OCCASIONS FOR UNIFORMS

Occasions.	Uniform.
1. For habitual garrison wear at all times when under arms, and until sundown when not under arms. 2. For duty in the field.	Service uniform, woolen or cotton depending upon the temperature.

Occasions.	Uniform.
3. For ordinary wear after retreat by officers not under arms. 4. For social uses before retreat. 5. When off post, except that when riding or taking physical exercise the service uniform may be worn. 6. When on duty with enlisted men for whom dress uniform is prescribed.	Dress uniform (in the Tropics and during hot weather in other places the white uniform may be worn).
7. When on duty with enlisted men for whom mounted dress uniform is prescribed. 8. When riding off the reservation.	Dress uniform (mounted).
9. State occasions at home or abroad. 10. When receiving the President of the United States. 11. When receiving or calling officially upon the President, sovereign or a member of the royal family of another country. 12. Ceremonies and entertainments when it is desired to do special honor to the occasion. 13. When full dress, dismounted, is prescribed for enlisted men. 14. Special or official functions of a general nature, when prescribed.	Full dress uniform.
15. When on duty with enlisted men for whom full dress, mounted, is prescribed. 16. Social or official functions of a general nature when prescribed. *On the following occasions when officers are required to be mounted.* 17. State occasions at home or abroad. 18. When receiving the President of the United States. 19. When receiving or officially calling upon the President, sovereign or a member of the royal family of another country.	Full dress uniform (mounted).

Occasions.	Uniform.
20. Ceremonies or entertainments when it is desired to do special honor to the occasion.	Full dress uniform (mounted).
21. Social or official functions of a general nature occurring in the evening. 22. For private formal dinners and other private formal social functions occurring in the evening. 23. For ordinary evening wear when desired.	Special evening dress uniform.
24. For private formal dinners and other private formal social functions occurring in the evening. 25. For ordinary evening wear when desired.	Blue mess dress uniform. In the Tropics and at other places in hot weather, the white mess dress uniform may be worn.
In the Tropics. 26. Until sundown when prescribed. 27. For ordinary wear after retreat. 28. For official occasions, under arms, when prescribed. *In the United States in warm weather.* 29. For ordinary wear after retreat. 30. For social use after retreat. 31. When off the post, or reservation.	White uniform.

Throughout the military and naval services of the United States when officers of the Army, Navy and Marine Corps appear together in uniform upon occasions of ceremony the following are the uniforms designated for each of the three services:

Designation of Uniform	Composition of Uniforms for		
	Army	Navy	Marine Corps
Uniform A	Full dress	Special full dress, or white special full dress.	Special full dress (with full dress trousers if in line with troops), or white special full dress.
Uniform B	Dress	Undress, or white undress.	Undress or white undress.
Uniform C	Full dress or evening dress.	Evening full dress; or evening full dress without swords or belts, and with blue caps; or dinner dress.	Special full dress, or mess dress.

The service uniform consists of a single breasted sack coat extending to one-third of the distance from the point of the hip to the knee, fitting tightly at the waist, with a standing collar, buttoned down the front with a row of five army buttons of dull finish bronze, having four patch pockets closed by pocket flaps buttoned with small size army buttons of bronze, one pocket on each breast and one on each side of the front below the waist, the shoulders having straps of the same material as the coat extending from the shoulder seam to the base of the collar secured with a small size bronze button at the collar end (the insignia of rank are worn on these straps), and the sleeves being trimmed with one row of half-inch braid three inches above the end of the sleeve, the braid being black for officers of the General Staff Corps and brown for all other officers; breeches of the same color and material as the coat; tan leather shoes and tan leather strap puttee leggings; the service hat, commonly

U. S. Army officer
Olive drab service uniform

known as the "campaign hat," a wide brimmed drab felt hat worn to a peak at the center of the crown and having the officers' hat cord around the base of the crown; or the service cap, a bell crowned cap of the same material as the coat with a sloping visor of tan leather and a one-half inch tan leather chin strap above the visor secured by a bronze button at each end of the visor. Olive-drab woolen gloves are worn with this uniform when required. For garrison wear a white shirt, collar and cuffs are worn with this uniform, but in the field a flannel olive-drab shirt is worn.

In garrison the saber is worn suspended by tan leather slings from a tan leather waist belt, but for war service in the field the saber is worn with a wide tan leather belt having a suspender strap of tan leather worn from the right shoulder diagonally across the body to rings in the belt in front and in rear of the left hip. This belt was recently adopted from the British Army and is known as the "Sam Browne" belt. In the trenches and on ordinary duty in the field, officers of the Army wear the pistol belt on which the service automatic pistol is carried in a leather or webbing holster.

Insignia of dull bronze metal indicating the arm of the service or the staff corps to which the wearer belongs are worn upon both sides of the collar of the service coat and the insignia of rank in bright metal, silver or gold according to rank are worn upon each shoulder strap of the coat.

For certain drills and for service in the field the coat may be dispensed with, in which case the olive-drab flannel shirt is worn and the corps insignia and insignia of rank are then worn upon the collar of the shirt.

The hat cord worn on the service hat by General Officers is a double cord of gold bullion with acorns of the same material at the ends, and that worn by other commissioned officers is the same except that it has black silk intermixed with the gold.

Army Field Clerks and Field Clerks Quartermaster Corps wear hat cords made of black and silver twisted strands.

Members of the Officers Training Corps undergoing training in the camps provided for that purpose wear a hat cord made of red, white and blue twisted strands.

The overcoat is worn with the service uniform when necessary.

Mounted officers wear tan boots, spurs and drab leather riding gloves with the service uniform.

The dress uniform consists of a dark blue cloth, single-breasted coat extending to one-third of the distance from the point of the hip to the knee; blue cloth trousers (the shade depending upon the rank and corps of the wearer as later described); a bell crowned cap, of dark blue cloth having the coat of arms of the United States embroidered in gold on the front of the crown at the center, with a sloping visor of black patent leather and a chin strap of gold braid three-eighths of an inch in width and eight inches long attached above the visor by a small gilt Army button at each end of the visor; black shoes; white shirt, collar and cuffs; and white gloves.

The dress coat for General officers (officers of the rank of General, Lieutenant General, Major General and Brigadier General) is double breasted with a standing and falling collar, two rows of buttons down the front as follows: for a General twelve buttons in each row arranged in three groups of four, for a Lieutenant General ten in each row arranged in three groups, the upper and lower groups of three and the central group of four, for a Major General nine in each row arranged in three groups of three each, and for a Brigadier General eight in each row arranged in groups of two; and the cuffs trimmed with three small size gilt army buttons on each back seam. The collar has on each side the proper insignia indicating staff corps, and on each shoulder there is a shoulder strap four inches long and one and seven-eighths inches wide with a border of raised gold embroidery three-eighths of an inch wide, the field of the strap being of dark blue cloth and bearing the stars indicating the rank of the General officer. These shoulder straps are worn with one of the sides touching the shoulder seam of the sleeve.

The dress coat for all other officers is a single breasted sack coat of dark blue cloth, with a standing collar, closed in front by buttons or hooks concealed by a fly, having a vertical opening on each side at the hip six inches high, the collar, front edges, bottom edge of the coat and the vertical side openings being trimmed with lustrous black mohair braid one and one-half inches wide. On each shoulder a shoulder strap of the same size as that described for General officers is worn, the field of the strap being the distinctive color of the arm of the service to which the wearer belongs and having the insignia of rank embroidered upon it. On each side of the collar the corps insignia are worn to indicate the corps or branch of the service to which the wearer belongs.

The dress trousers for General officers (except Chief of Coast Artillery, Chief of Engineers, Quartermaster General and General Officers of the Quartermaster Corps) are made of dark blue cloth without stripes or other trimming. For the General officers excepted in the last sentence the trousers are of dark blue cloth trimmed down the outer leg seams with stripes as follows:

Chief of Coast Artillery.— Stripes of scarlet cloth one and one-half inches wide.

Chief of Engineers.— Stripes of scarlet cloth one and one-half inches wide with a one-eighth inch piping of white cloth in the center of each stripe.

Quartermaster General and General Officers of the Quartermaster Corps.— Stripes of buff cloth one and one-half inches wide.

For officers below the rank of Brigadier General the dress trousers are of blue cloth with stripes of cloth one and one-half inches wide down the outer leg seams, the color of the cloth for the trousers and stripes depending upon the corps of the officer as follows:

Officers having permanent appointments in the Staff Corps and Departments (except Engineer and Quartermaster officers), dark blue cloth without any stripes.

Officers of the Engineer Corps.— Dark blue cloth with scarlet stripes having a one-eighth inch piping of white through the center of each stripe.

Officers holding permanent appointments in the Quartermaster Corps.— Dark blue cloth with buff stripes.

Officers of cavalry.— Sky blue cloth with stripes of yellow.

Officers of Artillery.— Sky blue cloth with stripes of scarlet.

Officers of Infantry.— Sky blue cloth with stripes of white.

The dress cap for General officers (except the Quartermaster General, Brigadier Generals of the Quartermaster Corps and the Chief of Coast Artillery) has a band of blue-black velvet one and three-quarters inches

U. S. Army. Officer, full dress uniform

Rank: Major, indicated by the three stripes in the sleeve decorations
Corps: Coast Artillery, indicated by the Corps insignia on the sleeves below the knot decoration

wide, upon which is embroidered in gold a design of oak leaves, and upon the visor there are two sprays of oak leaves embroidered in gold. The dress caps for the Quartermaster General and Brigadier Generals of the Quartermaster Corps and for the Chief of Coast Artillery are the same as for other General officers except that the cap for the Chief of Coast Artillery has the band of scarlet velvet and that for the Quartermaster General and Brigadier Generals of the Quartermaster Corps have the band of buff velvet.

The dress cap for Field officers (Colonels, Lieutenant Colonels and Majors) of all branches is the same as that for General officers, except that the band is decorated with two bands of gold lace braid one-half an inch wide, one at the top and one at the bottom of the band with a strip of cloth three-quarters of an inch in width between the two gold bands, the color of the cloth being the distinctive color of the arm of the service or staff corps to which the wearer belongs, these distinctive colors being the same as those for the " facings " of the uniforms.

When the saber is worn with the dress uniform the belt is worn under the coat, with full dress slings.

The overcoat is worn with the dress uniform when necessary, and the cloak, or blue cape, may be worn when the officer is not on duty with troops under arms.

When mounted officers in dress uniform wear dress breeches of cloth of the same color as their dress trousers and with the same stripes, black boots, white leather gloves and spurs.

The full dress uniform consists of a double-breasted coat of dark blue cloth extending to about three-fourths of the distance from the point of the hip to the knee, with a standing collar, two rows of large gilt buttons down the front between the line of the collar and the waist; epaulets or shoulder knots, as ordered, for General officers and shoulder knots for all other officers; dark blue cloth trousers for General officers, chaplains and officers holding permanent appointments in the Staff Corps (except officers of the Quartermaster Corps), and the same as dress trousers for all other officers; a chapeau or the dress cap for General officers and the dress cap for all other officers; black shoes; white shirt, collar and cuffs; white gloves; full dress belt and saber.

The full dress coat for General officers (except the Chief of Engineers, the Quartermaster General and the Brigadier Generals of the Quartermaster Corps) has collar and cuffs of blue-black velvet, the collar being ornamented with a band of oak leaves embroidered in gold, and the cuffs having a band of oak leaves embroidered in gold near the top. The full dress coat for the Chief of Engineers has a narrow piping of scarlet velvet down the front, that for the General officers of the Quartermaster Corps has buff collars and cuffs. The rank of the General officer is indicated by the insignia of rank (the appropriate number of stars) upon the cuffs.

The buttons on the front of the full dress coat for General officers are arranged in groups as described for the dress coat.

The full dress coat for all officers below the rank of Brigadier General (except officers of Engineers and officers holding permanent appointments in the Quartermaster Corps) has two rows of large size gilt army buttons down the front, nine in each row equally spaced, two rows of one-half inch gold lace braid around the collar, one at the top and one at the bottom, with the distinctive color of the "facings" of the corps, depart-

Copyright, 1908, by Brig. Gen. J. B. Aleshire, Qr.-Master General, U. S. A.

U. S. Army. Officers' winter uniforms

ment or arm of the service filling the space between the two rows. Officers of Engineers have a narrow piping of scarlet cloth down the front of the full dress coat and officers holding permanent appointments in the Quartermaster Corps have this piping of buff cloth and also cuffs of buff cloth two and one-half inches deep. For all officers below the rank of Brigadier General the full dress coat has one row of one-half inch gold lace braid around the sleeve two and one-half inches from the bottom and above this the gold braided designs indicating the rank of the wearer. These ornamentations are in the form of three loops, one large vertical loop with two smaller horizontal loops below it. The insignia indicating the corps, department or arm of the service to which the wearer belongs are worn in the angle at the bottom of the knot.

These knots are made up of from one to five rows of gold soutache braid one-eighth of an inch wide, the number of rows of braid indicating the rank of the wearer.

When mounted all officers wear the breeches described for dress uniform, black boots, white leather gloves and spurs.

The white uniform consists of a single-breasted sack coat of white duck of the same general design as the blue dress coat but trimmed with white braid and having straps of the same material as the coat upon the shoulders reaching from the shoulder seams to the base of the collar, white trousers and a white cap. The insignia indicating the corps, department or arm of service are worn upon the collar of the coat in bright metal and the insignia of rank are worn upon the shoulder straps. The white cap is of the same design and description as the dress cap except that the crown is made of white duck and the band is of white braid.

The special evening dress uniform consists of a dark blue cloth coat cut on the lines of the civilian evening dress coat, having regulation gilt buttons and the sleeves decorated as described for the full dress coat; trousers of dark blue cloth for officers of cavalry, artillery and infantry and full dress trousers for all other officers; white shirt, collar and cuffs; black silk necktie; white evening dress waistcoat with regulation gilt buttons; the dress cap; and black shoes.

The blue mess uniform consists of a dark blue mess jacket cut like the special evening dress coat but without tails, the collar and lapels being faced with silk of the color of the "facings" prescribed for the corps, department or arm of the service and the sleeves trimmed as described for the full dress coat; dress trousers for officers of infantry, cavalry, artillery, quartermaster corps and engineers, and full dress trousers for all other officers; white or blue waistcoat with small regulation gilt buttons; dress cap; white shirt, collar and cuffs; black silk necktie; and black shoes.

The white mess uniform consists of a white mess jacket cut on the same design as the blue mess jacket but with the sleeve trimmings of white braid; white waistcoat; white trousers; white shirt, collar and cuffs; the white cap; and white shoes.

The overcoat for officers is a double-breasted ulster of olive-drab cloth extending to about ten inches below the knee (overcoats reaching to the knee only are authorized for field service), with pleated back and a wide rolling collar, buttoning to the neck, with two rows of large flat horn buttons of the same color as the coat, five in each row, having a pocket with vertical opening on each side at the waist. The rank of the wearer is indicated by the trimmings on the sleeves. The overcoat for Gen-

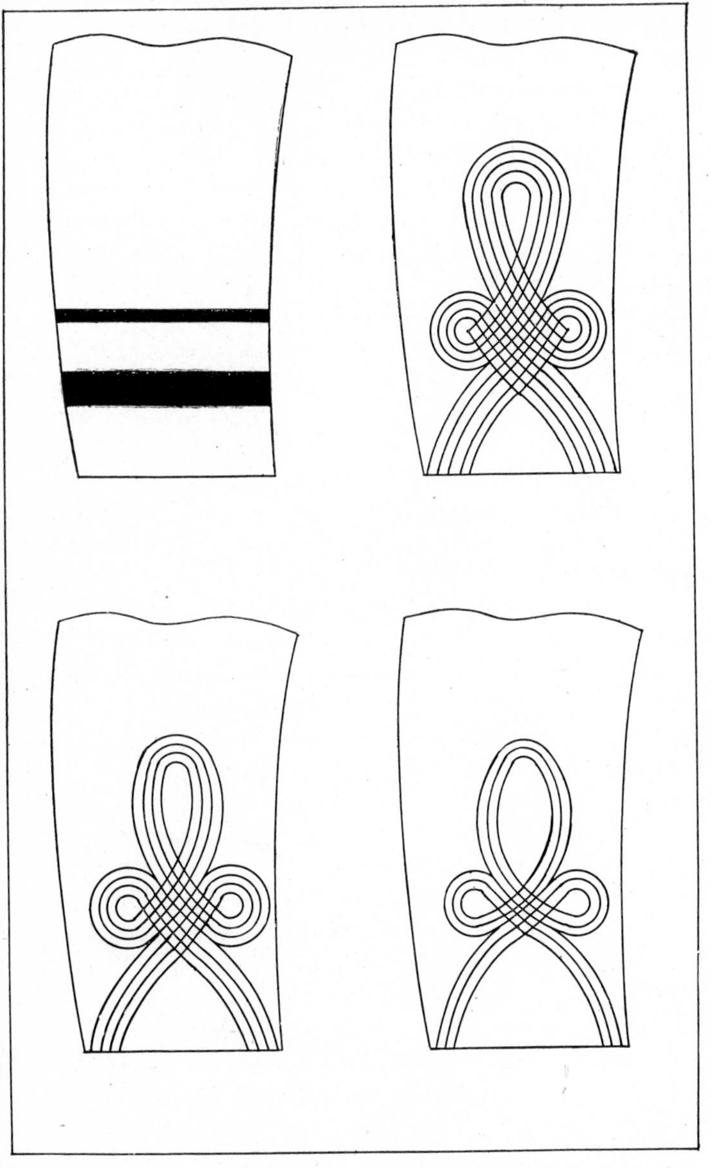

U. S. Army. Officers' overcoat sleeve braiding (in black) indicating rank

1. All General Officers
2. Colonel
3. Lieutenant Colonel
4. Major

U. S. Army. Officers' overcoat sleeve braiding indicating rank
Black braid for all except Second Lieutenant

1. Captain
2. First Lieutenant
Second Lieutenant (brown braid)
3. Field clerk
4. Lieutenant Colonel, General Staff Corps

eral officers has a band of black mohair braid one and one-quarter inches wide around the sleeve two and one-half inches above the end and another band of black mohair braid one-half of an inch wide placed one and one-half inches above the lower band. The overcoats for officers below the rank of Brigadier General have the ornamentations indicating rank as shown by the accompanying illustrations. For officers of the General Staff Corps the bands of black braid below the sleeve knot are seven-eighths of an inch wide.

The cape for officers is of dark blue cloth, extending to the knee, with a blue-black velvet rolling collar, lined with cloth depending upon the corps or arm of the service as follows:

General officers and officers of the Staff Corps and Departments (except Quartermaster General)	Dark blue.
Officers of the Quartermaster Corps	Buff.
Officers of Infantry	Light blue.
Officers of Artillery	Scarlet.
Officers of Cavalry	Yellow.
Chaplains	Black.

The chapeau for General officers is a cocked hat of black silk plush, having on the right side a rosette of black silk five inches long and three inches wide with a strip of gold lace in the center, the coat of arms of the United States being embroidered upon the upper end of the strip. Over the center of the chapeau two black ostrich plumes extend from front to rear, and there are gold bullion tassels at the front and back.

Aiguilettes of braided gold cord three-sixteenths of an inch in diameter are worn by officers of the General Staff Corps, officers of the Adjutant General's and Inspector

General's Departments, officers of the Bureau of Insular Affairs, aides-de-camp, regimental adjutants, adjutants of Artillery Districts, the Adjutant of the Military Academy at West Point, and Military Attaches at American Embassies and Legations in foreign countries.

Full dress belts for Major Generals are of red Russia leather with three stripes of gold embroidery, for Brigadier Generals of black webbing, for Field Officers (Colonels, Lieutenant Colonels and Majors) of black enamel leather with one wide stripe of gold lace, for officers holding permanent appointments in the staff corps and departments below the rank of major (except Engineers) of black enamel leather covered with a wide stripe of gold lace interwoven with three narrow stripes of black silk, for officers of Engineers the same but with gold stripes interwoven with three narrow stripes of scarlet silk, and for officers of cavalry, infantry and artillery below the rank of major the same but with the gold stripes interwoven with three narrow stripes of silk of the distinctive color of the arm of the service, cavalry yellow, infantry light blue and artillery scarlet.

A *sash* of buff silk is worn by General officers, the one for Brigadier Generals being worn around the waist over the belt and the ones for all Generals of higher rank being worn across the right shoulder under the epaulet or shoulder knot and diagonally across the body to the left side at the waist and terminating in heavy tassels which hang below the belt.

Epaulets, worn by General officers with full dress uniform, are of gold with heavy gold fringe. On the top is the coat of arms of the United States and the stars indicating rank.

Shoulder knots worn by all officers with full dress uniforms are five and one-half inches long and two and

U. S. Army officers

1. Insignia worn on caps
2. Full dress belt clasp
3. Service buttons

one-half inches wide, made of plaited gold cord and bearing the insignia of rank upon the upper surface.

The sword for officers of the Army is a saber with a slightly curved bright steel blade, a half-basket hilt with the guard of bright steel, and an ebony grip. The scabbard is of bright steel with two plain bands and rings for attaching the saber to the slings.

The saber knot worn on the hilt of the saber for attaching the sword to the wrist, for wear with full dress uniform is of heavy gilt cord ending in a gilt braided acorn for General officers and for other officers a strap of flat gold braid with a row of black silk interwoven in it near each edge; and for wear with service uniform it is made of plaited leather cord ending in a leather tassel.

INSIGNIA OF RANK AND CORPS

The rank of an officer of the Army is indicated in two ways, first, by insignia of rank placed upon the epaulets and shoulder knots worn with full dress uniform, upon the shoulder straps worn with dress uniform, upon the cloth shoulder straps of the service coats and white coats and upon the collar of the olive-drab flannel shirt when it is worn without the coat; second, by the insignia upon the sleeves of the full dress coat, the special evening dress coat, the overcoat and the blue and white mess jackets, this braiding being of gold on the full dress coat, special evening dress coat and blue mess jacket, black upon the overcoat and white upon the white mess jacket.

The insignia of rank referred to above for the various ranks of officers, as shown in the illustrations, are as follows:

General — Four silver stars.

Lieutenant General — One large silver star and two smaller ones, one on each side of the larger star.

Major General — Two silver stars, one inch in diameter.

Brigadier General — One silver star, one inch in diameter.

Colonel — A silver spread eagle, three quarters of an inch high and two inches from tip to tip of wings.

Lieutenant Colonel — A silver oak leaf, one inch high and one inch wide.

Major — A gold oak leaf, one inch high and one inch wide.

Captain — Two silver bars, one inch long and one quarter of an inch wide.

First Lieutenant — One silver bar, one inch long and one quarter of an inch wide.

Second Lieutenant — One gold bar, one inch long and one quarter of an inch wide.

The insignia of rank upon the sleeves of the full dress coat, special evening dress coats, and blue mess jacket, are as follows:

General — A band of oak leaves in gold at the top of the cuff and four silver stars below the band.

Lieutenant General — A band of oak leaves in gold at the top of the cuff and one large silver star and two smaller silver stars, one on each side of the large star, below the band.

Major General — A band of oak leaves in gold at the top of the cuff and two silver stars one inch in diameter, below the band.

Brigadier General — A band of oak leaves in gold at the top of the cuff and one silver star one inch in diameter, below the band.

Colonel — A gold band one-half of an inch wide around the sleeve with a knot of three loops, one large loop placed vertically and two smaller loops placed horizontally at each side below the large loop, the knot being placed above the gold band, the dimensions of the knot being height eight inches and width six and three quarters inches. The knot for the rank of colonel is composed

U. S. Army. Officers' shoulder straps worn on blue dress coats

1. General
2. Lieutenant General
3. Major General
4. Brigadier General

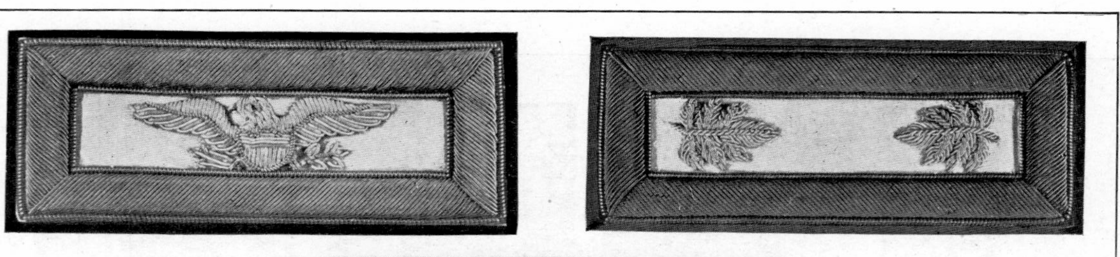

U. S. Army. Officers' shoulder straps worn on blue dress coats

1. Colonel

2. Lieutenant Colonel (Silver leaf)
Major (Gold leaf)

3. Captain

of five rows of braid one-eighth of an inch wide spaced one quarter of an inch apart. The insignia indicating the corps, department or arm of the service is worn in the center of the space formed by the lower curves of the knot and the gold band around the sleeve. For chaplains this insignia is a Latin cross of silver.

Lieutenant Colonel — The same as for a colonel except that the knot is composed of four rows of braid.

Major — The same as for a colonel except that the knot is composed of three rows of braid.

Captain — The same as for colonel except that the knot is composed of two rows of braid.

First Lieutenant — The same as for a colonel except that the knot is composed of one row of braid.

Second Lieutenant — There is no knot, the one-half inch band of gold braid around the sleeve with the insignia indicating the corps, department or arm of the service being the only ornamentation on the sleeves.

The sleeves of the white mess jackets have the same insignia to indicate rank and corps as those of the full dress coat but the band around the sleeve and the knot are made of white braid.

The rank of General officers is indicated on the overcoat by silver stars placed between the two bands of black braid on each sleeve.

The corps, department or arm of the service to which an officer belongs is shown in two ways; first, by the color of the "facings," or distinctive color trimmings of the uniform, and second, by the insignia of the different corps, departments and arms of the service worn upon the collars and also upon the sleeves of the full dress coat, special evening dress coat, mess jackets and overcoat.

Facings.— The facings or distinctive colors for the various corps, departments and arms of the service are as follows:

General Officers (except the Quartermaster General and Brigadier Generals of the Quartermaster Corps)	dark blue.
Quartermaster General and Brigadier Generals of the Quartermaster Corps	buff.
Adjutant General's Department ..	dark blue.
Inspector General's Department ..	dark blue.
Judge Advocate General's Department	dark blue.
Quartermaster Corps	buff.
Ordnance Department	black piped with scarlet.
Signal Corps	orange piped with white.
Medical Corps	maroon.
Corps of Engineers	scarlet piped with white.
Cavalry	yellow.
Artillery	scarlet.
Infantry	light blue.
Chaplains	black.

The insignia to designate the corps, department or arm of the service to which an officer belongs, as shown in the illustrations, are made of bright metal, gold or silver according to the corps, for blue and white uniforms and dull finish bronze for service uniforms. They are worn on the sleeves of the full dress coat, special evening dress coat, blue mess jacket and white mess jacket, and on each side of the collars of the dress coat, service coats and olive-drab flannel shirt.

The bright metal insignia are as follows:

All officers.— The letters "U. S." in Gothic design, five-eighths of an inch high, each letter followed by a period, are worn on each side of the collar of the dress and service coats. For officers of the Reserve Corps the letter "R" is added and for officers of the Volunteers the letter "V" is added. These letters are of

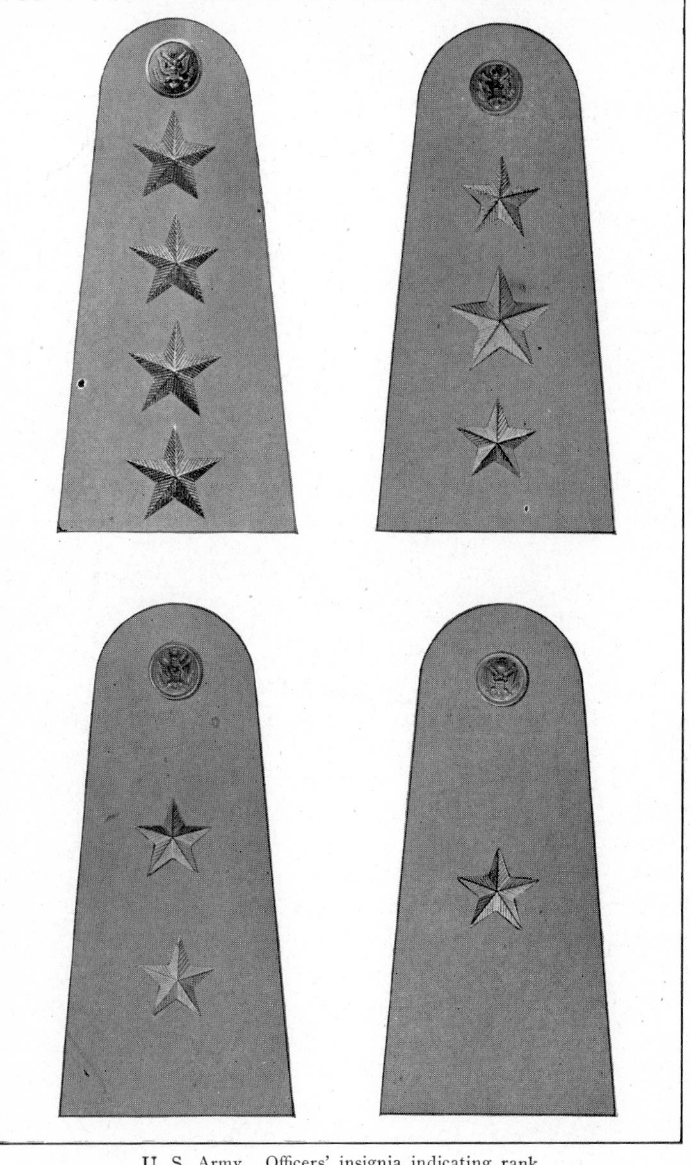

U. S. Army. Officers' insignia indicating rank

Shoulder straps worn on the olive drab service coats and the white coat

1. General
2. Lieutenant General
3. Major General
4. Brigadier General

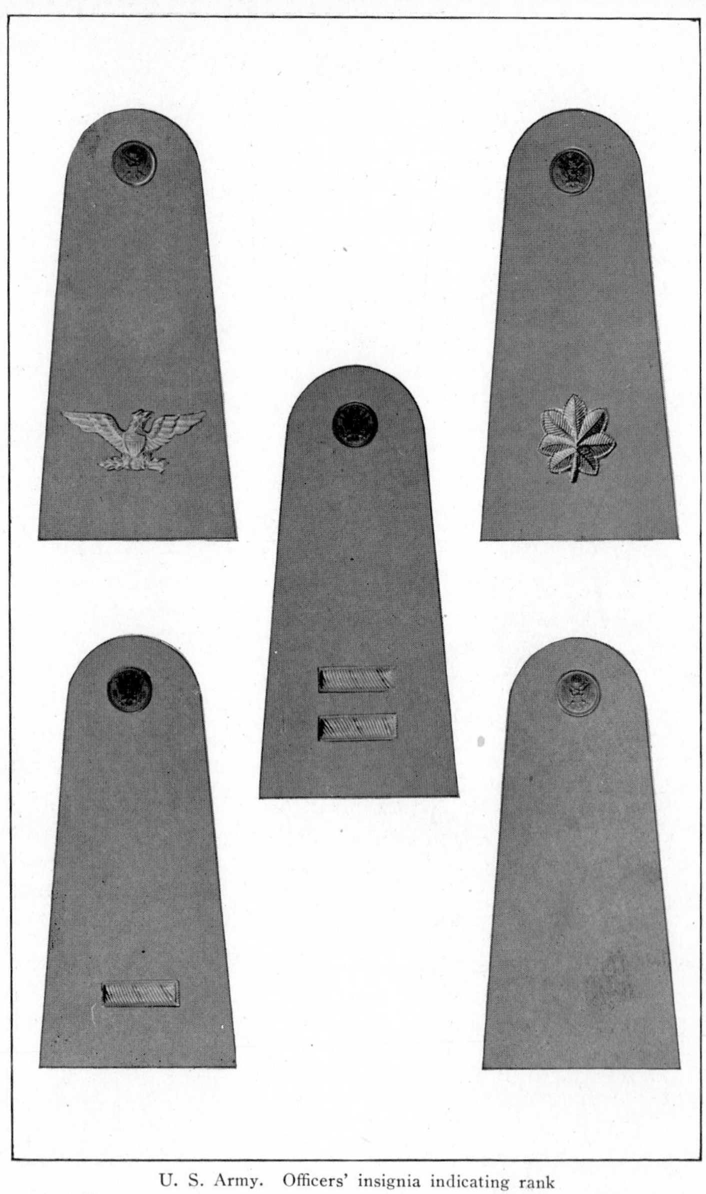

U. S. Army. Officers' insignia indicating rank

Shoulder straps worn on the olive drab service coats and the white coat

1. Colonel
2. Lieutenant Colonel (Silver Leaf), Major (Gold Leaf)
3. Captain
4. First Lieutenant (Silver Bar), Second Lieutenant (Gold Bar)
5. Field Clerk

gold except for officers of the Engineer Corps who wear them in silver.

General Staff Corps.—A gold five-pointed star one and a quarter inches in diameter surmounted by the coat of arms of the United States in gold and enamel.

Corps of Engineers.— The letters "U. S." of silver and a turretted castle of silver.

Chaplains.— A silver Latin cross.

Adjutant General's Department.— A gold shield one inch high.

Inspector General's Department.— A sword and fasces of gold, crossed and surmounted by a gold wreath with the inscription "Droit et Avant" in blue enamel on the wreath.

Judge Advocate General's Department.— A sword and pen crossed and surmounted by a wreath, all of gold.

Quartermaster Corps.— A sword and a key crossed on a wheel surmounted by an eagle, in gold except the rim of the wheel which is in blue enamel set with thirteen gold stars.

Medical Corps.— A caduceus of gold.

Medical Reserve Corps.— The same surmounted by the letters "R. C." in bronze.

Sanitary Corps.— The same surmounted by the letters "S. C."

Dental Surgeons.— The same surmounted by the letters "D. C." in bronze.

Acting Dental Surgeons.— The same in silver with gold letters.

Ordnance Department.—A flaming spherical shell of gold.

Signal Corps.— Two crossed signal flags with a vertical torch at the center, all of gold.

Cavalry.— Two sabers of gold crossed with the number of the regiment in the angle above them.

Field Artillery.— Two field guns of gold crossed with the number of the regiment in the angle above them.

Coast Artillery.— Two gold cannons crossed, surmounted at the center by an oval of red enamel with a gold projectile point up.

Infantry.— Two gold rifles crossed with the number of the regiment in the angle above them.

Philippine Scouts.— The same as for infantry but with the letter " P " in the angle above the crossed rifles.

Porto Rico Regiment.— The same but with the letters " P. R."

Aides-de-camp.—A shield of the United States surmounted by a spread eagle of gold, the stripes of the shield red and white and the field blue enamel with gold stars, the number of which correspond to the rank of the General officer upon whose staff the aide-de-camp is serving.

Regimental Staff Officers.— Regimental adjutants and quartermasters have the devices of the insignia of the Adjutant General's Department or of the Quartermaster Corps respectively in the angle below the insignia of their arm of the service.

Veterinarians.— An insignia consisting of a caduceus surcharged with the letters V. C.

Assistant Inspectors of small arms practise for regiments of the Organized Militia wear the insignia of the arm of the service to which the regiment belongs with the number of the regiment above it and a bursting shell below it.

U.S. U.S. N.A.

U.S.R. U.S. N.G.

U. S. Army. Officers' collar insignia indicating arm of the Service, Corps or Department

1. All officers of the Regular Army
2. All officers of the National Army
3. All officers of the Reserve
4. All officers of the National Guard
5. Quartermaster Corps
6. Signal Corps
7. Inspector General's Department
8. Judge Advocate General's Department

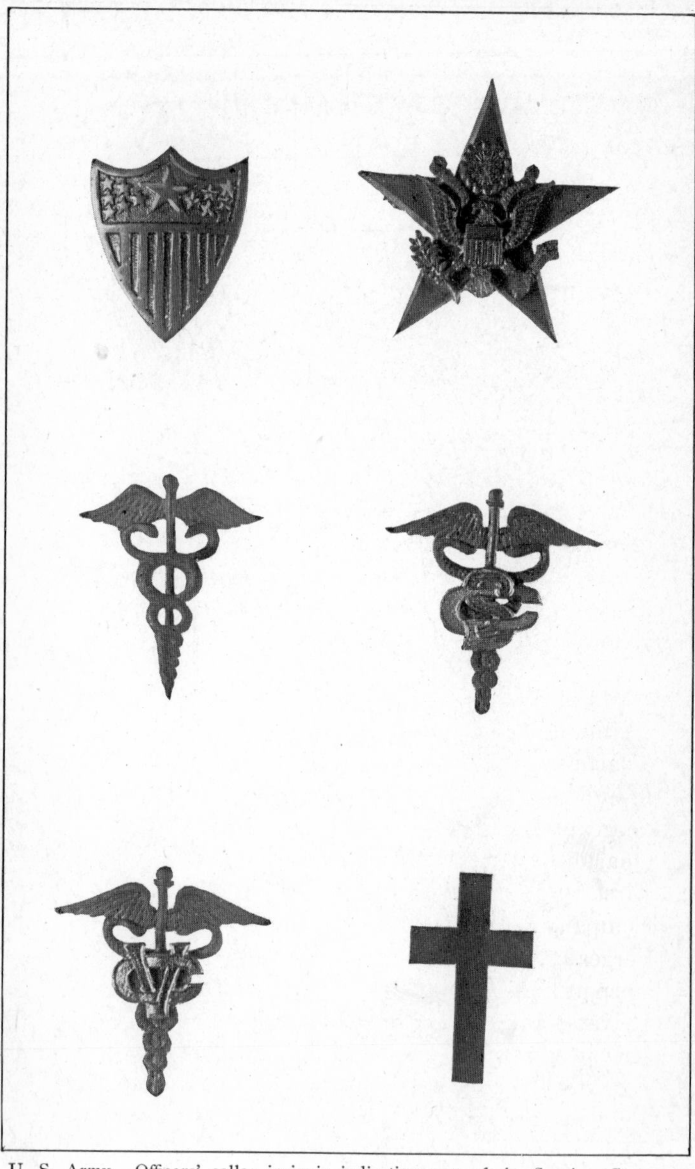

U. S. Army. Officers' collar insignia indicating arm of the Service, Corps or Department

1. Adjutant General's Department
2. General Staff Corps
3. Medical Corps
4. Sanitary Corps
5. Veterinary Corps
6. Chaplain

Uniform and Insignia of the Cadets at the U. S. Military Academy, West Point, N. Y.

The Corps of Cadets at the U. S. Military Academy at West Point, N. Y., is organized into Battalions of four companies each. The Corps of Cadets is commanded by an officer of the Army especially detailed for this duty, who, unless of actual higher rank, has the local rank and pay of a Lieutenant Colonel while performing this duty.

The Battalions are commanded by officers of the Army detailed from the Department of Tactics of the Military Academy and while performing the duty of Battalion Commanders they have the rank and pay of Majors.

The other officers of the Corps of Cadets are selected from the cadets at the Academy, the grades of rank being as follows:

Captain.
Adjutant.
Quartermaster.
Lieutenant.
Sergeant Major.
Quartermaster Sergeant.
First Sergeant.
Company Quartermaster Sergeant.
Sergeant.
Corporal.
Privates First Class, according to class standing.
Privates Second Class, according to class standing.
Privates Third Class, according to class standing.
Privates Fourth Class, according to class standing.

The insignia of these various ranks, worn on the full dress coat, are as follows:

Captains.— Chevrons of four stripes of single gold lace braid on a black background, on each arm above the elbow, points up.

Adjutant.— Chevrons of three stripes of single gold lace braid on a black background with three arcs of the same braid beneath, on each arm above the elbow, points up.

Quartermaster.— Chevrons of three stripes of single gold lace braid with three horizontal stripes of the same braid beneath on a black background, on each arm above the elbow, points up.

Lieutenants.— Chevrons of three stripes of single gold lace braid on a black background, on each arm above the elbow, points up.

Sergeant Major.— Chevrons of two stripes of single gold lace braid with two arcs of the same braid beneath on a black background, on each arm above the elbow, points up.

Quartermaster Sergeant.— Chevrons of two stripes of single gold lace braid with two horizontal stripes of the same braid beneath on a black background, on each arm above the elbow, points up.

First Sergeants.— Chevrons of two stripes of single gold lace braid with a diamond shaped lozenge in the angle beneath, on a black background, on each arm above the elbow, points up.

Company Quartermaster Sergeants.— Chevrons of two stripes of single gold lace braid with one horizontal stripe beneath, on a black background, on each arm above the elbow, points up.

Sergeants.— Chevrons of two stripes of single gold lace braid on a black background, on each arm above the elbow, points up.

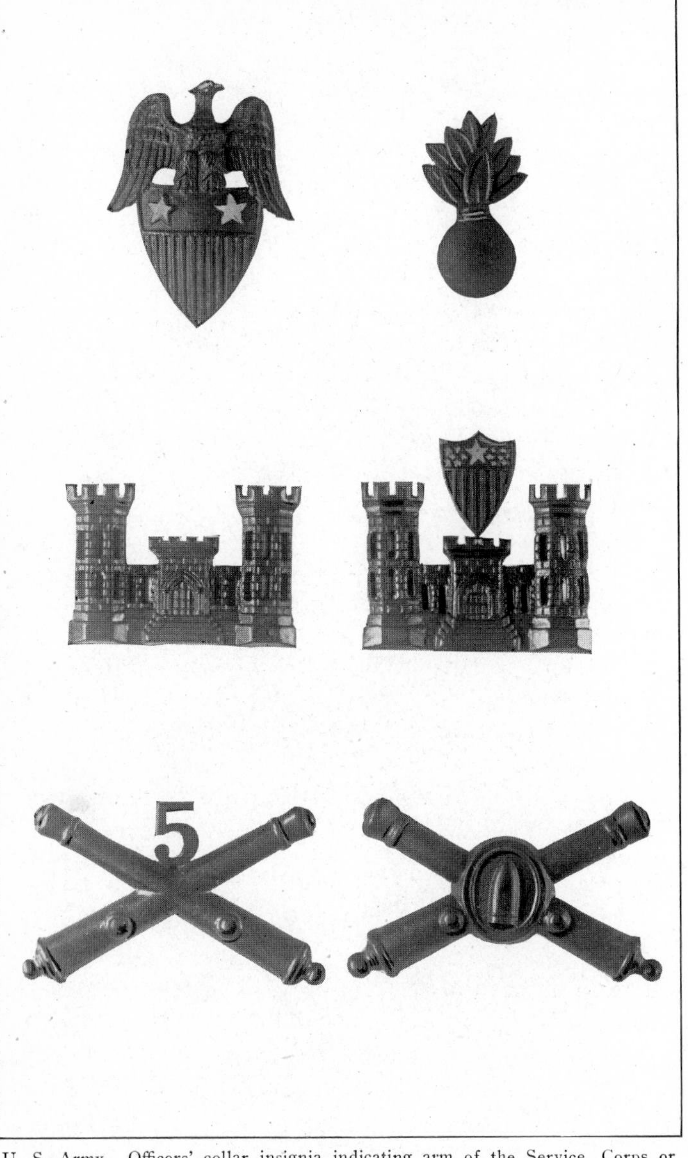

U. S. Army. Officers' collar insignia indicating arm of the Service, Corps or Department

1. Aide-de-camp to General Officer
2. Ordnance Corps
3. Engineer Corps
4. Adjutant of Engineer Corps
5. Field Artillery
6. Coast Artillery

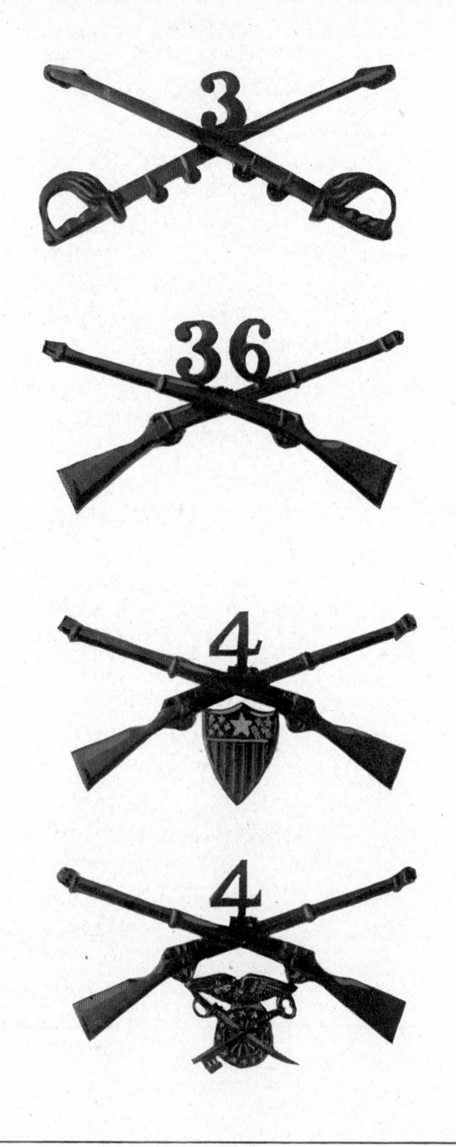

U. S. Army. Officers' collar insignia indicating arm of the Service, Corps or Department

1. Cavalry
2. Infantry
3. Adjutant of Infantry
4. Quartermaster of Infantry

Color Bearer.— Chevrons the same as for sergeants with a star in the angle beneath.

Corporals.— Chevrons of two stripes of single gold lace braid on a black background, on each arm below the elbow, points up.

Color Corporals.— Chevrons the same as for corporals with a star in the angle beneath.

On the dress coats and overcoats the chevrons worn by the Cadet Officers are of the same designs as those above described for the full dress coats except that they are made of black cloth on a gray background and those worn on the overcoats are of only one-third the size of those for the full dress and dress coats.

The Cadets are divided into four classes according to the year's course they are pursuing, the first class corresponding to the seniors at a college, the second class corresponding to the juniors, the third class corresponding to the sophomores and the fourth class corresponding to the freshmen.

The class to which a Cadet belongs is indicated by stripes worn upon the sleeves of the full-dress and dress coats and the overcoat, three stripes for the first class, two stripes for the second class, one stripe for the third class and none for the fourth class, thus each stripe shows one year of service as a Cadet.

On the sleeves of the full-dress coat these stripes are of gold soutache braid placed diagonally across the outer side between the wrist and the elbow; on the sleeves of the overcoat they are the same as for the full-dress coat except that they are made of black soutache braid; and for the dress coat the stripes are of black soutache braid placed across the outer side of the sleeve parallel to the broad black braid on the cuff.

Cadets who are classed as "Distinguished" on account of high standing in their studies and drills wear a five-pointed gold star on each side of the collar of the full-dress and dress coats.

The uniforms of the West Point cadets are of gray cloth for wear during the winter and of white duck for wear during the summer, the color of the winter uniforms being that which is usually known as "cadet gray." Each cadet is required to have complete outfits of full-dress, dress and white uniforms.

Their full-dress uniform consists of a full-dress coat, gray or white trousers, full-dress hat, black leather shoes, white waist-belt and white cross-belts. Cadet officers wear a plume of black feathers in the hat, a white sword belt and a red silk sash. The Cadet Sergeant Major, Cadet Quartermaster Sergeant and Cadet First Sergeants wear a white sword belt and a red silk sash.

The full-dress coat is of gray cloth, fitting closely, single breasted, with three rows of gilt bell buttons down the front, eight buttons in each row, one row in the center and one row on each side, the coat being cut away just below the waist line across the front and having short skirts behind. The skirts of the coat have twelve gilt bell buttons, three down the plait of each skirt, the upper one at the waist, and three placed lengthwise on each skirt. The coat has a square standing collar with one bell button on each side. Each cuff has three bell buttons. The collar, front of the coat, the cuffs and the skirt of the coat are trimmed with black silk cord in designs as shown in the illustration.

The trousers for winter wear with both the full-dress and dress uniforms are of gray cloth with black stripes one and one-half inches wide down the outer seams.

The full-dress hat is of black felt, bell crowned, six inches high, with a sloping visor. It is trimmed with

Copyright, 1908, by Brig. General J. B. Aleshire, Qr. Master General, U. S. A.

Cadets, U. S. Military Academy
Full dress, dress and service uniforms

1. Cadet, Sergeant (Dress)
2. Cadet, Private (Campaign Uniform)
3. Cadet, Corporal (Dress)
4. Cadet, First Sergeant (Full Dress)
5. Cadet, Captain (Full Dress)
6. Cadet, Adjutant (Full Dress)
7. Cadet, Private (Full Dress)
8. Captain of Infantry (Full Dress)

gilt decorations, bears the insignia of the Military Academy on a gilt plate in front, has a black pompon set in a gilt socket on the front at the center (a black plume being worn by cadet officers, instead of the pompon), and a gilt scale chain strap worn above the visor.

When mounted the cadets wear gray cloth breeches and riding leggins instead of trousers.

The dress uniform of the cadets consists of a dress coat, dress cap, gray or white trousers, black leather shoes, white waist-belt and white cross-belts and leather gloves. Cadet officers wear a white sword belt and a worsted sash.

The dress coat is of gray cloth, single breasted, with a straight standing collar, closed down the center of the front by buttons concealed beneath a fly, the coat reaching to about nine inches below the waist. The coat is trimmed around the collar, down the front, around the bottom edge and up the side seams of the back with black mohair braid one inch wide, the braid down the front being double. There is also one stripe of the same braid around each sleeve two and one-half inches from the lower edge of the cuff.

The dress cap is of gray cloth, bell crowned, three and one-half inches high, with a band of black mohair braid one and three-quarter inches wide and a sloping visor of black patent leather. In the front and center of the cap is worn the insignia of the United States Military Academy in gilt metal one and three-quarter inches high.

The overcoat is of gray kersey, double breasted, with six buttons on each side down the front, coat to reach within ten inches of the ground when the wearer is standing. It has a stand and fall collar five inches deep. There are also two buttons at the hip and one at the bottom of each plait behind. All of the buttons are gilt, seven-eighths of an inch in diameter, and bear the arms of the U. S. Military Academy with the word " Cadet " around the margin at the top and the letters " U. S. M. A." around the margin at the bottom. There is also a cape of the same material as the coat, cut circular, extending to the hip buttons. The coat and cape are lined with gray woolen material.

The raincoat is a sleeveless sack overcoat of gray water-proof material with a cape attached to the coat, the skirts of the coat extending to within eight inches of the ground.

The cadets are also furnished with a gray woolen shirt which is sometimes worn at drills without the coat.

At certain of the drills and exercises a service hat of felt similar to the " campaign hat " is worn.

UNIFORM AND INSIGNIA OF FIELD CLERKS, U. S. ARMY

By the Act of Congress of August 29, 1917, the grades of Army Field Clerk and Field Clerk Quartermaster Corps were established in the United States Army. These officers are appointed by the Secretary of War and take precedence in rank next after Cadets and before all noncommissioned officers, so that their position is similar in relative rank to that of Warrant officers in the United States Navy and Marine Corps.

The Army Field Clerks belong to the Adjutant General's Department and the Field Clerks Quartermaster Corps are a part of that corps.

They wear the same uniform as commissioned officers, omitting all insignia of rank and the brown bands of braid around the cuffs of the service coat. On their service hats they wear a hat cord of black and silver twisted strands.

Army Field Clerks wear on each side of the collar of the service coat a bronze insignia consisting of two quill pens crossed with a miniature adjutant general's shield in the lower angle.

Field Clerks Quartermaster Corps wear on each side of the collar of the service coat a bronze insignia consisting of two quill pens crossed with a miniature Quartermaster Corps insignia in the lower angle.

ENLISTED MEN'S UNIFORMS, U. S. ARMY

The enlisted men of the Army are required to have complete outfits of service uniform for winter and summer, dress uniform and fatigue uniform, and in addition cooks and bakers, members of the Hospital Corps and members of the general recruiting service have white uniforms.

The occasions upon which the different uniforms are worn are given in the regulations as follows:

TABLE OF OCCASIONS

Occasion.	Uniform
1. For habitual garrison wear until retreat, when not under arms. 2. For habitual garrison wear under arms. 3. For inspection and guard mounting, when ordered by the commanding officer. 4. For all other ceremonies when the weather or climate will not permit the wearing of dress or full dress. 5. When changing station by rail or water.	Service uniform with the service cap.

Occasion.	Uniform
6. For field duty.	Service uniform with the service hat. In the trenches the steel helmet is worn.
7. For habitual wear in garrison after retreat and when on leave. 8. For parade and ceremonies except inspection and guard mounting, when weather and climate permit.	Dress uniform. In the Tropics and in hot weather the cotton service uniform (khaki) is worn instead.
9. For parade and other ceremonies garrison (except inspection and guard mounting) when ordered. 10. For all ceremonies other than garrison when ordered.	Full dress uniform.
11. For cooks and bakers when at work in kitchen or bakery. 12. For Hospital Corps men on duty in hospital wards, operating rooms, etc. 13. For members of the general recruiting service when on duty at recruiting stations, etc., when prescribed.	White uniform.
14. On fatigue duty in stables, at mountain battery drills, at work or drill at emplacements of the Coast Artillery.	Fatigue uniform.

The service uniform for enlisted men of the Army consists of a single breasted sack coat of olive drab woolen or cotton material, extending to about ten inches below the waist, with a standing collar, buttoned down the front with one row of five regulation bronze buttons, having four outside patch pockets, one on each breast and on each side below the waist line, each pocket

U. S. Army. Non-commissioned officers, olive drab service uniform

1. Color Sergeant, Infantry
2. First Sergeant, Field Artillery
3. Company Quartermaster Sergeant, Cavalry
4. Sergeant, Signal Corps
5. Sergeant Major, Infantry

U. S. Army. Enlisted men, Infantry, full dress uniform

1. Corporal 2. First Sergeant 3. Private 4. Musician 5. Sergeant

being closed with a shield shaped flap buttoned by a small regulation button, and a strap of the same material as the coat on each shoulder sewed in at the shoulder seam and buttoned at the collar end by a small regulation button; breeches of the same material as the coat, khaki colored canvas leggings, tan leather shoes; and a service cap or service hat. The service cap is a bell crowned cap with a sloping tan leather visor and a tan leather chin strap across the front above the visor secured by a small bronze button at each end of the visor. The service hat is the brown felt wide brimmed hat universally called the "campaign hat" and is worn with what is known as the "Montana peak," that is, brought to a point at the center of the top of the crown by making four dents in the top of the crown. A hat cord of the distinctive color of the corps or arm of the service to which the wearer belongs is worn around the base of the crown of the service hat. During war the steel helmet is worn when on duty in the trenches or on the battle line. In garrison the tan leather belt is worn with the service uniform, and in the field the webbing cartridge belt of the same color as the uniform is worn.

Mounted men wear spurs and tan leather leggings with this uniform.

In the tropics and in hot weather the service uniform of cotton material is worn, and at drills and in the field, the coat is sometimes dispensed with and the olive drab flannel shirt is worn.

The overcoat and gloves of olive-drab wool are worn when the weather requires.

During time of war this is the only uniform worn by the men or carried by them into the field of operations.

The dress uniform for enlisted men consists of a single breasted coat of dark blue cloth, extending to about ten inches below the waist, with a standing collar, buttoned down the front with one row of six gilt regulation buttons and having a strap of dark blue cloth on each shoulder; the dress cap of dark blue cloth; sky-blue cloth trousers; a white collar; and tan leather shoes. When under arms in this uniform white gloves are worn except when the overcoat is worn, in which case olive-drab gloves are worn. The dress coat is trimmed around the top and base of the collar and down the front edges of the collar, around the edges of the shoulder straps and around each sleeve four inches from the bottom edge by a narrow piping of the distinctive color of the arm of the service or corps to which the wearer belongs, and there are three small regulation gilt buttons on each cuff and one at the collar end of each shoulder strap.

The trousers of noncommissioned officers have stripes of the same distinctive color down the outer leg seams, the stripes for corporals being one-half inch wide and those for higher noncommissioned officers being one and one-quarter inches wide, those for musicians being double, each part one-half inch wide.

The dress caps for enlisted men are made of a dark blue cloth with a bell crown, a black patent leather sloping visor and a half-inch chin strap of patent leather worn above the visor and secured by a gilt button at each end of the visor. There is one stripe around the band of the cap at the upper edge of the band and one at the lower edge of the band, each stripe being one-half inch in width and of the distinctive color of the corps or arm of the service to which the wearer belongs, these distinctive colors being those as given for the "facings."

The tan leather or garrison belt is worn with the dress uniform.

U. S. Army. Non-commissioned officers' chevrons

1. Regimental Sergeant Major
2. Battalion or Squadron Sergeant Major
3. Color Sergeant
4. Drum Major

U. S. Army. Non-commissioned officers' chevrons

1. Regimental Supply Sergeant
2. Sergeant of Field Music
3. Mess Sergeant
4. Lance Corporal

The overcoat is worn with it when the weather requires it.

Mounted men wear breeches with this uniform, the color and trimmings being the same as for the trousers, and riding gloves, riding leggings and spurs.

The full dress uniform for enlisted men is the same as their dress uniform with the addition of a breast cord of the distinctive color of the corps or arm of the service to which they belong. This breast cord is a double plaited loop of round cord worn from one shoulder to the other across the breast with a single cord passing across the back and the front loop ending on the right side in two plaited plates and two tassels.

The fatigue uniform consists of brown canvas or duck working coat and trousers. This is a working uniform. A fur cap is furnished for wear in very cold weather.

The overcoat for enlisted men is a double breasted ulster made of olive-drab cloth, extending eight to ten inches below the knee (overcoats extending to the knee are authorized for wear in the field), buttoning to the neck with two rows of large flat buttons of the same color as the coat, and having a wide rolling collar. It has a pleat down the center of the back.

Rain clothes for enlisted men are olive-drab waterproof coats or the poncho or rubber blanket worn in the fashion of a cape. Rubber boots are used when required, as in wet trenches.

INSIGNIA OF RANK FOR ENLISTED MEN

The rank of the various noncommissioned officers of the United States Army and Marine Corps and the rating of the corresponding petty officers of the Navy is usually indicated by chevrons, a form of badge derived from the days when heraldry played a great part in the world's affairs.

"Chevron" is an architectural term denoting the rafters of a roof meeting at an angle at the upper apex, and it is derived from the French word "*chevre,*" a goat, and so used on account of the fancied resemblance of a pair of such rafters to the horns of a goat.

The chevron in heraldry was employed as a badge of honor to mark the main supporters of the head of the clan, "the top of the house," and it came to be used in various forms as an emblem of rank for the knights and men-at-arms in feudal days, and from this resulted its common use as an insignia of rank in the armies and navies of the present day.

In some countries chevrons are used as insignia of rank for commissioned officers as well as for noncommissioned officers, but in the United States service the use of chevrons is confined to the latter class.

In the United States Army and Marine Corps the chevrons are worn with the point up but in the Navy they are worn with the point down.

The chevrons indicating the rank of noncommissioned officers are worn midway between the shoulder and the elbow on both sleeves of the service coats, full dress coat and overcoat.

The chevrons for the dress coat are 3¼ inches wide made of stripes of cloth of the distinctive color of the corps, department or arm of the service, each stripe being ⅜ of an inch wide.

These distinctive colors for the chevrons for noncommissioned officers of the various corps, departments and arms of the service are:

U. S. Army. Non-commissioned officers' chevrons

1. First Sergeant
2. Company Supply Sergeant
3. Sergeant
4. Corporal

U. S. Army. Non-commissioned officers' chevrons

1. Electrician Sergeant, First Class
2. Electrician Sergeant, Second Class
3. Battalion Supply Sergeant
4. Stable Sergeant

U. S. Army. Non-commissioned officers' chevrons
Coast Artillery Corps

1. Master Electrician
2. Engineer, Coast Artillery Corps
3. Master Gunner
4. Fireman, Coast Artillery Corps

U. S. Army. Non-commissioned officers' chevrons
Coast Artillery Corps

1. Gun Commander
2. Gun Pointer
3. Casemate Electrician
4. Chief Planter and Chief Loader
5. First Class Gunner
6. Second Class Gunner
7. First Class Observer and Plotter
8. Second Class Observer

Field Artillery and Coast Artillery scarlet.
Cavalry .... yellow.
Infantry .... white.
Engineers .... scarlet piped with white.
Ordnance .... black piped with white.
Hospital Corps .... maroon piped with white.
Quartermaster Corps .... buff.
Army Service Detachment, U. S.
Military Academy .... green piped with white.
Army Service School Detachment. green.

The chevrons for the service coats, the overcoat and the olive drab shirt are of the same size and design as those for the dress coat except that they are made of olive-drab material, the shade being slightly darker than that of the coat.

There are also a number of special badges to designate certain men assigned to special duties, such as cook, chief mechanics, artificer, farrier, saddler, horseshoer, first and second class gunners, electricians, engineer, gun commander and gun pointer. These special badges are of the same color as the chevrons and are worn in the same manner.

The chevrons and special badges for the different ranks and duties in the various corps, departments and arms of the service are as follows:

Regimental Sergeant Major — Chevron of three stripes and three arcs of a circle below them.
Sergeant Major Senior Grade, Coast Artillery — The same.
Quartermaster Sergeant, Senior Grade — The Quartermaster Corps insignia with a wreath below and a star above it.
Master Hospital Sergeant — The caduceus insignia of the Medical Corps with a wreath below and a star above it.
Master Engineer, Senior Grade — The castle insignia of the Engineer Corps with a wreath below and a star above it.
Master Electrician, Coast Artillery — A design representing

forked lightning with a wreath below it and a star above.

Master Electrician, Signal Corps — A wreath with forked lightning at the top and the Signal Corps insignia in the center.

Master Electrician, Quartermaster Corps — A wreath with forked lightning at the top and the Quartermaster Corps insignia in the center.

Band Leader — Chevron of three stripes and two arcs of a circle below them with a trumpet in the center.

Hospital Sergeant, First Class — Chevron of three stripes and one arc of a circle below them with a caduceus in the center.

Hospital Sergeant — Chevron of three stripes with a caduceus below them.

Engineer Coast Artillery Corps — A design representing an engine governor with a wreath below it and a star above.

Ordnance Sergeant — Chevron of three bars with one arc below it and the insignia of the Ordnance Corps in the center.

Sergeant Quartermaster Corps — Chevron of three stripes with the insignia of the Quartermaster Corps below them.

Supply Sergeant, Regimental — Chevrons of three stripes with three horizontal bars below them.

Battalion or Squadron Sergeant Major — Chevron of three stripes with two arcs of a circle below them.

Sergeant Major Junior Grade, Coast Artillery — Chevron of three stripes with two arcs of a circle below them.

Supply Sergeant, Battalion — Chevron of three stripes with two horizontal bars below them.

First Sergeant — Chevron of three stripes with a diamond shaped lozenge below them.

Sergeant First Class, Medical Department — Chevron of three stripes and an arc below them with the caduceus device in the center.

Sergeant, First Class, Quartermaster Corps — Chevron of three stripes with one horizontal stripe below and the Quartermaster Corps insignia in the center.

Sergeant, First Class, Corps of Engineers — Chevron of three stripes with one arc of a circle below them and the Engineer Corps insignia in the center.

U. S. Army. Non-commissioned officers' chevrons
Quartermaster Corps

1. Quartermaster Sergeant
2. Sergeant, First Class
3. Sergeant
4. Corporal

U. S. Army. Non-commissioned officers' chevrons
Signal Corps

1. Sergeant, First Class
2. Sergeant
3. Corporal
4. Lance Corporal

Sergeant First Class, Signal Corps — Chevron of three stripes with one arc of a circle below and the Signal Corps insignia in the center.

Electrician Sergeant, First Class, Coast Artillery— Chevron of three stripes with a wreath below it and a device representing forked lightning in the center and a short stripe between the wreath and the lightning.

Assistant Engineer, Coast Artillery — A device representing an engine governor with a wreath below it.

Master Gunner, Coast Artillery — A projectile placed vertically with a wreath below it and a star above it.

Band Sergeant and Assistant Leader of U. S. Military Academy Band — Chevron of three stripes and two arcs of a circle below them and a lyre in the center.

Assistant Band Leader — Chevron of three stripes and one arc of a circle below them and a trumpet in the center.

Sergeant Bugler — Chevron of three stripes with a bugle below them.

Electrician Sergeant Second Class, Coast Artillery — Chevron of three stripes with a wreath below them and a device representing forked lightning in the center.

Radio Sergeant — Chevron of three stripes with a device representing forked lightning below them.

Color Sergeant — Chevron of three stripes with a star below.

Sergeant — Chevron of three bars.

Company Supply Sergeant — Chevron of three stripes with one horizontal bar below them.

Mess Sergeant — Chevron of three stripes with a crescent below them.

Stable Sergeant — Chevron of three stripes with a horse's head below them.

Fireman, Coast Artillery — Chevron of one stripe with one arc of a circle below it and a device representing the governor of an engine in the center.

Corporal — Chevron of two stripes.

Lance Corporal (Acting Corporal) — Chevron of one stripe.

Chief Mechanic — Two hammers crossed with a wreath below them.

Cook — A device representing a cook's hat.
Artificer — Two hammers crossed.
Horseshoer — A horseshoe, toe up.
Mechanic — Two hammers crossed.
Saddler — A saddler's round knife, edge up.
Wagoner — An eight spoke wheel.
Musician — A lyre.
Trumpeter — A bugle.
First class Private of Engineers — The castle insignia of the Engineer Corps.
First class Private, Signal Corps — The Signal Corps insignia, two crossed flags and a vertical torch.
First class Private Ordnance Corps — The Ordnance Corps insignia, a bursting spherical shell.
First class Private Hospital Corps — The Hospital Corps insignia, a caduceus.
First class Private, Quartermaster Corps — The insignia of the Quartermaster Corps.
Casemate Electrician, Coast Artillery — A mine case with a bar below it, enclosed in a circle.
Badge for Excellence at Target Practice, Coast Artillery — The figure "1."
Chief Planter, Coast Artillery — A mine case enclosed in a circle.
First class Gunner, Gun Company, Coast Artillery — A projectile, point up, with a bar below it.
Second class Gunner, Gun Company, Coast Artillery — A projectile, point up.
First class Gunner, Mine Company, Coast Artillery — A mine case with a bar below it.
Second class Gunner, Mine Company, Coast Artillery — A mine case.
Gun Commander, Coast Artillery — Two crossed cannon with a bar below, enclosed in a circle.
Gun Pointer, Coast Artillery — Two crossed cannon enclosed in a circle.
Observer and plotter, Coast Artillery — An equilateral triangle with a bar below it, enclosed in a circle.
Observer, Second Class, Coast Artillery — An equilateral triangle enclosed in a circle.

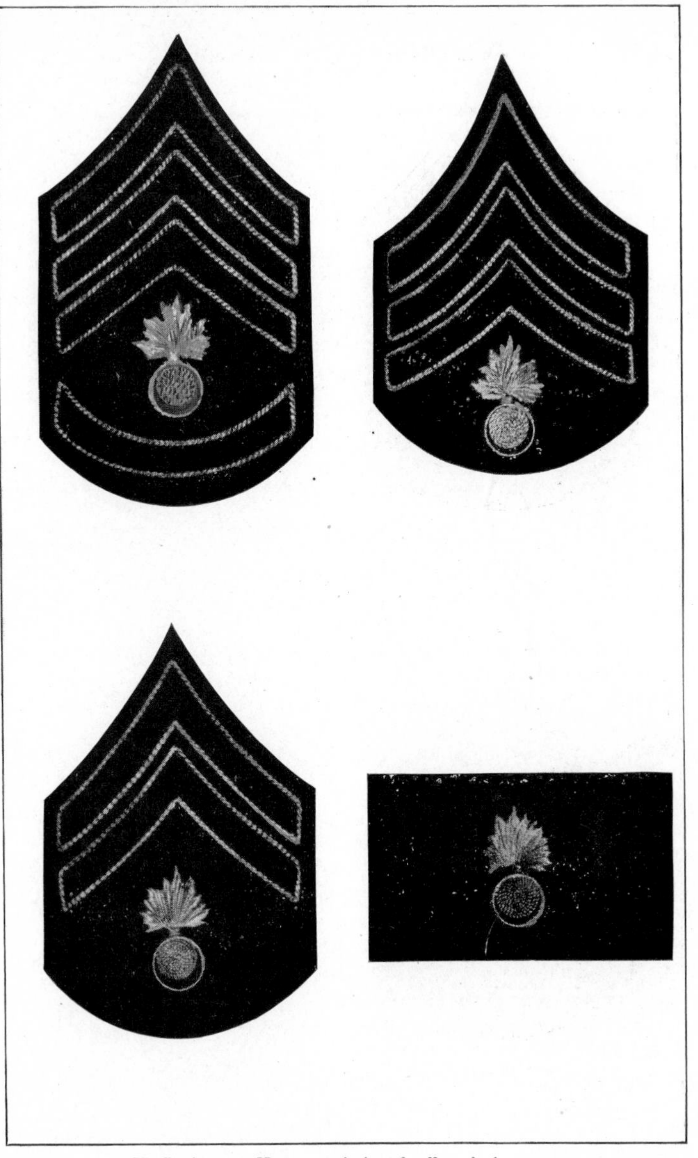

U. S. Army. Non-commissioned officers' chevrons

Ordnance Corps

1. Ordnance Sergeant
2. Sergeant of Ordnance Corps
3. Corporal of Ordnance Corps
4. First Class Private of Ordnance Corps

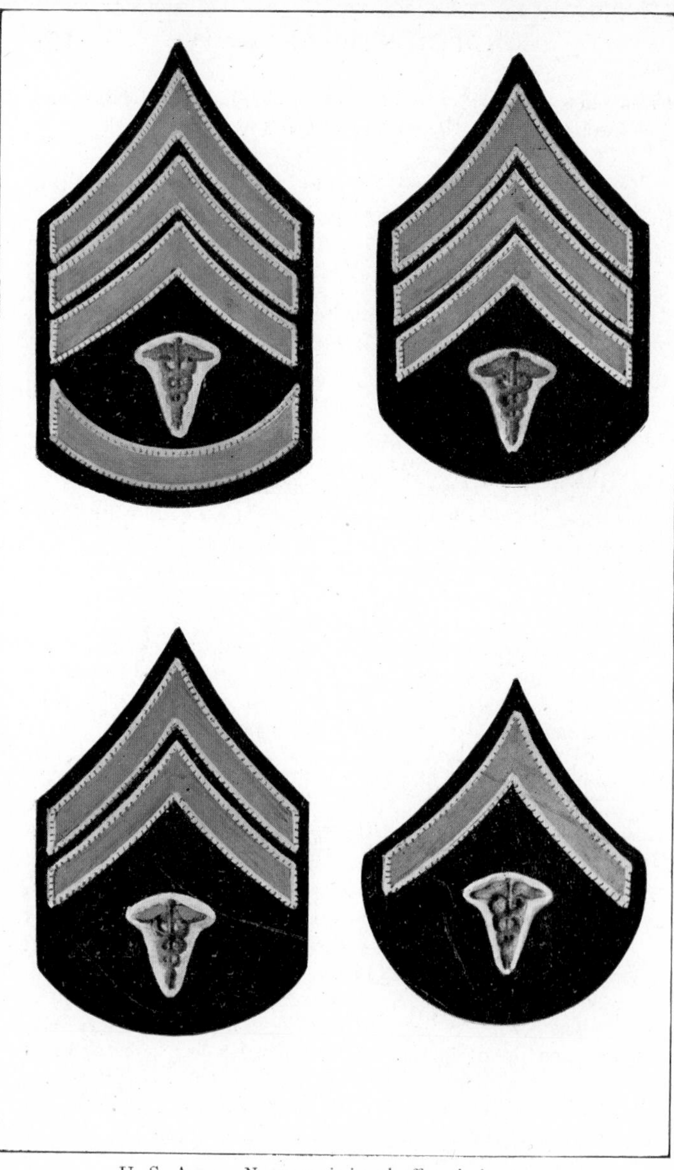

U. S. Army. Non-commissioned officers' chevrons
Medical Corps

1. Sergeant, First Class
2. Sergeant
3. Corporal
4. Lance Corporal

First class Private, Signal Corps — The crossed flags and torch device of the Signal Corps.

The corps, detachment or arm of the service of an enlisted man of the United States Army is indicated by the special devices worn upon the front of the cap and upon the collars of the coats. The devices for caps are of gilt metal for the blue cap and of dull finish bronze metal for the olive drab service cap. They are, as shown in the illustrations, as follows:

Cavalry — Two sabers in their scabbards, crossed with the edges up, with the number of the regiment in the upper angle and the letter of the troop in the lower angle.

Artillery — Two cannon, crossed with their muzzles up, with the number of the regiment in the upper angle and the letter of the battery in the lower angle for the Field Artillery and the number of the company in the lower angle for the Coast Artillery.

Infantry — Two rifles, crossed with the muzzles up, the number of the regiment in the upper angle and the letter of the company in the lower angle, for the Porto Rico Regiment the letters "P. R." in the upper angle, and for the Philippine Native troops the letter "P" in the upper angle.

Engineers — The turretted castle device of the Engineer Corps with the number of the regiment above it and the letter of the company below it.

Hospital Corps — The caduceus device of the Hospital Corps.

Quartermaster Corps — A sword and a key crossed on a wheel surmounted by a spread eagle.

Signal Corps — Two signal flags crossed with a torch placed vertically in the center.

Band Musician — A lyre with the number or letters surcharged upon the face indicating the corps or regiment to which the band belongs; for the coast artillery the number of the band, for the Engineer band a castle, for Infantry, Cavalry and Field Artillery bands the number of the regiment, for the Military Academy band the letters "M. A.", for bands of the Native troops in the Philippines the letter "P", for the band of the Porto Rico Regiment the letter "P. R.", for the bands of the Disciplinary Barracks the letters "D. B. G.", and for the Recruiting Service the letters "R. S."

Field Musician (Trumpeter) — A trumpet, with the number of the regiment above and the letter of the company in the center.

Master Signal Electrician, Master Electrician and Electrical Sergeants — A wreath enclosing a device representing forked lighting.

Ordnance Corps — A wreath enclosing the bursting shell device of the Ordnance Corps.

Quartermaster Sergeants — A wreath enclosing the device of the Quartermaster Corps.

Master Hospital Sergeant and Sergeant First Class, Hospital Corps — A wreath enclosing a caduceus.

Noncommissioned officers of the Signal Corps (except Master Signal Electrician) — A wreath enclosing the flag and torch device of the Signal Corps.

General Recruiting Service — A wreath enclosing the letters "R. S."

U. S. Military Academy Detachments — A cogged wheel enclosing a hammer and a quill crossed.

U. S. Army Disciplinary Barracks Guard. — A wreath enclosing the letters "D. B. G."

Noncommissioned Staff officers do not wear the letters of the company, battery or troop as they are not attached to any company but they do wear the numbers of the regiment when attached to a regiment.

The permanent detachments at the U. S. Military Academy at West Point wear the following cap devices according to the arm of the service:

Artillery ....Two cannon crossed with the letters "M. A." in the upper angle and the letters "D. E. T." in the lower angle.

U. S. Army. Non-comm.ssioned officers' chevrons

1. Band Leader
2. Assistant Leader, West Point Band
3. Chief Trumpeter
4. Sergeant, Band

U. S. Army. Non-commissioned officers' chevrons

1. Master Electrician, Quartermaster Corps
2. Master Signal Electrician
3. First Class Private, Signal Corps
4. Wagoner
5. First Class Private, Quartermaster Corps
6. Farrier
7. Chief Mechanic
8. Mechanic or Artificer

Cavalry ....Two sabers crossed with the letters "M. A." in the upper angle and the letters "D. E. T." in the lower angle.

Engineers ....A castle with the letters " M. A." above it and the letters " D. E. T." across the center of the castle.

Field Musician ....A trumpet with the letters " M. A." (Trumpeter) above it and the letters " D. E. T." in the center.

Collar Insignia.— The insignia worn on each side of the collar of the blue dress coat to indicate the corps, detachment or arm of the service are of gilt metal and of the same description as given above for the cap insignia, with the exception that in the case where the cap insignia have a wreath encircling them it is omitted from the collar insignia.

Army Aviation Corps Insignia.— Distinguishing marks are provided for the officers and enlisted men of the Aviation Corps in order that they may be readily recognized. These insignia are embroidered in silver on a blue background and are worn upon the left breast of the coat or shirt and consist of the following devices for the various ranks:

Aviator.— A shield with an eagle's wing on each side extending horizontally to the right and to the left of it, and a five-pointed star above it, the shield having the letter " U. S." upon it.

Junior Aviator and Reserve Aviator.— The same without the star.

Observer.— The same without the right wing.

Enlisted Aviators.— A design representing the propeller of an airplane with an eagle's wing extending to the right and left of it.

Student Aviators.— The distinctive mark is a white

band worn around the service cap and around the left sleeve.

Aviation Mechanics.— A circle surrounding an airplane propeller, the number of the squadron being placed above the circle.

Enlisted men on duty in the Aviation Corps.— A design representing an airplane propeller with the number of the squadron above it.

The letters designating the nationality of the enlisted men of the United States Army are worn upon each side of the collar of the blue dress coat one inch from the neck opening in front, with the devices indicating the corps, department or arm of the service five-eighths of an inch in rear of the letters. These letters are of Gothic design five-eighths of an inch in height and are,

" U. S." for the regular service.

" U. S. R." for the reserves.

" U. S. V." for the volunteers.

" U. S. S." for enlisted scouts.

" U. S." surcharged with the letters " N. A." for the National Army.

" U. S." surcharged with the letters " N. G." for the National Guard of the several states and territories taken into the service of the United States.

The insignia worn on the collars of the service coats consist of dull bronze metal discs one inch in diameter, the one worn on the right side of the collar bearing in relief the letters " U. S." and the one worn on the left side of the collar bearing in relief the distinctive insignia of the corps, department or arm of the service, as shown in the illustrations.

Brassards are bands of white or colored cloth worn upon the arms to designate officers and enlisted men assigned to certain special duties.

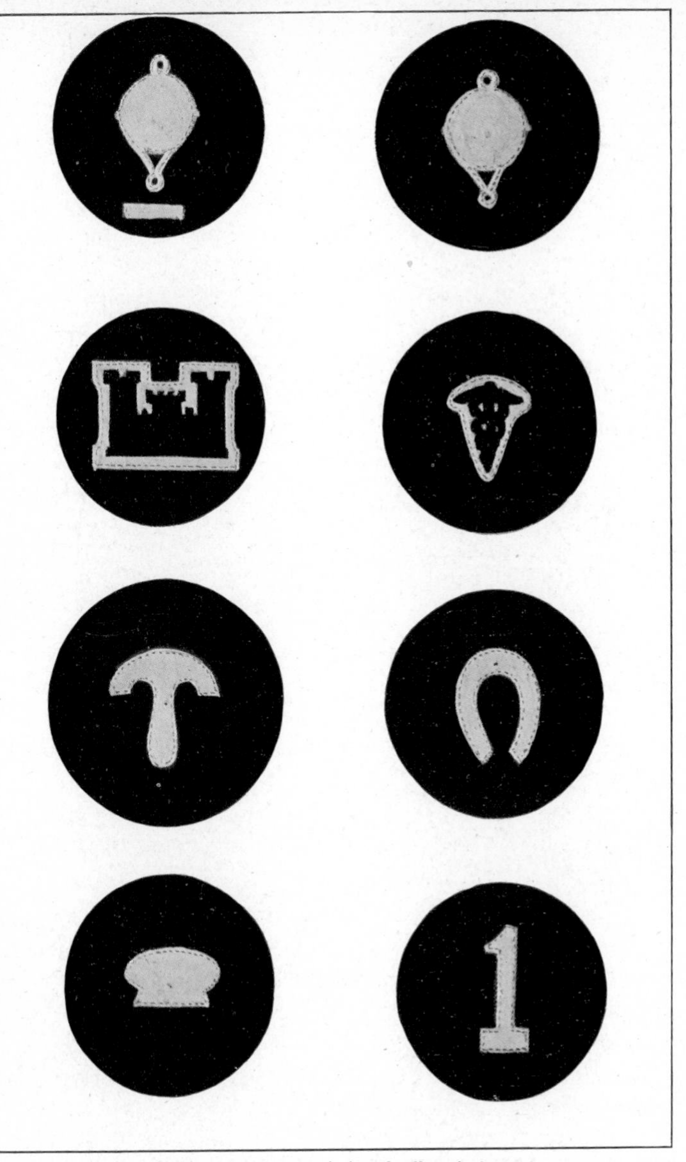

U. S. Army. Non-commissioned officers' chevrons

1. First Class Gunner, Mine Company
2. Second Class Gunner, Mine Company
3. First Class Private, Engineer Corps
4. First Class Private, Hospital Corps
5. Saddler, Cavalry
6. Horseshoer, Cavalry
7. Cook
8. Badge for Excellence in Target Practice, Coast Artillery

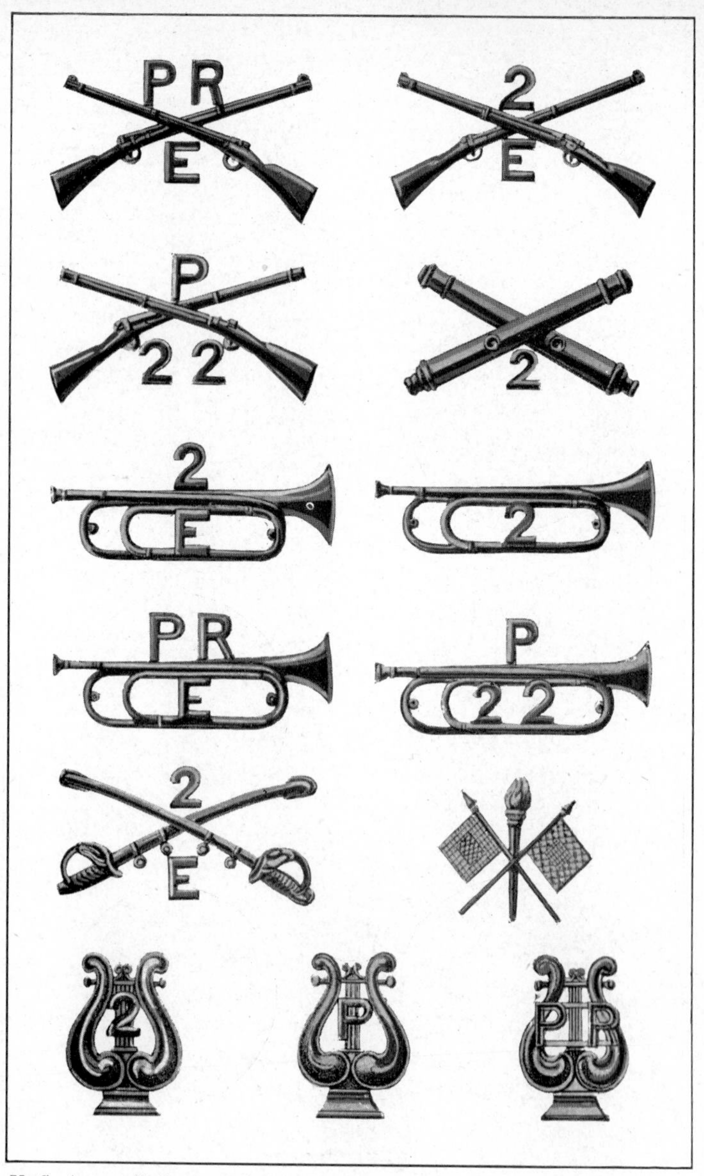

U. S. Army. Enlisted men's insignia worn on front of caps indicating arm of the Service, Corps or Department

1. Infantry, Porto Rico Regiment
2. Infantry
3. Native Philippine Troops
4. Artillery
5. Musician, Infantry; Trumpeter, Cavalry
6. Musician, Artillery
7. Musician, Porto Rico Regiment
8. Musician, Philippines
9. Cavalry
10. Signal Corps
11. Band Musician
12. Band, Philippines
13. Band, Porto Rico

Red Cross Brassard.— In time of war with signatories of the Geneva Convention all persons in the military services who are rendered neutral by the terms of that convention wear upon the left arm above the elbow a brassard of white cloth bearing upon it a Geneva cross in red cloth while on duty in the field of operations. The persons entitled to wear this brassard are surgeons, members of the hospital corps, nurses, chaplains and the personnel engaged exclusively with the removal and transportation of the sick and wounded.

Red Brassard.— The authorized mounted orderlies of infantry and cavalry regiments, the mounted men assigned as orderlies to general officers in command of brigades and higher units and the agents of communication of field artillery while on duty in the field wear a red brassard on the right forearm.

White Brassard.— Student aviators undergoing instruction in flying (sometimes called flying cadets) wear a white brassard on the arm.

Field Clerk's Brassard.— Field clerks of Engineers wear upon the left arm above the elbow a brassard of maroon colored cloth with white edges.

Service Stripes.— All enlisted men of the Army who have served one or more enlistments in the Army, Navy or Marine Corps wear one stripe for each such enlistment on each sleeve of the dress coat midway between the wrist and the elbow. These service stripes are three-eighths of an inch in width and are placed diagonally across the outside of the sleeve.

The color of the stripe is that of the branch of the service in which the enlistment that it represents was served, as follows:

Cavalry, yellow.

Artillery, scarlet.

Engineers, scarlet piped with white.

Infantry, white.

Hospital Corps, maroon piped with white.

Ordnance, black piped with scarlet.

Signal Corps, orange piped with white.

Quartermaster Corps, buff.

Service School Detachment, green.

Service Detachment, Military Academy, green piped with white.

U. S. Navy, scarlet piped with yellow.

U. S. Marine Corps, yellow piped with scarlet.

Buttons.— The buttons worn by enlisted men of the Army on the dress coat are of gilt metal and bear the coat of arms of the United States in relief; those worn on the service coats are of the same size and design but are made of dull finish bronze metal, and those worn on the overcoat are large bronze flat buttons of the same design.

Identification Tag.— Each officer and enlisted man of the U. S. Army is required to wear two aluminum identification tags about the size of a silver half dollar whenever the field kit is worn, one tag to be suspended from the neck underneath the clothing by a cord or thong of leather passed through a hole in the tag, the second tag being suspended from the first one by a cord or thong. Each tag bears stamped upon it the name, rank, company, regiment and corps of the wearer. This tag is for use in identifying the wearer in case of death or serious wounds. In case of death one tag is buried with the body and the duplicate is kept with the record of the place of burial and the cause and date of death.

Identification Patch.— In order that the men in an advance line of attack upon the battlefield may be recog-

U. S. Army. Enlisted men's insignia worn on front of caps indicating arm of the Service, Corps or Department

1. Quartermaster Sergeant
2. Mess Sergeant
3. Sergeant, First-class, Hospital Corps
4. Ordnance Sergeant
5. Master Signal Electrician, Master Electrician, Electrician Sergeant
6. Non-commissioned officer, Signal Corps
7. Hospital Corps
8. Engineer Corps
9. Quartermaster Corps
10. Band Musician, Engineers
11. Musician, Engineers
12. Ordnance Corps

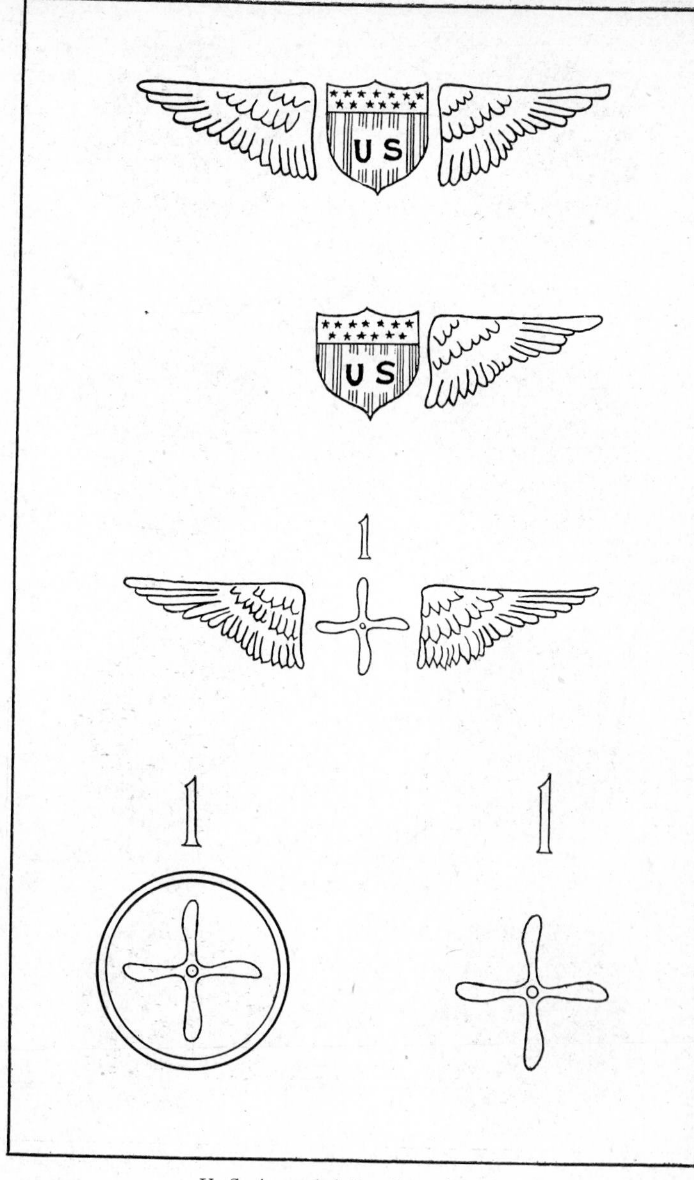

U. S. Army Aviation Corps insignia

1. Aviator (Regular aviators have a silver star above the shield. Junior and Reserve aviators have no star)
2. Observer
3. Enlisted Aviator
4. Aviation Mechanic
5. Other enlisted men

U. S. Army. Enlisted men's insignia worn on collars of service coats

1. All enlisted men, right side of collar
2. Cavalry
3. Infantry
4. Field Artillery
5. Coast Artillery
6. Engineer Corps
7. Quartermaster Corps
8. Signal Corps

U. S. Army. Enlisted men's insignia worn on collars of service coats

1. Hospital Corps
2. Ordnance Corps
3. Band Musician
4. Electrician
5. Infantry, Porto Rico Regiment
6. Infantry, Native Troops, Philippines
7. Recruiting Service
8. Prison Guard

nized by the officers who are controlling their advance and accurately placing the curtain of shrapnel fire ahead of them, it has become necessary to prescribe identification patches upon the backs of the men's coats between the shoulders. These identification patches are of different designs and colors to mark the different regiments and brigades, circles, triangles, squares and other shapes being used. The shape and color of these patches is not laid down in uniform regulations in the United States Army, but these details are prescribed from time to time in orders from Headquarters of the Field Armies.

SEAL OF THE U. S. NAVY DEPARTMENT

CHAPTER V

UNIFORMS AND INSIGNIA OF THE U. S. NAVY

THE uniforms of the officers and enlisted men of the United States Navy are made of dark blue cloth for wear in cold or temperate weather and of white duck for wear in hot or tropical weather.

U. S. NAVAL OFFICERS' UNIFORMS

Commissioned officers of the Navy are required to have complete outfits of special full dress, evening dress, full dress, undress, blue service dress and white service dress uniforms; the occasions upon which the various uniforms are required to be worn by officers of the Navy and the Marine Corps being given in the official regulations as follows:

Copyright, Harris & Ewing, Washington, D. C.

Admiral William S. Benson
Chief of Naval Operations, United States Navy

Occasion.	Uniform.
1. State occasions, at home or abroad. 2. Receiving or being received by the President, an ex-President, the Vice-President, or the Secretary of the Navy of the United States, or the sovereign, chief executive or ruler of any country, or any member of a royal family, or an ambassador of the United States or of any country, at home or abroad. 3. At ceremonies, solemnities, or entertainments, when desirable to do special honor to the occasion. 4. At general inspection on the first Saturday in the month. In inclement weather, service dress may be prescribed.	Navy.— Special full dress, or white special full dress. Marine Corps.— Special full dress (with full dress trousers, if in line with troops), or white special full dress.
5. First visits to officers of flag rank, or exchanging visits of ceremony with foreign officials. 6. Ceremonies, solemnities, or entertainments where dress uniform is not sufficient.	Navy.— Full dress, or white full dress. Marine Corps.— Special full dress (with full dress trousers, if in line with troops), or white full dress.
7. Reception of — (a) Assistant Secretary of the Navy. (b) Member of the President's Cabinet other than the Secretary of the Navy. (c) Chief Justice of the United States. (d) Governor general of islands or groups of islands occupied by the United States, visiting a ship or station officially, within the waters or limits of his government.	Navy.—Dress, or white dress. Marine Corps.— Special full dress (with full dress trousers, if in line with troops), or white undress.

Occasion.	Uniform.
(e) Governor of one of the States or Territories of the United States, visiting a ship or station within the waters or limits of his government. (f) President of the Senate. (g) Speaker of the House of Representatives. (h) Committee of Congress. (i) Envoy extraordinary and minister plenipotentiary, minister resident, or other diplomatic representative of or above the rank of chargé d'affaires, within the waters of the nation to which he is accredited. (j) Flag officer going aboard his flagship to assume command; also when he relinquishes command.	Navy.— Dress, or white dress. Marine Corps.— Special full dress (with full dress trousers, if in line with troops), or white undress.
8. First visit in port to commanding officers, and ordinary occasions of duty and ceremony on shore. 9. At Saturday morning inspection, except the first in the month. In inclement or hot weather, service dress or white service dress may be prescribed, in either case with swords.	Navy.—Dress, or white dress. Marine Corps.— Special full dress (with full dress trousers, if in line with troops), or white undress.
10. Reporting for duty.	Navy.— Undress, or white undress. Marine Corps.— Undress, or white undress.
11. Serving as member of a general court-martial, court of inquiry, examining or retiring board.	Navy.— Undress, or white undress. Marine Corps.— Undress, white undress, or field dress.

U. S. Naval officers' special full dress uniform
Gunner Rear Admiral

U. S. Naval officer. Full dress uniform

Rank: Lieutenant, indicated by the stripes on the sleeve; the tops of the epaulets also bear the insignia of rank.

Corps: The Line of the Navy, indicated by the star on the sleeve.

Occasion.	Uniform.
12. Serving as member of a summary court-martial.	Navy and Marine Corps.—The uniform of the day with side arms.
13. Serving as judge advocate of a general court-martial, or court of inquiry, recorder of a summary court-martial, deck court officer, member of a board other than an examining or retiring board, witness before a court or board, counsel for the accused.	Navy and Marine Corps.—The uniform of the day.
14. Upon occasions of special ceremony, by officers on duty with enlisted men under arms on shore, when the uniform prescribed for other officers is special full dress or full dress.	Navy.— Undress with leggings, or white undress with leggings. Marine Corps.—Full dress, or white undress. (No leggings ever to be worn with full dress.)
15. Visiting foreign officers other than commanding officers. 16. At informal daytime receptions, to which officers are invited in their official capacity, when frock coats are appropriate.	Navy.— Undress, or white undress, without swords. Marine Corps.—undress or white undress, without swords.
17. At all times not otherwise provided for.	Navy.— Service dress (or white service dress when suitable). Marine Corps.—Undress (or white undress when suitable) without swords.

Occasion.	Uniform.
18. On duty with enlisted men under arms ashore, except as specified in No. 14.	Navy.—Service dress, blue or white, as prescribed, and leggings, with swords (or revolvers or both). Marine Corps.—Undress, or field dress, with or without leggings, as prescribed; revolvers also if prescribed.
19. When prescribed by the senior officer present. 20. At the option of and under restrictions imposed by the commanding officer, when the uniform of the day is white service dress; to be worn only by officers on board their own ship, or at exercise in boats.	Navy.—White service dress with blue trousers. Marine Corps.—White undress with blue undress trousers, without swords.
21. Ceremonies in the evening to which officers are invited in their official capacity, such as public balls, dinners, and evening receptions. In hot weather, and in other circumstances where appropriate, dinner dress may be prescribed.	Navy.—Evening full dress. Marine Corps.—Special full dress or mess dress.
22. At informal evening occasions to which officers are invited in their official capacity. In hot weather, or in other circumstances where appropriate, mess dress may be prescribed.	Navy.—Evening dress. Marine Corps.—Mess dress.

Photo by Harris & Ewing, Washington, D. C.

U. S. Naval officer. Blue service uniform

Rank: Lieutenant Commander, shown by the gold leaf on the collar and the stripes on the sleeve.

Corps: Line of the Navy, shown by the anchor on the collar and the star on the sleeve.

Photo by G V. Buck, Washington, D. C.

U. S. Naval officer. White service uniform

Rank: Lieutenant Junior Grade, indicated by the stripes on the shoulder marks.
Corps: The Line of the Navy, indicated by the stars on the shoulder marks.

Occasion.	Uniform.
23. On occasions of ceremony, as in No. 19, or in hot weather and other circumstances where appropriate, as a substitute for Uniform C.	Navy.— Dinner dress. Marine Corps.— Mess dress, with white mess jacket.
24. On ordinary social occasions in the evening to which officers are invited in their official capacity, and where hot weather and other circumstances make it appropriate. 25. When authorized under No. 21 by the commanding officer.	Navy.— Mess dress. Marine Corps.— Mess dress, with white mess jacket. White trousers may be prescribed for both Navy and Marine Corps.

In time of war the uniform prescribed for all ordinary occasions of duty is service dress, blue or white depending upon the temperature and weather.

The special full dress uniform consists of the cocked hat, a double breasted coat with tails at the back only as is the case in the ordinary civilian evening dress coat, trousers with gold stripes down the outer leg seams, black shoes, gold epaulets and the sword carried from a belt and slings of black cloth having gold stripes through it.

The full dress uniform consists of the same trousers, cocked hat, sword and belt as for special full dress, with a double breasted frock coat with a rolling collar and lapels, and gold epaulets.

The evening dress uniform consists of a dark blue cloth evening dress coat and a white waistcoat cut after the prevailing style for civilian evening dress but fitted with gilt navy buttons, plain dark blue trousers, black patent leather shoes and the blue or white cap. Epaulets and full dress trousers (with the gold stripes on them) may be prescribed, in which case the uniform is known as *evening full dress* and the cocked hat is worn with it. For wear in hot weather a *mess jacket* of white is prescribed, cut after the fashion of the evening dress coat but without tails. The shoulder marks are worn with the mess jacket to indicate corps and rank, and either white or blue trousers may be worn with it.

The undress uniform consists of the frock coat without epaulets, plain dark blue or white trousers, the blue or white undress cap, black shoes and the sword carried from a black leather belt and slings.

The blue service dress uniform consists of a dark blue single breasted coat extending to about eight inches below the waist, with standing collar, buttoned up the front with the buttons concealed by a fly-front, and trimmed around the collar, down the front, around the bottom and up the side seams of the back with one and a quarter inch black mohair braid, the undress cap, plain dark blue trousers and black shoes. The white cap and white trousers are sometimes worn with the blue service dress coat.

The white service dress uniform consists of a single breasted white duck coat extending to about eight inches below the waist, with standing collar, buttoned up the front with five large size gilt navy buttons, with a patch pocket on each breast closed by a flap at the top buttoned by a small size gilt navy button, without braid trimming, and having on each shoulder a shoulder strap (known in the service as a "shoulder mark") about five inches long and two and a quarter inches wide bearing the in-

Photo by G. V. Buck, Washington, D. C.

U. S. Navy. Officer in overcoat

Rank: Lieutenant, indicated by the stripes on the shoulder marks and on the sleeves

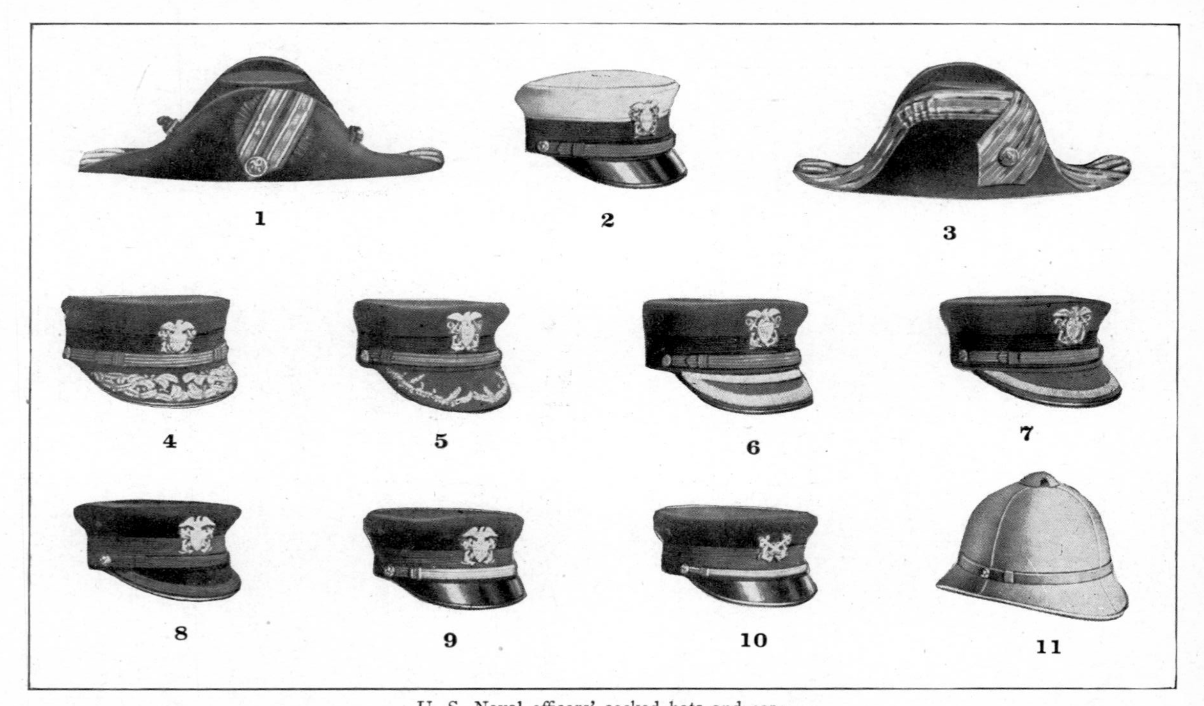

U. S. Naval officers' cocked hats and caps

1. Cocked hat, commissioned officers below Flag rank. 2. White cap, officers below rank of Commander. 3. Cocked hat, Flag officers. 4. Flag Officers' cap. 5. Cap, Captain and Commander. 6. Cap, Staff Officers of Flag rank. 7. Staff Officers, rank of Captain and Commander. 8. Chaplain, rank of Captain and Commander. 9. Cap of officers below rank of Commander. 10. Cap, Warrant Officers. 11. Tropical helmet (not worn at present).

signia which indicates the corps or branch of the Navy to which the wearer belongs and his rank as an officer, plain white trousers, white cap and white shoes.

The winter service aviation uniform consists of a cap, coat, breeches and spiral wrap puttees of forestry-green woolen cloth, and tan leather shoes. The cap is exactly the same design and style as the white service cap except that the material of the crown above the black mohair band is of forestry-green cloth. The coat is the same as the white service uniform coat except that the material is forestry-green cloth. Standard navy gilt buttons are worn on this coat and the rank is shown by shoulder marks the same as those worn with the white service coat.

NAVAL AVIATION CORPS INSIGNIA

The Naval Aviation Corps insignia consist of a vertical foul anchor surcharged with a shield of the United States with eagle's wings extending to the right and left of it as shown in the above illustration. These insignia are made of gilt metal and are worn upon the left breast by all Aviators in the Naval Service, that is by all officers and enlisted men of the Navy and Marine Corps who have qualified as Aviators and are detailed to duty with the Naval Aviation Corps.

The summer service flying uniform for officers of the Navy detailed for aviation duty and for officers of the Naval Reserve Flying Corps consists of a khaki coat of the same style as the white service coat, with which the shoulder marks indicating rank are worn, khaki breeches, woolen wrap puttees of drab color, tan shoes, and a khaki cap of the same style as the white cap.

The working uniform for officers detailed for aviation duty and for officers of the Naval Reserve Flying Corps is a one-piece overall suit of khaki colored cotton duck, canvas or moleskin.

Dungarees (or overalls), consisting of a blue denim jacket and pair of trousers, are worn by officers when working in engine and fire-rooms and in turrets and magazines.

When the sword is worn with the service dress uniforms the belt is worn under the coat unless the pistol is worn on the belt, in which case the belt is worn outside of the coat.

White gloves are worn with all uniforms on dress occasions or when the sword is worn except at battle drills or with landing forces on shore expeditions.

The overcoat is a dark blue ulster-coat, reaching about midway from the knee to the foot, double breasted, buttoning to the neck with seven large flat black buttons on each side, with a wide rolling collar, with a pocket having a vertical opening on each side above the waist, and fitted with waist straps at the back. Shoulder marks of the same design as those for the white service coat are worn with the overcoat and the rank of the wearer is indicated by stripes of black mohair braid on the lower part of the sleeve. The overcoat is lined with black, and a hood is provided to be worn over the head in very cold weather.

A boat cloak or cape of dark blue cloth, cut full, with a rolling collar of black velvet is also provided for officers of the Navy.

The rain coat is a black mackintosh with a cape reaching to the tips of the fingers when the arms hang naturally; and in rainy and wet weather at sea officers usually wear rubber boots, oilskin coats and "sou-wester" hats.

The cocked hat for officers of flag rank (admirals, vice admirals, rear admirals and commodores) is of black silk beaver trimmed with gold lace braid as shown in the illustration, figure 3; and for all other commissioned officers, except chaplains and chief warrant officers, it is trimmed around the outer edge of the top of the crown with black silk lace braid as shown by figure 1.

The blue cap for flag officers is shown by figure 4, and for captains and commanders by figure 5, the cap for officers of the Staff Corps of the rank of rear admiral is shown by figure 6, and for the same classes of officers of the ranks of captain and commander by figure 7. The decorations on the visor shown in the illustrations are embroidered in gold, with the exception of caps for chaplains of the ranks of captain and commander, which have black embroidered bands as shown by figure 8.

The chin strap for all commissioned officers except chaplains is of black leather covered with gold lace braid one-half inch wide; for chaplains it is made of lustrous black mohair, as shown by figure 8. The chin strap for warrant officers' caps is one-quarter of an inch in width, figure 10.

The cap device embroidered on the center and front of the caps of all commissioned officers consists of a silver shield emblazoned paleways of thirteen pieces, with chief strewn with stars, surmounted by a silver spread eagle, the whole placed upon two crossed foul anchors in gold, as shown by the illustration. The cap device for warrant officers' caps consists of the two crossed foul anchors in gold, as shown by figure 10.

The blue cap for all commissioned officers below the rank of commander has a plain black patent leather visor, figure 9.

The white caps for all officers are similar in shape to the blue caps, the band, cap devices, chin straps and visor decorations for the different corps and ranks being the same as for the blue caps of the same officers, figure 2.

The cap for Warrant officers is the same as that for commissioned officers except that the device worn on the front consists of two gold foul anchors crossed and the chin strap of gold braid is but one-quarter of an inch wide, figure 10.

INSIGNIA OF RANK AND CORPS

The rank of officers of the Navy is indicated in four ways: first, by stripes upon the sleeves of the special full dress coat, frock coat, evening dress coat, blue service coat and overcoat; second, by rank insignia on each side of the front opening of the collar of the blue service coat; third, by stripes upon the shoulder marks (or straps) worn on the white service coat, the mess jacket and the overcoat; and fourth, by rank insignia on the upper surface of the epaulets worn with special full dress, full dress and evening dress. These stripes indicating rank encircle the sleeves, the lower one being two inches above the edge of the sleeve and parallel to it; on all blue coats except the overcoat they are of gold lace braid, except for chaplains who wear black braid stripes; and on the overcoats of all commissioned officers they are of black mohair braid.

The number, width and arrangement of the sleeve

U. S. Navy. Officers' sleeve braiding indicating rank

Gold braid on special full dress, full dress, evening dress and blue service coats. Black braid on overcoats, without the stars

1. Admiral of the Navy
2. Admiral
3. Vice Admiral
4. Rear Admiral

U. S. Navy. Officers' sleeve braiding indicating rank
Gold braid on special full dress, full dress, evening dress and blue service coats. Black braid on overcoats, without the stars

1. Commodore
2. Captain
3. Commander
4. Lieutenant Commander

stripes indicating the rank of officers, as illustrated, are as follows:

Admiral of the Navy, two stripes two inches wide with one stripe one inch wide between them, the stripes being one quarter of an inch apart.

Admiral, one stripe two inches wide with three stripes one-half an inch wide above it, the stripes being one quarter of an inch apart.

Vice Admiral, one stripe two inches wide with two stripes one-half an inch wide above it, the stripes being one quarter of an inch apart.

Rear Admiral, one stripe two inches wide with one stripe one-half an inch wide above it, the stripes being one quarter of an inch apart.

Commodore, one stripe two inches wide.

Captain, four stripes each one-half of an inch wide, set one quarter of an inch apart.

Commander, three stripes each one-half of an inch wide, set one quarter of an inch apart.

Lieutenant Commander, two stripes one-half of an inch wide with one stripe one quarter of an inch wide between them, the stripes being set one quarter of an inch apart.

Lieutenant, two stripes one-half of an inch wide set one quarter of an inch apart.

Lieutenant Junior Grade, one stripe one-half of an inch wide with one stripe one quarter of an inch wide set one quarter of an inch above it.

Ensign, one stripe one-half of an inch wide.

The sleeve stripes for Chief Boatswain, Chief Gunner, Chief Machinist, Chief Carpenter, Chief Sailmaker, Chief Pay Clerk and Chief Pharmacist of the rank of Lieutenant Junior Grade or Ensign are of the same number and widths as those prescribed for Lieutenants Junior Grade or Ensign, except that when made of gold they are woven with dark-blue silk thread for widths of one-half inch at intervals of two inches.

The Corps or branch of the service to which the officer belongs is indicated in connection with the rank stripes on the sleeves as follows:

All Line Officers wear a star embroidered in gold, one and one-eighth inches in diameter, on the outside of each sleeve of the special full dress coat, frock coat, evening dress coat and blue service coat, one quarter of an inch above the rank stripes.

For Line Officers of the Naval Militia the gold star is surrounded by a gold circle one and three-eighths inches in diameter.

Staff Officers wear the same sleeve rank stripes as those worn by the Line Officers of the same rank but they do not wear the gold star. The Corps to which Staff Officers belong is indicated by bands of colored cloth around the sleeves filling the intervals between the gold rank stripes, the colors and material of the stripes for the different corps being as follows:

Medical Officers — dark maroon velvet.

Pay Officers — white cloth.

Professors of Mathematics — olive green cloth.

Naval Constructors — dark violet cloth.

Civil Engineers — light blue velvet.

Medical Reserve Officers — crimson cloth.

Dental Officers — orange colored velvet.

When but one stripe is worn, that is for officers of the rank of ensign, the colored cloth is made to show one quarter of an inch on each side of the stripe.

For Staff Officers of the Naval Militia the colored corps stripes are broken for a distance of one and one quarter inches at the center of the front of the sleeve.

U. S. Navy. Officers' sleeve braiding indicating rank

Gold braid on special full dress, full dress, evening dress and blue service coats. Black braid on overcoats, without the stars

1. Lieutenant
2. Lieutenant, Junior Grade
3. Ensign
4. Lieutenant, Naval Militia

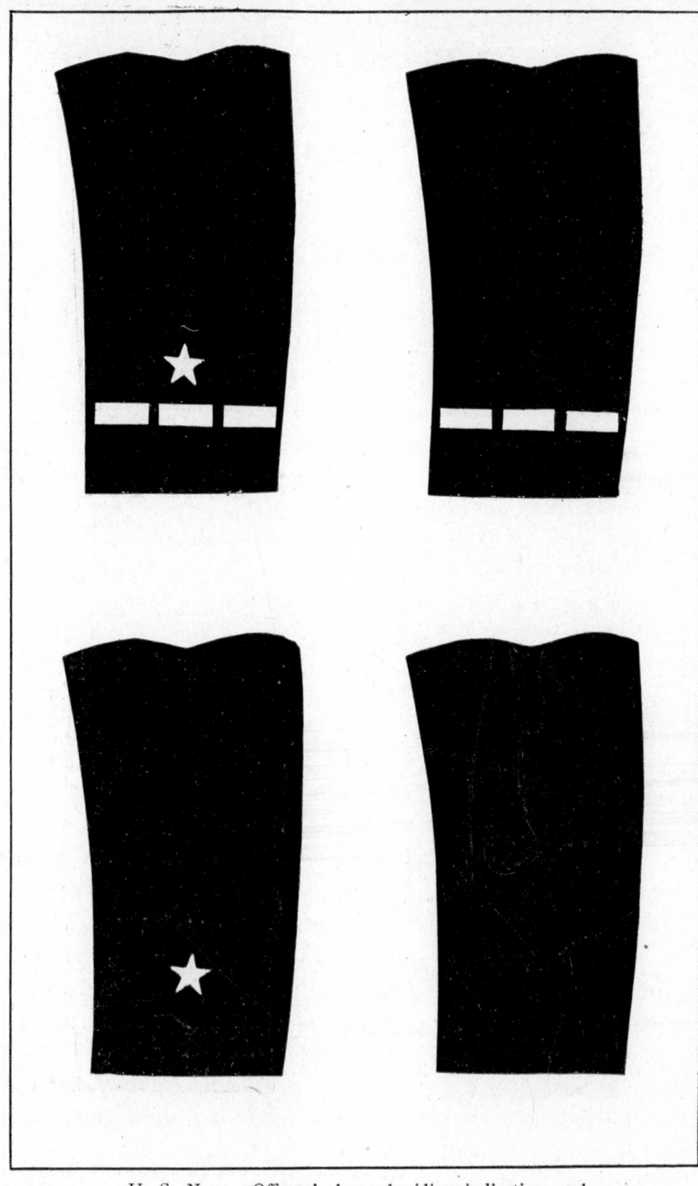

U. S. Navy. Officers' sleeve braiding indicating rank

Gold braid on special full dress, full dress, evening dress and blue service coats. Black braid on overcoats, without the stars

1. Chief Boatswain, Chief Gunner, Chief Machinist
2. Chief Carpenter, Chief Sailmaker, Chief Pharmacist, Chief Pay Clerk
3. Boatswain, Gunner, Machinist
4. Carpenter, Sailmaker, Pharmacist, Pay Clerk, Mate

The rank and corps of officers is shown on the blue service coat in two ways: first, by the stripes on the sleeves as above described; second, by rank and corps insignia worn on each side of the standing collar, to the right and left of the front opening at the neck.

These collar insignia are as illustrated, and consist of the insignia of rank in combination with the device indicating the corps of the wearer.

The Corps device or insignia, indicating to what corps or branch of the service the officer belongs, are:

Line Officers: a silver foul anchor, one and five-eighths inches long over all, one inch wide from tip to tip.

Medical Corps Officers: a silver acorn embroidered upon a gold spread oak leaf, stem to tip one and three-quarters inches, width one inch.

Pay Corps Officers: a silver oak sprig of three leaves and three acorns, one and three-quarters inches long by one inch wide.

Professors of Mathematics: a silver oak leaf and an acorn, one and three-quarters inches long and one inch wide.

Naval Constructors Corps: a gold sprig of two live-oak leaves and an acorn, one and five-eighths inches long and one and three-eighths inches wide.

Civil Engineers Corps: two crossed silver sprigs, each of two live-oak leaves and an acorn, one and three-quarter inches long and one inch wide.

Chaplains: a Latin cross embroidered in silver.

Medical Reserve Corps: a gold acorn embroidered upon a silver spread oak leaf, one and three-quarters inches long and one inch wide.

Dental Corps: a gold spread oak leaf with a silver

acorn on either side of the stem, one and three-quarter inches long and one inch wide.

The rank insignia, indicating the rank of the wearer, are practically the same as those for the Army and the Marine Corps, and are as follows:

Admiral — four silver stars.

Vice Admiral — three silver stars.

Rank of Rear Admiral — two silver stars.

Rank of Commodore — one silver star.

Rank of Captain — a silver spread eagle.

Rank of Commander — a silver oak leaf.

Rank of Lieutenant Commander — a gold oak leaf.

Rank of Lieutenant — two silver bars.

Rank of Lieutenant Junior Grade — one silver bar.

Rank of Ensign — no insignia.

Midshipman — a gold anchor.

The insignia indicating the rank and corps of officers are worn on each side of the collar of the blue service coat as illustrated; for Line Officers they are as follows:

Admiral of the Navy — four silver stars, the two end stars being surcharged upon gold foul anchors.

Admiral — four silver stars, the star nearest the back being surcharged upon a gold foul anchor.

Vice Admiral — three silver stars with a silver foul anchor in rear of them.

Rear Admiral — two silver stars with a silver foul anchor in rear of them.

Commodore — one silver star with a silver foul anchor in rear of it.

Captain — a silver spread eagle with a silver foul anchor in rear of it.

Commander — a silver oak leaf with a silver foul anchor in rear of it.

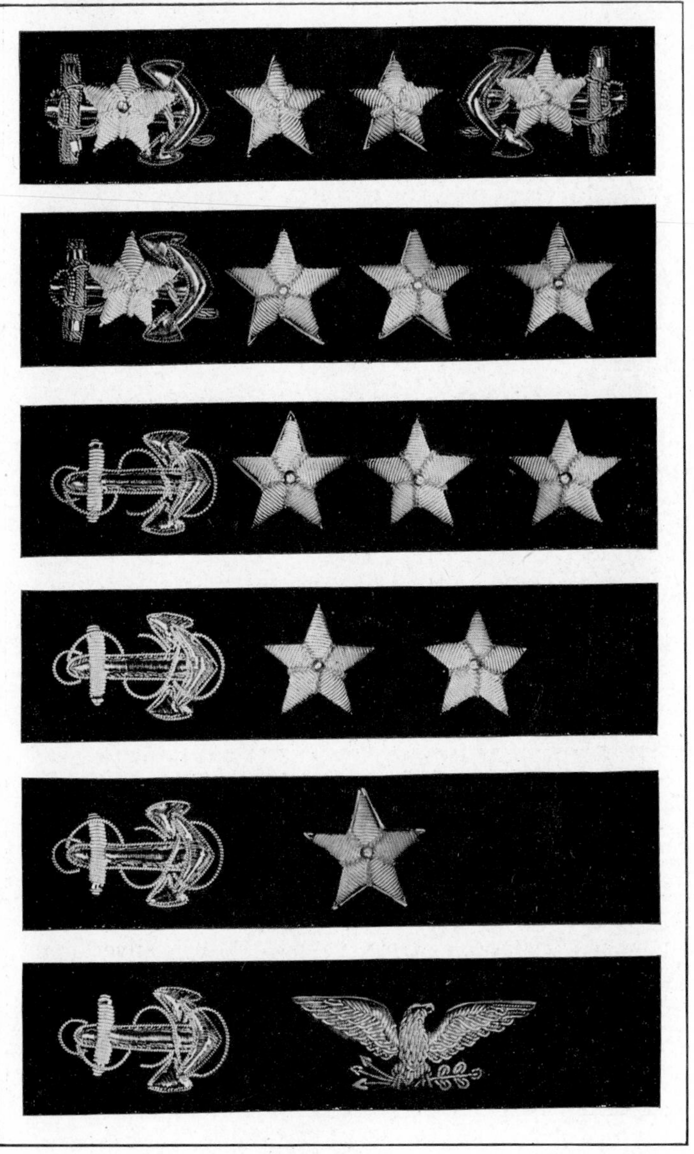

U. S. Navy. Officers' insignia of rank and Corps on collar of blue service coat, showing right side of collar

1. Admiral of the Navy
2. Admiral
3. Vice Admiral
4. Rear Admiral
5. Commodore
6. Captain

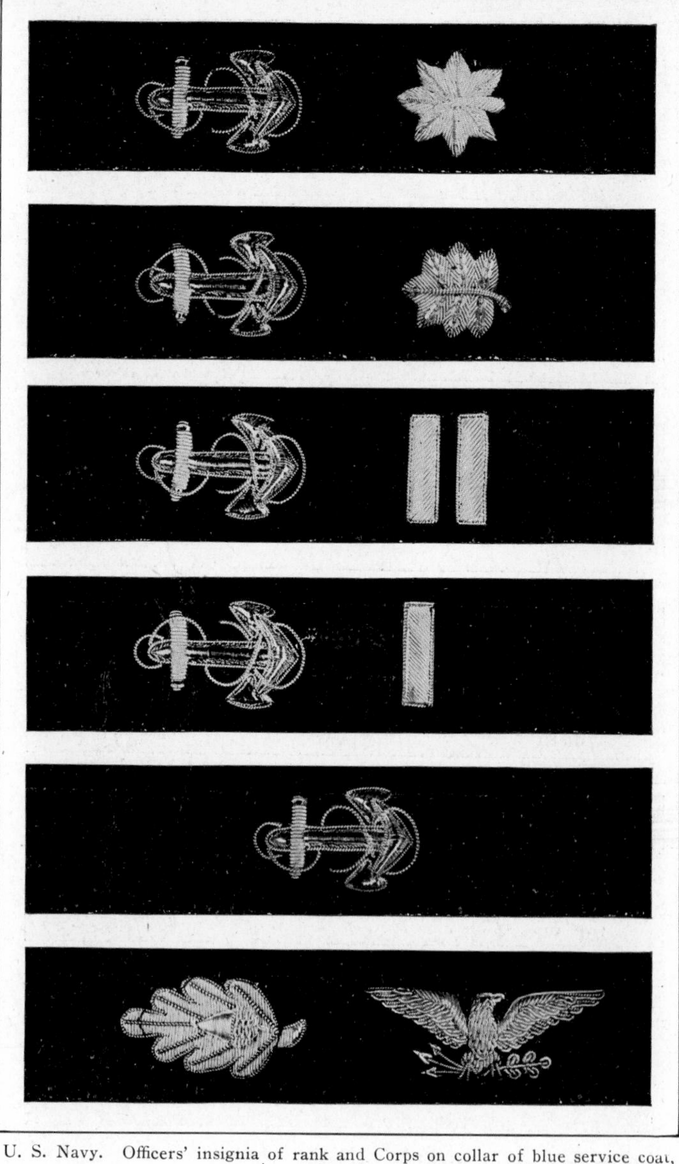

U. S. Navy. Officers' insignia of rank and Corps on collar of blue service coat, showing right side of collar

1. Commander (Silver leaf)
2. Lieutenant Commander (Gold leaf)
3. Lieutenant
4. Lieutenant, Junior Grade
5. Ensign
6. Medical Officer with the rank of Captain

Lieutenant Commander — a gold oak leaf with a silver foul anchor in rear of it.

Lieutenant — two silver bars vertical with a silver anchor in rear of them.

Lieutenant, Junior Grade — one silver bar vertical with a silver foul anchor in rear of it.

Ensign — a silver foul anchor.

Staff Officers of all ranks wear the Corps device or insignia indicating the particular corps to which they belong (as described on page 121) in place of the silver foul anchor above described and the same rank insignia for the different ranks as described for Line Officers. Thus, a Medical Director with the rank of Captain wears the silver spread eagle indicating the rank and the Medical Corps device of the silver acorn upon the gold leaf indicating the Medical Corps; a Pay Director with the rank of Captain wears the silver spread eagle indicating the rank and the silver oak sprig of three leaves and three acorns indicating the Pay Corps; a Chaplain with the rank of Commander wears the silver leaf indicating the rank and the silver Latin cross indicating his corps; a Professor of Mathematics with the rank of Commander wears the silver leaf indicating the rank and the silver oak leaf and acorn indicating the corps; a Naval Constructor with the rank of Commander wears the silver leaf indicating the rank and the silver two live-oak leaves and acorn indicating the Construction Corps; a Civil Engineer with the rank of Commander wears the silver leaf indicating the rank and the silver crossed live-oak leaves indicating the Corps of Civil Engineers; and a Dental Surgeon with the rank of Lieutenant wears the two silver bars indicating the rank and the gold oak leaf and silver acorns indicating the Dental Corps.

The insignia showing the corps of the Chief Boatswain, Chief Gunner, Chief Machinist, Chief Carpenter, Chief Sailmaker, Chief Pharmacist and Chief Pay Clerk consist of devices worn on each side of the collar of the frock coat just above the V notch in the lapel, as follows:

Chief Boatswain — two foul anchors crossed, embroidered in silver, surcharged at the center by a gold five-pointed star.

Chief Gunner — a flaming spherical shell, embroidered in silver, surcharged at the center by a gold five-pointed star.

Chief Machinist — a three-bladed propeller embroidered in silver, surcharged at the center by a gold five-pointed star.

Chief Carpenter — a carpenter's square, embroidered in silver with the point down.

Chief Sailmaker — a diamond embroidered in silver.

Chief Pharmacist — a caduceus, embroidered in silver.

Chief Pay Clerk — an oak sprig of three leaves and three acorns, embroidered in silver.

The Corps of Warrant Officers is also shown by corps devices worn on each side of the collar of the frock coat just above the V notch in the lapel, as follows:

Boatswain — two foul anchors crossed, embroidered in gold, surcharged at the center by a silver five-pointed star.

Gunner — a flaming spherical shell, embroidered in gold, surcharged at the center by a silver five-pointed star.

Machinist — a three-bladed propeller, embroidered in gold, surcharged at the center by a silver five-pointed star.

Carpenter — a carpenter's square embroidered in gold with the point down.

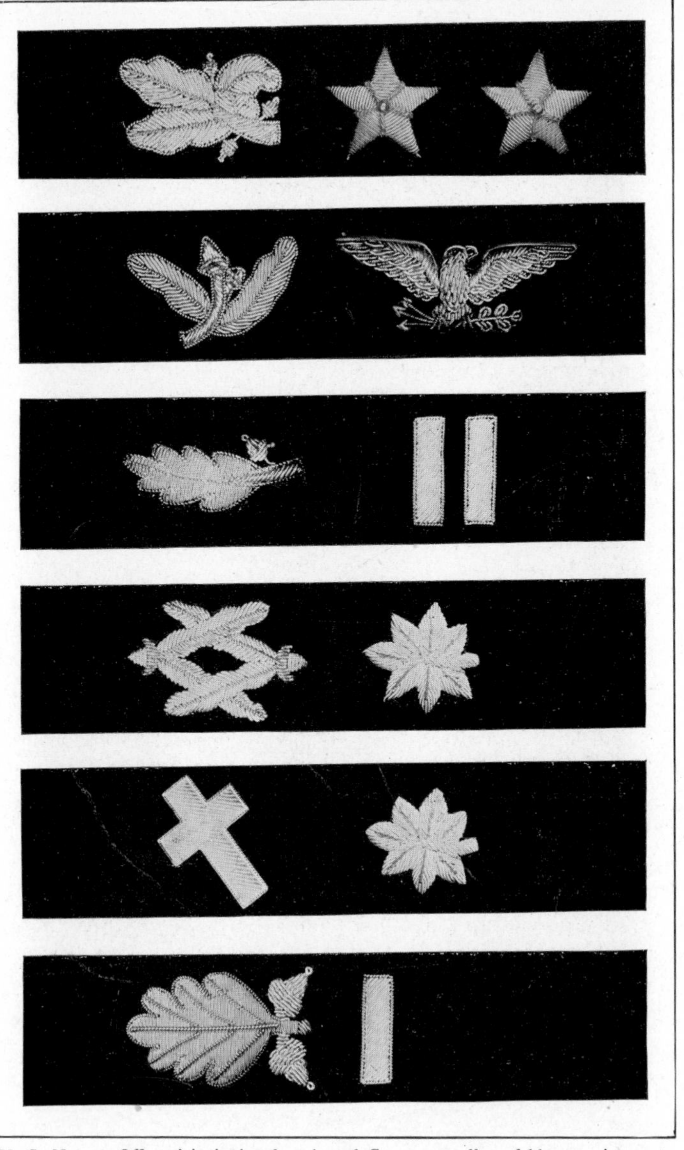

U. S. Navy. Officers' insignia of rank and Corps on collar of blue service coat, showing right side of collar

1. Officer of the Pay Corps with the rank of Rear Admiral
2. Naval Constructor with the rank of Captain
3. Professor of Mathematics with the rank of Lieutenant
4. Civil Engineer with the rank of Commander
5. Chaplain with the rank of Commander
6. Dental Surgeon with the rank of Lieutenant, Junior Grade

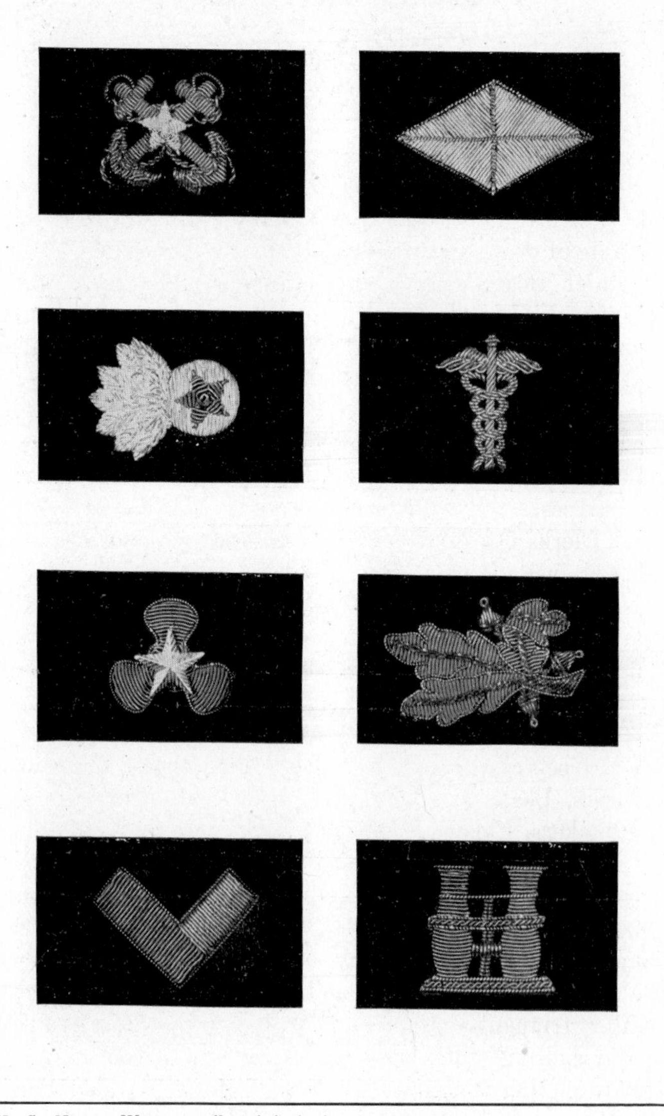

U. S. Navy. Warrant officers' insignia on collars of blue service and dress coats, showing right side of collar

1. Chief Boatswain and Boatswain
2. Chief Sailmaker and Sailmaker
3. Chief Gunner and Gunner
4. Chief Pharmacist and Pharmacist
5. Chief Machinist and Machinist
6. Chief Pay Clerk and Pay Clerk
7. Chief Carpenter and Carpenter
8. Mate

Sailmaker — a diamond embroidered in gold.

Pharmacist — a caduceus embroidered in gold.

Pay Clerk — an oak sprig of three leaves and three acorns embroidered in gold.

Mate — a binocular glass, embroidered in gold for a Mate of less than twenty years' service and in silver for a Mate of over twenty years' service.

Chief Boatswains, Chief Gunners and Chief Machinists, being Line Officers, wear the gold star above the sleeve stripes; while Chief Carpenters, Chief Sailmakers, Chief Pharmacists and Chief Pay Clerks, being Staff Officers, do not wear the star on the sleeve.

Boatswains, Gunners and Machinists, being Warrant Officers of the Line wear the gold star on the sleeve, but no stripes. Carpenters, Sailmakers, Pharmacists and Pay Clerks have the sleeves of the coat without decoration or insignia.

Chief Boatswains, Chief Gunners, Chief Machinists, Chief Carpenters, Chief Sailmakers, Chief Pharmacists and Chief Pay Clerks wear on the collars of their blue service coats the same devices showing their corps as those already described to be worn upon the collars of their frock coats; and the same is true of the Warrant Officers, Boatswains, Gunners, Machinists, Carpenters, Sailmakers, Pharmacists, Pay Clerks and Mates.

Shoulder marks for officers are worn on the white service coat, mess jacket and overcoat to indicate the corps and rank of the wearer. These marks are of dark blue cloth lined with black silk, stiffened so as to lie flat, 4½ to 5¼ inches long and 2¼ inches wide, finished with a triangular point and a gilt Navy button at the collar end, and they are worn on the top of each shoulder extending from the base of the collar to the shoulder seam.

The designs for the different ranks are as shown in the illustrations. For officers of the Line they are as follows:

Admiral of the Navy — covered with gold lace braid two inches wide, with four silver stars, the two end stars being surcharged upon gold foul anchors.

Admiral — covered with gold lace braid two inches wide, with four silver stars, the one nearest the collar end being surcharged upon a gold foul anchor.

Vice Admiral — covered with gold lace braid two inches wide, with a silver foul anchor and three silver stars, the anchor being nearest the collar end.

Rear Admiral — covered with gold lace braid two inches wide, with two silver stars and a silver foul anchor between them.

Commodore — covered with gold lace braid two inches wide, with one silver star and a silver foul anchor, the anchor being nearest the collar end.

Captain — a gold star at the collar end and four stripes of gold lace braid one-half of an inch wide, set one-quarter of an inch apart.

Commander — a gold star and three stripes of gold lace braid one-half of an inch wide, set one-quarter of an inch apart.

Lieutenant-Commander — a gold star and two stripes of gold lace braid one-half of an inch wide with one such stripe one-quarter of an inch wide, between them, stripes set one-quarter of an inch apart.

Lieutenant — a gold star and two stripes of gold lace braid one-half of an inch wide, set one-quarter of an inch apart.

Lieutenant Junior Grade — a gold star and one stripe of gold lace braid one-half of an inch wide and

U. S. Navy. Officers' shoulder marks indicating rank

Worn on the white service uniform coat, the white mess jacket and the overcoat

1. Admiral of the Navy
2. Admiral
3. Vice Admiral
4. Rear-admiral
5. Commodore
6. Captain
7. Commander
8. Lieutenant-Commander
9. Lieutenant

U. S. Navy. Officers' shoulder marks indicating rank
Worn on the white service uniform coat, the white mess jacket and the overcoat

1. Lieutenant, Junior Grade	2. Ensign	3. Chief Boatswain
4. Chief Gunner	5. Chief Machinist	6. Chief Carpenter
7. Chief Pharmacist	8. Chief Pay Clerk	9. Chief Sailmaker

one stripe one-quarter of an inch wide, set one-quarter of an inch apart.

Ensign — a gold star and one stripe of gold lace braid one-half of an inch wide.

For officers of the Staff Corps of the rank of Rear Admiral or Commodore the shoulder marks are the same as those for Rear Admiral or Commodore of the Line, except that in place of the silver anchor the corps device indicating the corps to which the officer belongs is used.

For officers of the Staff Corps below the rank of Commodore the stripes for the different ranks are the same as those described for officers of the Line but the star is omitted, the Corps to which the officer belongs being indicated by stripes of colored cloth filling the spaces between the gold stripes, the colors and materials being as follows:

Medical Corps Officers — dark maroon velvet.
Pay Corps Officers — White cloth.
Professors of Mathematics — olive green cloth.
Naval Constructors — dark violet cloth.
Civil Engineers — light blue velvet.
Medical Reserve Officers — crimson cloth.
Dental Officers — orange colored velvet.

The shoulder marks for Chief Boatswain, Chief Gunner, Chief Machinist, Chief Carpenter, Chief Sailmaker, Chief Pharmacist and Chief Pay Clerk, bear the gold stripes indicating their rank of the same width and position as in the case of other officers of their rank, except that the gold stripe is broken at the center by a section of one-half of an inch embroidered in dark blue silk, and the corps is shown by the insignia as described for each on page 124 to be worn on the collars of the frock coats. The insignia in each case are placed on the center of the strap above the stripe.

The shoulder marks for Warrant Officers, Boatswains, Gunners, Machinists, Carpenters, Sailmakers, Pharmacists and Pay Clerks, bear the same insignia indicating the corps of the wearer as those for the Chief Boatswains, Chief Gunners, Chief Machinists, Chief Carpenters, Chief Sailmakers, Chief Pharmacists and Chief Pay Clerks, but the gold stripes indicating rank are omitted.

The shoulder marks for Mates bear a binocular glass embroidered in gold for mates of less than twenty years' service and in silver for those of over twenty years' service.

The rank and corps of officers of the Navy is shown upon the gold epaulets worn with special full dress, full dress and evening full dress uniforms by the regular rank and corps insignia placed upon the top of the epaulet. These insignia are the same for the different ranks or grades as those worn on the collars of the blue service coats.

For Officers of the Staff the epaulets have the same insignia for indicating the rank as in the case of the corresponding rank of officers of the Line, but to indicate the particular corps to which the wearer belongs the proper Corps insignia or devices are substituted in the place of the silver foul anchors worn by officers of the Line.

The gilt buttons worn by officers of the Navy upon the coats for which they are prescribed bear in relief an eagle with wings lifting above an anchor placed hori-

U. S. Navy. Officers' shoulder marks indicating rank
Worn on the white service uniform coat, the white mess jacket and the overcoat

1. Boatswain	2. Gunner	3. Machinist
4. Carpenter	5. Pay Clerk	6. Sailmaker
7. Pharmacist	8. Mate	9. Lieutenant Commander, Naval Militia

U. S. Navy. Cap insignia

1. Commissioned officers
2. Warrant officers

Service Buttons for Officers

3. U. S. Navy
4. U. S. Naval Reserve
5. U. S. Coast Guard
6. U. S. Public Health Service
7. Collar insignia, Lieutenant, U. S. Naval Reserve, showing left side of collar

zontal; surrounded by thirteen five-pointed stars and a plain circle.

Aiguilettes worn by Naval Officers are loops of plaited blue and gold cord terminating in gilt metal ornaments decorated with silver anchors. They are worn by personal aids to the President and the Secretary of the Navy, aids at the White House, members of the personal staff of a Flag Officer in command of a fleet or subdivision of a fleet, and by aids to the Commandants of Naval Stations and the Superintendent of the Naval Academy.

The personal aids to the President wear the aiguilettes on the right side and all other officers for whom they are prescribed wear them on the left side.

They are worn with all uniforms to indicate the special duty of the wearer as an aid entitled to convey the orders of the officer to whose staff he is assigned.

The Sword knot for naval officers is a loop of gold braid ending in a bullion tassel, worn on the hilt of the sword. The original purpose of this loop was to wear it around the right wrist when the sword was carried in the hand to prevent the loss of the sword if it should be accidentally dropped or knocked from the hand in combat. The sword knot is worn by commissioned officers only.

Officers of the Line and of the Staff Corps of the Naval Reserve Force wear the same rank marks as those described for the officers of the regular Navy, but, instead of the silver anchor for the Line Officers and the various Corps devices and insignia to indicate the Corps or branch of the service of the Staff officers of the Staff of the regular Navy, they wear the Naval Reserve Force device on the collar of the blue service coat.

The Naval Reserve Force Device or insignia is of

the same design as the device worn on the front of the cap by commissioned officers of the Navy. It is one inch in height, made of metal, the shield and eagle being of silver and the crossed anchors of gold.

The gilt buttons worn by officers of the Naval Reserve Force are of the same sizes as those worn by the officers of the regular service but the design is different, and by this design the fact that an officer is a member of the Naval Reserve Force is shown when he is wearing any uniform having gilt buttons. The Naval Reserve Force gilt button for officers bears a plain vertical anchor and the letters U. S. N. R., as illustrated.

UNIFORMS AND INSIGNIA OF MIDSHIPMEN

The Corps of Midshipmen at the Naval Academy is organized into a regiment of four battalions of four companies each for military formations and drills, with Midshipmen Officers and Petty Officers, as follows:

Midshipman Commander.....Commanding the Regiment.
Midshipman Lieutenant Commander ....Commanding a Battalion.
Midshipman Lieutenant......Regimental Adjutant and Company Commander.
Midshipman Junior Lieutenant ....Regimental Commissary and Regimental Signal Officer, Battalion Adjutant, and junior Company officer.
Midshipman Ensign ....Regimental Aid, Battalion Commissary, and junior Company officer.
Midshipman Regimental Staff Petty Officer.
Midshipman Battalion Staff Petty Officer.
First Petty Officer.
Second Petty Officer.
First-Class Petty Officer.

Second-Class Petty Officer.

The Midshipmen are provided with uniform as follows:

Full dress — consisting of a dark blue double breasted jacket cut to reach just below the waist, roached at the sides over the hips, pointed at front and back, with standing collar and two rows of gilt buttons down the front and three gilt buttons on each cuff; dark blue trousers, a blue cap similar to that worn by other naval officers, white gloves and black shoes.

Service dress — consisting of a dark blue blouse coat similar in cut and design to the blue service coat of other officers; dark blue trousers, the blue cap and black shoes.

White service dress — consisting of a white duck coat with gilt buttons similar in cut and style to the white service coat of other officers, white duck trousers, white cap and white shoes.

Khaki undress — consisting of a khaki blouse, trousers and cap.

Working dress — consisting of khaki blouse and trousers and white hat.

Working undress — consisting of khaki shirt and trousers and white hat.

The overcoat is an ulster of dark blue cloth, double breasted, buttoning to the neck with two rows of gilt buttons on the front with a wide rolling collar.

The insignia of the Corps of Midshipmen are a gold anchor worn on the full dress jacket and blue service coat on each side of the collar near the front. All Midshipmen attaining above 85 per cent in standing also wear a gold star on each side of the collar.

The rank of Midshipman Officers is indicated by

stripes of gold braid one-eighth of an inch wide sewn around the sleeves of the full dress jacket, service coat and overcoat, the lower stripe being about two inches from the lower edge of the sleeve, the number of stripes for the different grades being:

Midshipman Commander.....	Five stripes one quarter of an inch apart.
Midshipman Lieutenant Commander	Four stripes one quarter of an inch apart.
Midshipman Lieutenant	Three stripes one quarter of an inch apart.
Midshipman Junior Lieutenant	Two stripes one quarter of an inch apart.
Midshipman Ensign	One stripe.

All Midshipman Officers also wear a gold star one inch in diameter three-fourths of an inch above the upper stripe on each sleeve.

The rank of Midshipman Petty Officers is indicated by devices embroidered in gold upon the sleeves, above the elbow, of the full dress jacket, undress coat and overcoat, indicating the different grades as follows:

Regimental staff petty officer — an eagle and an anchor, surmounted by three stars placed pyramidally, with a chevron of three stripes below the anchor.

Battalion staff petty officer — the same as for regimental staff petty officer except there are but two stars.

First and Second Petty Officers — the same as for staff petty officers except there is but one star.

First-class Petty Officer — the same as for first and second petty officers except that the chevrons are omitted.

Second-class Petty Officer — the same as for first-class petty officers except that the star is omitted.

The midshipmen are divided into four classes, accord-

U. S. Navy. Midshipmen. Sleeve stripes indicating class
Gold stripes on the sleeves of the dress coat, undress coat and overcoat

1. First Class
2. Second Class
3. Third Class
4. Fourth Class

ing to the year's course, the first class corresponding to seniors at college, the second class corresponding to juniors at college, the third class corresponding to sophomores at college and the fourth class corresponding to freshmen at college.

To distinguish the class to which they belong all midshipmen, except Midshipman Officers and petty officers and fourth classmen, wear service stripes of gold braid one-eighth of an inch wide diagonally across the outside of each sleeve of the full dress jacket, service coat and overcoat from front seam to rear seam, each stripe indicating one year of service at the Naval Academy; thus, the first classmen have three stripes, the second classmen two stripes, the third classmen one stripe, and the fourth classmen plain sleeves with no stripes.

ENLISTED MEN'S UNIFORMS, U. S. NAVY

Enlisted men of the Navy are required to have complete outfits of blue dress, white dress, blue undress, white undress and working dress. Dungaree suits are prescribed for the engineers force and for men of the Artificer Branch. Rain clothes are allowed for the deck force and men who are required to do duty where they would require them.

The occasions upon which the different uniforms of the United States Navy and Marine Corps are worn by the enlisted men are laid down in the regulations as follows:

1. Occasions of ceremony, parades or reviews, unless otherwise ordered.	NAVY.— Dress. MARINE CORPS.— Dress.
2. On liberty or leave.	NAVY.— Dress. MARINE CORPS.— Dress or field dress.

3. On ordinary occasions, either on or off duty.	NAVY.— Undress. MARINE CORPS.— Dress or field dress.
4. At battery drills, and by details of men or individuals engaged in work for which this dress is necessary.	NAVY.—Working dress. MARINE CORPS.— Field dress.
5. When prescribed for physical and battery drills, boat exercise under oars, or handling stores or ammunition alongside.	NAVY.—Undress without jumpers. MARINE CORPS.—Dress or field dress, without coats, with flannel shirts.
6. In the Tropics in isolated anchorages, or at sea, when prescribed.	NAVY.— White undress without jumpers. MARINE CORPS.— Dress or field dress, without coats.

The blue dress uniform for chief petty officers and for officers' cooks and stewards consists of a double breasted blue cloth coat with rolling lapel collar and two lower and one breast pocket with flaps, the coat to be worn buttoned, blue cloth trousers, black shoes, a dark blue cloth cap with patent leather visor, white shirt and collar and black bow tie, as illustrated. For all other enlisted men (except bandsmen whose uniform is described later, the blue dress uniform consists of a blue overshirt with a rolling collar, blue cloth trousers, blue flat cap, black neckerchief and black shoes, as illustrated. The overshirt collar falls down the back about nine inches for a width of from fourteen to eighteen inches and is trimmed around the edges with three stripes of narrow white braid and a white five-pointed star in each corner. The overshirt is cut to fit loosely with a shield shaped yoke at the top and a draw string at the waist, the length being such that when the draw string is tightened at the waist the shirt will fall two to four inches below it. The sleeves have tight buttoned cuffs and these are trimmed with stripes of narrow white braid, three stripes

U. S. Navy. Chief petty officer

Blue dress uniform
Seaman Branch, indicated by rating badge on right arm
Ex-apprentice, indicated by mark on right arm below elbow
Third Enlistment, indicated by two enlistment stripes on left arm

White dress uniform
Artificer Branch, indicated by rating badge on left arm
Second Enlistment, indicated by one enlistment stripe on left arm

U. S. Navy. Enlisted men

Blue dress uniform
Rating, Petty officer first class, indicated by rating badge with chevron of three stripes
Seaman Branch, indicated by rating badge being on right arm

White dress uniform
Rating, Seaman first class, indicated by three stripes on cuffs
Seaman Branch, indicated by branch mark being on right shoulder seam

for petty officers of the first, second and third classes, and men of the seaman first class; two stripes for men of the seaman second class, and one stripe for men of the seaman third class and mess attendants, the men of these different classes being enumerated in the table in Chapter II. The trousers for chief petty officers are cut after the style for civilian trousers, but for other enlisted men they are made to fit snug over the hips with a black ribbon lacing at the back, closed in front by a square flap front with small black buttons at the sides and top, and cut bell shaped at the bottom in order that they may be rolled up easily. The blue cap for all enlisted men except chief petty officers, officers' stewards and cooks, and bandsmen, is of the style known as the "flat cap." It has a band two inches wide around which is sewn a black silk cap ribbon bearing the name of the ship or station of the wearer in plain gold letters, the ribbon being tied in a double bow knot at the left side. Above the band the crown is about four inches greater in diameter than the band and is stretched out flat by a "grommet" or ring worn inside of the edge of the crown.

The white dress uniform for chief petty officers and officers' stewards and cooks consists of a white duck coat, white duck trousers, white cap, white shirt and collar, black tie and white shoes, the coat and trousers being made after the same style as the blue dress coat, and the cap having a black visor and band and a white crown. For all other enlisted men (except bandsmen) the white dress uniform consists of a white dress "jumper" shirt with blue cloth collar and cuffs, white trousers, black neckerchief, black shoes and a white hat. The white dress jumper is not tightened at the waist like the blue overshirt but is cut off square about six inches below the waist and allowed to hang free.

The blue undress uniform for chief petty officers and officers' stewards and cooks is the same as the blue dress uniform for these men except that the material of which it is made is blue serge and a blue flannel shirt may be worn. For all other enlisted men (except bandsmen) the blue undress uniform consists of a blue undress jumper, blue cloth or flannel trousers, blue cap or white hat and black shoes. The blue undress jumper is the same as the overshirt except that there are no stripes of braid or stars on the collar or cuffs and the sleeves are not buttoned at the cuff but cut off square and hemmed.

The white undress uniform for chief petty officers and officers' stewards and cooks is the same as the white dress for these men. For all other enlisted men (except bandsmen) it consists of a white undress jumper of the same style as the blue undress jumper and white trousers and white hat, the jumper and trousers being made of white navy drill.

The working dress uniform, blue or white, for all enlisted men is the same as undress, blue or white as the case may be, except that chief petty officers and officers' stewards and cooks may go without the coat and wear the blue flannel shirt if in blue, and other enlisted men do not wear the neckerchief and may wear the watch cap when in blue. The watch cap is a dark blue knitted cap without visor or brim that may be pulled down over the ears for cold weather.

Winter Service Uniform.— At various times in the past when vessels of the Navy have been detailed for long periods of duty in the Arctic regions or where the weather conditions are particularly cold and severe, spe-

U. S. Navy. Chief petty officer

Blue working dress uniform *Rank:* Chief Master-at-Arms

U. S. Navy. Winter uniform

Wind and rain proof uniform worn by crews of U. S. Destroyers and Patrol Vessels during winter in northern waters

cial uniforms have been authorized to be worn by the officers and enlisted men making up the personnel of such expeditions. For the Arctic expeditions these special uniform suits have usually been made of fur similar in pattern to the garments worn by the natives of the Far North.

The conditions under which the Destroyer Flotillas and Patrol Squadrons must operate off the coasts of Northern Europe during the severe weather of the winter months has necessitated the design of a special uniform for their crews. This winter storm uniform consists of heavy waterproof boots of the style known as "Arctics"; wind and rain proof trousers of heavy material; an overshirt of specially heavy wool with a hood; and a wind and rain proof coat with a hood to be worn over all.

While the appearance of a sailor dressed in this uniform is very different from that which we are accustomed to see upon the decks of the trim and smart vessels of the United States Navy, it is made necessary by the severe conditions of the service demanded and adds to efficiency in that it serves to keep the men dry and warm and able to perform their duties when the little vessels of the patrol fleet are swept by heavy seas and chilling gales.

Dungaree suit consists of a jumper and trousers made of blue denim drill.

Gloves for enlisted men are made of dark gray wool.

Bathing trunks of dark blue material are required to be worn by all men bathing "over the side" from a ship.

Pajamas consisting of a shirt and trousers of light weight white cotton drill are provided for enlisted men.

Overcoats for chief petty officers are of dark blue cloth, double breasted, buttoning to the neck with two rows of large black buttons, with a rolling collar, two vertical breast pockets and two lower side pockets with flaps. For all other enlisted men (except bandsmen) the overcoat is the same style but reaches only to the tips of the fingers when the arms hang at the sides.

Uniforms for bandsmen of the navy consist of a blue dress coat, white dress coat, sky-blue trousers, white trousers, blue cap, and white cap, all of the same design and cut as those for the enlisted men of the U. S. Marine Corps (described in Chapter VI) except that navy buttons are worn instead of marine corps buttons, a lyre device is worn on the cap, instead of the marine corps device, and the navy "rating badges" are worn by the bandmaster and first musicians instead of the chevrons worn by the noncommissioned officers of the marine corps.

The overcoat for bandsmen is of sky-blue cloth, double breasted, buttoning to the neck with two rows of gilt navy buttons, lined with red flannel, falling collar five inches deep, cut to reach about six inches below the knee, and provided with a circular cape of the same color.

The rank and special duty (or "rating" as it is styled in the navy) of the petty officers of the first, second and third classes, as given in the table on page 38, is shown by a "rating badge" which is worn on the right sleeve between the elbow and the shoulder by petty officers of the Seaman Branch and in the corresponding position on the left sleeve by all other petty officers.

The rating badge consists of a spread eagle above a

"specialty mark" showing the duty and a chevron showing the "class" or rank of the wearer. These badges are three and one-quarter inches broad.

The chevrons are made of stripes of cloth three-eighths of an inch wide, placed one-quarter of an inch apart as shown in the illustrations. A peculiarity of the navy chevrons is that they are worn with the apex of the angle formed by the two bars of each stripe pointing down instead of up as in the army and marine corps.

The specialty marks are placed in the center of the angle formed by the upper stripe of the chevron and the spread eagle is placed just above the specialty mark.

For use on blue clothing the chevrons are made of scarlet cloth and the eagle and specialty marks are embroidered in white; while for white clothing the chevrons are of blue cloth and the specialty marks and eagle are embroidered in blue.

For petty officers holding three consecutive good-conduct badges (namely, the good-conduct medal and two bars, representing three full enlistments served with efficiency and good conduct) the chevrons are made of gold lace braid and the eagle and specialty marks are embroidered in silver.

The specialty marks indicating the different ranks or "ratings" are, as shown in the illustrations, as follows:

NUMBER OF FIGURE IN ILLUSTRATION.	RANK OR "RATING."
1.	Master at arms.
2.	Boatswain's mate, or coxswain.
3.	Quartermaster.
4.	Blacksmith, or shipfitter.
5.	Sailmaker's mate.
6.	Printer.

7. .... Carpenter's mate, plumber and fitter, painter.
8. .... Turret captain.
9. .... Gunner's mate.
10. .... Storekeeper.
11. .... Yeoman.
12. .... Electrician.
13. .... Machinist's mate, boiler maker, water tender, coppersmith, oiler.
14. .... Hospital corps (red cloth Geneva cross).
15. .... Bandmaster, musician.
16. .... Commissary steward.
17. .... Ship's cook and baker.
18. .... Bugler, worn on the left arm above the elbow.

Petty officers detailed to duty in the Naval Aviation Corps wear rating badges of the same design as those worn by other petty officers, the number of stripes in the chevron showing the class, three stripes with an arc of a circle above for chief petty officer class, three stripes for first class, two stripes for second class and one stripe for third class, and the specialty marks showing the various classes of duty being as follows:

Quartermaster Aviation..A steering wheel with one eagle's wing to the right of it and one to the left of it.

Machinists's Mate Aviation.............. A two bladed airplane propeller with one eagle's wing to the right of it and one to the left of it.

Carpenter's Mate Aviation............ Two axes crossed with one eagle's wing to the right of it and one to the left of it.

U. S. Navy. Petty officers' rating badges worn on sleeves of uniform coats, overshirts and jumpers. The special detail is indicated by the specialty mark worn in the angle of the chevron

1. Chief Master-at-Arms
2. Boatswain's Mate, First Class
3. Gunner's Mate, Second Class
4. Quartermaster, Third Class

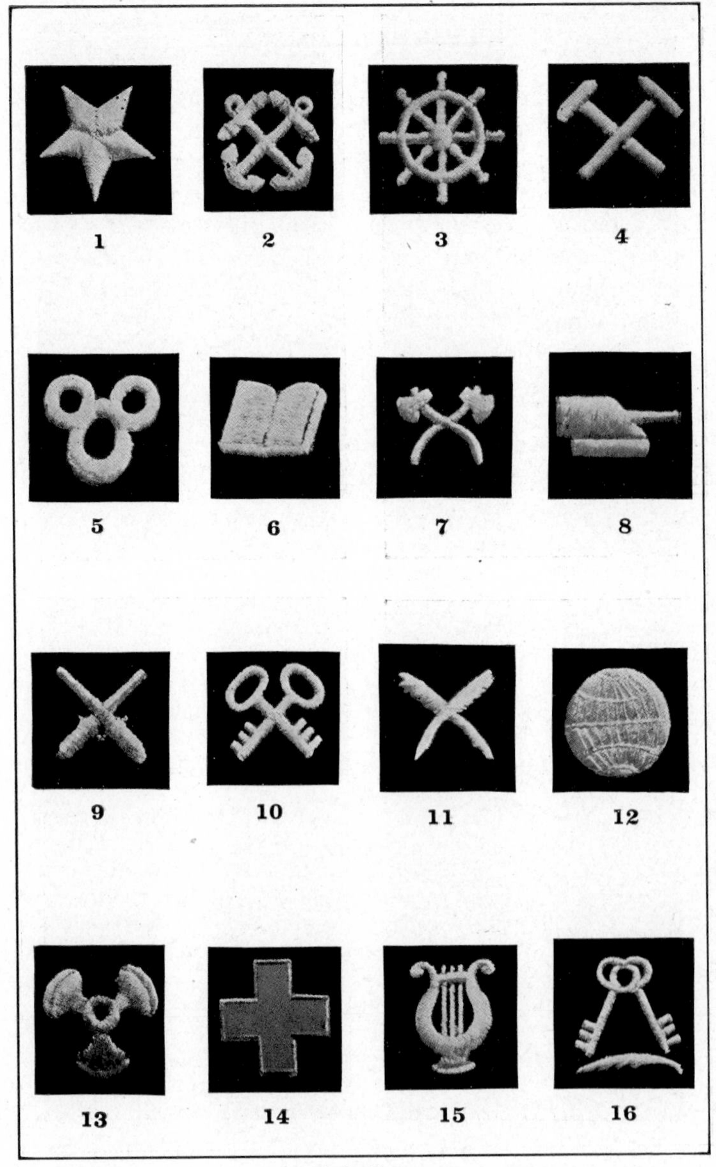

U. S. Navy
Petty officers' specialty marks

These specialty marks measure 2½ inches from tip to tip of the eagle's wings.

"Distinguishing marks" are worn by certain enlisted men to indicate special duties or stations to which they are detailed or to show certain qualifications. These marks are embroidered in white silk for blue clothing and in blue silk for white clothing and, as illustrated, are as follows:

NUMBER OF FIGURE IN ILLUSTRATION.	DUTY OR STATION.
19.	Seaman-gunner mark, worn below the chevron by petty officers and in place of the rating badge by other men who have qualified as seaman-gunners.
20.	Gun captain mark, worn by men detailed by the commanding officer as gun captains, on the opposite arm to that on which the rating badge is worn.
21.	Gun pointer mark, worn by men who have qualified as gun pointers on the opposite arm to that on which the rating badge is worn; gun pointers of the first class wear the mark with a star above it (Figure 22).
23.	The Navy "E," worn by members of the turret, gun and torpedo crews that make exceptionally high scores on record target practice, and men of the Engineer Division of the ship winning the trophy in the annual engineering competition.
	Expert rifleman's mark, worn by enlisted men of the Navy, Marine Corps and Naval Militia qualified as expert riflemen on the left sleeve midway between the wrist and the elbow, and consisting of a square, one inch, containing target rings three-quarters of an inch and one-half

NUMBER OF FIGURE IN ILLUSTRATION.	DUTY OR STATION.
	of an inch in diameter and a bull's-eye one-quarter of an inch in diameter, embroidered in blue on white for white clothing, in white on blue for blue clothing and in gray on khaki for khaki colored clothing.
24.	Radio operator, worn by electricians who are radio operators below the rating badge.
25.	Torpedoman mark, worn by gunner's mates who have qualified in torpedoes and mines below the rating badge.
7.	Shipwright's mark, worn by shipwrights in the same place as the rating badge.
14.	Hospital Corps mark (the Geneva cross), worn by hospital apprentices on the left arm above the elbow.
17.	Ship's cook of the third and fourth classes, bakers of the second class and officers' stewards and cooks, worn on the left arm above the elbow.
3.	Signalmen, first and second class, worn on the arm above the elbow in place of the rating badge.
15.	Musician's mark, worn by musicians of the first and second class on the left arm above the elbow.
26.	Ex-apprentice mark, worn by all men who have passed through the rating of apprentice in the navy; worn on the front of the overshirt and jumper just below the neck opening and on the sleeve of petty officers' coats on the same side as the rating badge, between the wrist and the elbow.

The Branch of the Navy to which all enlisted men not petty officers belong is shown by a *branch mark,* a

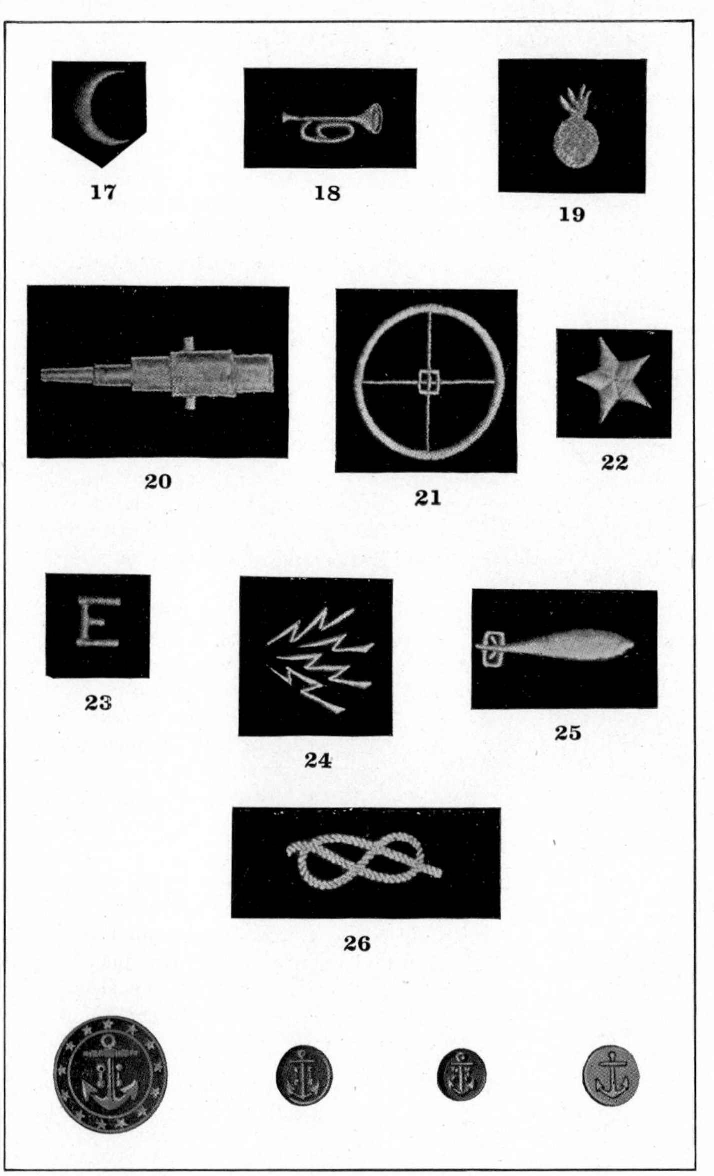

U. S. Navy
Enlisted men's specialty marks, distinguishing marks and buttons

stripe of braid three-eighths of an inch wide around the top of the sleeve at the shoulder seam.

For the Seaman Branch the *branch mark* is worn on the right arm, in blue for white clothing and white for blue clothing; for the artificer branch, engineer force, the branch mark is worn on the left arm in red. Hospital apprentices, shipwrights, musicians, buglers, commissary and messmen wear no branch mark.

Service stripes.— To show the number of enlistments that a man has served all enlisted men who have served one or more enlistments of three or four years wear service stripes, three-eighths of an inch wide, diagonally across the outer side of the left sleeve of the blue coat, white coat, overshirt or jumper. These service stripes are of scarlet cloth on blue clothing and of blue cloth on white clothes. One service stripe is worn for each enlistment of three or four years that the wearer has completed. For petty officers who hold three consecutive good-conduct badges the service stripes are made of gold lace braid.

Neckerchief.— The neckerchief worn by enlisted men with the blue overshirt and white dress jumper is of black silk thirty-six inches square, worn around the neck under the collar, tied in a square knot just below the collar opening in front.

Leggings.— For duty with landing forces ashore enlisted men of the navy wear khaki-colored canvas leggings.

ENLISTED MEN OF THE NAVAL MILITIA

Enlisted men of the Naval Militia wear the same uniforms as those prescribed for the regular Navy with the addition of the *distinguishing mark for the Naval Militia,* consisting of a vertical foul anchor enclosed in a diamond shaped lozenge. This mark being embroidered in white on a blue ground for blue clothing and in blue on a white ground for white clothing. It is worn on overshirts and jumpers just below the neck opening and on coats (except overcoats) on the same sleeve as the rating badge midway between the wrist and the elbow.

The cap ribbon worn by enlisted men of the Naval Militia bears the words "Naval Militia" followed by the authorized abbreviation for the state or territory to which they belong thus, for the Naval Militia of Massachusetts,

NAVAL MILITIA, MASS.

When United States ships are assigned for the use of the Naval Militia of any state such men of the organization as the Governor of the state may designate may wear on their cap ribbons the name of the ship so assigned with the distinguishing mark for the naval militia before and after the name of the ship.

The Naval Reserve enlisted men wear the same uniform as that prescribed for the various grades of the regular service, with the exceptions that all gilt buttons worn on the uniforms are of the special design prescribed for the Naval Reserve, that is, having upon them in relief a plain vertical anchor surrounded by the letters U. S. N. R., and the cap ribbons bear the words

U. S. NAVAL RESERVE FORCE

The Navy Sword.— The sword carried by all officers of the Navy has a bright steel cut and thrust blade from twenty-six to thirty-two inches long depending upon the height of the wearer, having a half-basket hilt and a grip covered with white shark skin wrapped with a spiral of gilt wire, the hilt being of brass gilded. It is carried in a scabbard of black leather with gilded tip ferrule and gilded straps and rings for attaching the slings which attach it to the belt. The under side of the guard has the letters " U. S. N." in relief, the upper ring strap is decorated with a foul anchor, the lower ring strap is decorated with scrolls, the rings are attached to the straps by bands representing knotted rope, the tip ferrule is decorated with a " figure of eight " knot and finished at the bottom with a carved dolphin.

The blade of the sword is etched on each side with designs typical of the naval service, and on one side near the hilt the name of the owner is engraved within a scroll.

The belt for naval officers is closed at the front and center by a circular belt plate ornament with a raised design of a wreath enclosing a circle of rope one inch in diameter inside of which is an American eagle on a horizontal anchor above a pyramid of cannon balls, the space between the rope circle and the eagle and anchor design having thirteen stars in a circle.

Identification tag.— Every officer and enlisted man of the U. S. Navy on active duty is required to wear an identification tag, which consists of an oval plate of monel metal, one and one-quarter inches by one and one-half inches in size, suspended from the neck by a monel metal wire encased in a cotton sleeve.

On one side of the tag is etched the finger print of the right index finger of the officer or man wearing the tag and on the other side, for officers the letters "U. S. N.," the surname and initials, the rank and the date of commission or appointment; for enlisted men the letters " U. S. N.," the surname and initials, the month, day and year of enlistment expressed in numerals thus "1.5.1916." and the month, day and year of birth similarly expressed.

A copy of the finger print of each officer and enlisted man in the Naval Service is also kept on file at the Bureau of Navigation of the Navy Department in Washington, D. C.

These tags are for the purpose of identification in case of death or wounds so serious as to produce unconsciousness.

SEAL OF THE U. S. MARINE CORPS

CHAPTER VI

UNIFORMS AND INSIGNIA OF THE U. S. MARINE CORPS

THE marines serve both on ship and ashore, while aboard ship their duties closely approximate those of the sailor in the line of the navy and while serving ashore their duties are of the same nature as those of the army soldier, but their uniform is distinctly military in style and appearance.

Both officers and enlisted men have uniforms of blue cloth corresponding to those of the navy and worn upon the same occasions, and the officers have white uniforms to be worn upon the occasions when officers of the navy wear white, while the enlisted men have no white uniform coats but wear uniforms of khaki colored cotton material upon the occasions when enlisted men of the navy wear white. This khaki uniform is officially known as "summer field" uniform, but commonly called "khaki."

Both officers and men are also provided with a "winter field" uniform for wear upon active service in the field whenever the weather is too cold for the khaki uniform. The winter field uniforms and the overcoats for officers and men are made of woolen cloth of a shade known as "forestry green," a grayish olive green.

In time of war the special full dress, full dress and mess dress uniforms are not worn unless especially ordered for a particular occasion.

UNIFORMS FOR OFFICERS OF THE MARINE CORPS

The commissioned officers of the Marine Corps are required to have complete outfits of special full dress, full dress, undress, white undress, mess dress, summer field and winter field uniforms.

The warrant officers of the Marine Corps are required to have the same uniforms with the exception of special full dress, full dress and mess dress.

The occasions upon which these uniforms are worn are given in the table of occasions for uniforms for officers of the Navy and Marine Corps, page 109, and the composition of the various uniforms is as follows:

Special Full Dress Uniform.— For officers of the Line, a double breasted frock coat of dark blue cloth, extending to about one foot below the waist, with two rows of gilt Marine Corps buttons down the front from the line of the collar to the waist, the buttons being arranged in groups of threes for the rank of Major General Commandant, in groups of twos for the rank of Brigadier General and equally spaced for all other ranks; with a standing collar embroidered with gold oak leaves for

Major General George Barnett
Major General Commandant of the United States Marine Corps

general officers and covered with gold lace braid for other ranks, the cuffs bearing ornamentations of gold embroidery to indicate the rank of the wearer (see illustrations at page 155), the cuffs for general officers being of dark blue velvet; dark blue cloth trousers, trimmed down the outer leg seams with one and a quarter inch wide gold lace braid having a quarter inch scarlet silk stripe through the center; a bell-crowned cap of dark blue cloth with a sloping visor with a gold chin strap above it and the silver and gold Marine Corps device at the center of the front of the crown, gold epaulets, black shoes, white gloves, and the Marine Corps sword suspended from a belt by slings, belt and slings covered with gold lace braid.

For officers of the Staff, the same as for officers of the Line except that the coat is single breasted with one row of buttons and gold shoulder knots are worn instead of epaulets, and aiguilettes of plaited gold cord are worn.

For the Major General Commandant, and officers of the Staff, there may be worn with this uniform a chapeau or "cocked hat" of black silk beaver with a two-inch strap of gold lace on the right side upon which is the silver and gold Marine Corps device and a plume of cock's feathers extending over the top of the crown from front to rear, the plume to be canary-yellow for the Major General Commandant and scarlet for officers of the Staff.

The Major General Commandant also wears with this uniform a sash of buff silk with bullion tassels diagonally across the body from the right shoulder to the waist at the left side, the tassels hanging below the belt.

Brigadier Generals wear with this uniform a sash belt with a bow at the left side, of two and a half inch gold lace with a three-eighths inch scarlet stripe through the center, from which the sword is suspended by gold lace trimmed slings.

When mounted, officers wear full dress breeches and black boots with this uniform.

The full dress cap for the Major General Commandant has a band of blue-black velvet decorated with gold embroidered oak leaves, and a wreath of oak leaves around the Marine Corps device.

The full dress cap for Brigadier Generals is the same as for the Major General Commandant, except that the wreath of oak leaves around the corps device is omitted.

The full dress cap for all other commissioned officers has a band of gold lace braid with a three-eighths inch scarlet stripe through the center, the visor being covered with dark blue cloth decorated with sprays of oak leaves for field officers (Colonels, Lieutenant-colonels and Majors) and with plain black patent leather for company officers (Captains, First Lieutenants and Second Lieutenants).

Full dress uniform.— The same coat as worn with special full dress, full dress trousers, gold shoulder knots, full dress cap, white gloves, and black shoes. The same sash and belt for the Major General Commandant, the same sash for Brigadier Generals and the same belt for other commissioned officers as those worn with the special full dress uniform.

The full dress trousers for the Major General Commandant and Brigadier Generals are of dark blue cloth with a stripe of black mohair braid one and one-half inches wide down the outer leg seams; for all Line officers below the rank of Brigadier General they are of sky-blue cloth with a stripe of scarlet cloth one and one-half inches wide down each outer leg seam; and for

Photo by Harris & Ewing, Washington, D. C.

U. S. Marine Corps. Officer, special full dress uniform
Rank: Lieutenant Colonel of the Staff

Photo by Harris & Ewing, Washington, D. C.

U. S. Marine Corps. Officer, full dress uniform
Rank: Major of the Line

Staff officers below the rank of Brigadier General they are of dark blue cloth with a stripe of scarlet cloth one and one-half inches wide down each outer leg seam.

The chapeau may be worn with this uniform by the Major General Commandant and officers of the Staff.

When mounted officers wear full dress breeches and black boots with this uniform, the breeches being of the same color and with the same stripes as the full dress trousers.

Undress uniform.— The blue undress coat, undress trousers (white trousers may be worn), undress cap (white undress cap may be worn), black shoes (white shoes with white trousers), white gloves, the sword worn suspended from a tan leather belt and slings. When mounted undress breeches and black boots are worn.

The undress coat for all officers is a single breasted sack coat of dark blue cloth or serge extending to about ten inches below the waist, with a standing collar, buttoned down the front by five Marine Corps gilt buttons. On the front it has four outside patch pockets, one on each breast and one on each side below the breast pockets with their tops at the waist line, all the pockets being closed by pointed flaps buttoned by small Marine Corps gilt buttons. On the shoulders there are shoulder straps of the same material as the coat extending from the shoulder seam to the base of the collar, the insignia of rank being worn thereon. The Marine Corps device indicating the corps and the staff corps device or aide-de-camp's device for indicating the staff corps or special assignment of officers being worn on the collar on each side of the neck opening in front. The sword belt is worn underneath this coat.

The undress trousers for General officers are of dark

blue cloth with stripes of black mohair braid down the outer leg seams, for Line officers below the rank of Brigadier General they are of sky-blue cloth or serge with one and a half inch scarlet stripes down the outer leg seams, and for Staff officers below the rank of Brigadier General they are of dark blue cloth or serge with one and a half inch scarlet stripes down the outer leg seams.

The undress cap is of dark blue cloth with a sloping visor having the same ornamentation for General officers and Field officers as the full dress cap, the Marine Corps device in the center of the front and a chin strap above the visor made of gold braid three-eighths of an inch wide with a narrow scarlet stripe through the center of it. For General officers the band of the cap is of blue-black velvet and for all other officers it is of black mohair braid.

The white undress cap is made of white duck and white braid of the same style as the blue undress cap and provided with the same visor, corps device and chin strap as the blue undress cap.

Undress breeches, worn when mounted, are of the same color as undress trousers and have the same stripes.

White undress uniform.— The white undress coat, white trousers, white cap, white shoes, white gloves and sword with tan leather sword belt and slings. The white undress coat is made of white duck or drill after the same style and design as the blue undress coat and bears the same rank, corps and staff devices.

Mess dress uniform.— Blue mess jacket, special full dress trousers, white dress waistcoat with gilt buttons, gold shoulder knots, full dress cap, white shirt and collar, black necktie, black patent leather shoes. The white mess jacket is worn in hot weather and white trousers

Photo by Harris & Ewing, Washington, D. C.

U. S. Marine Corps. Officer, blue undress uniform
Field officer of the Line

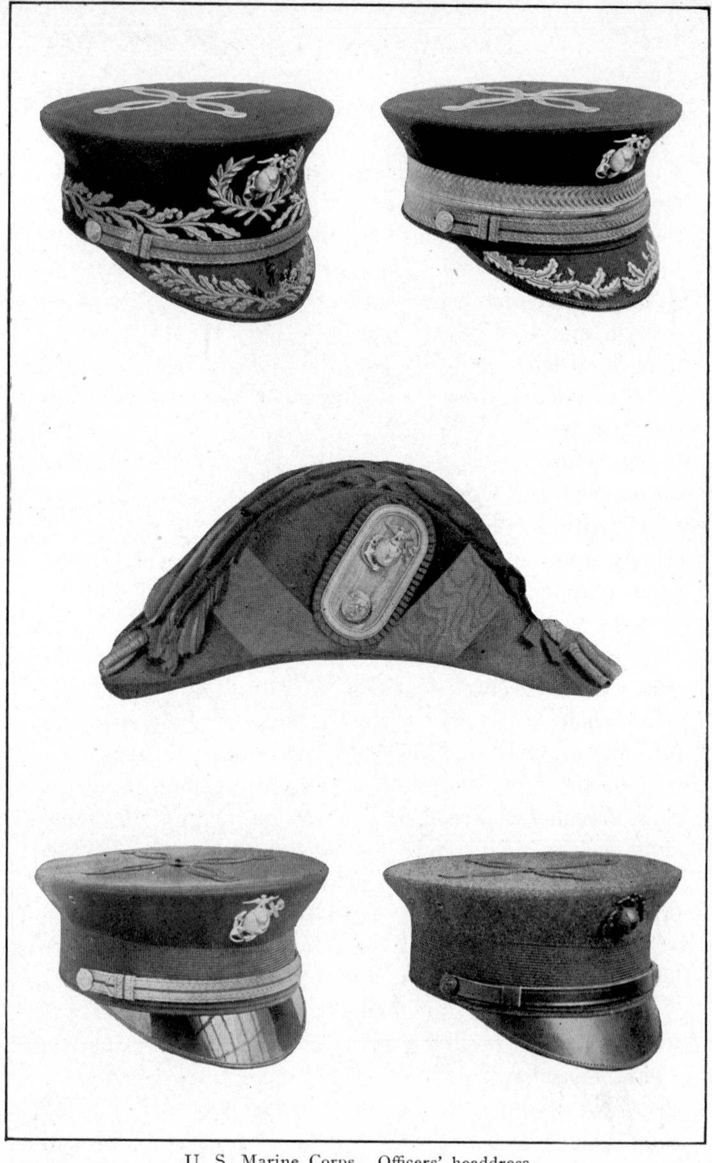

U. S. Marine Corps. Officers' headdress

1. Full dress cap, Major General Commandant
2. Full dress cap, field officers
3. Chapeau, Major General Commandant
4. Undress cap, company officers
5. Winter field cap, all officers

may be worn with it, in which case the white cap is worn.

The mess jacket is a round shell jacket of dark blue cloth, with standing collar, extending to the points of the hip bones at the sides and curving downward slightly to the front and back. The jacket is worn hooked at the collar but open down the front which has one row of sixteen small Marine Corps gilt buttons. The collar is covered with gold lace braid and the sleeves bear the same ornamentations indicating rank as those worn on the full dress coat.

The white mess jacket is of the same style as the blue mess jacket but has no sleeve ornamentation, and is provided with shoulder straps of the same material as the jacket, upon which the insignia of rank are worn in the same manner as on the shoulder straps of the undress coats.

The mess dress is worn on occasions when naval officers wear their evening dress uniform.

Summer field uniform.— The summer field uniform is made of khaki colored cotton drill and consists of a coat of the same style and design as the white undress coat, breeches, field hat or khaki colored cap of the same style as the white cap, tan leather shoes, tan leather strap puttee leggings, and the sword suspended from the tan leather belt and slings, the belt being worn outside of the coat. Mounted officers may wear tan leather boots.

The field hat is the wide brimmed brown felt hat worn with the peaked crown, commonly known as the "campaign hat." It has the Marine Corps device on the front of the crown to indicate the corps, and in the case of officers a hat cord woven of gold and red and finished at the ends with gold and red acorns is worn around the base of the crown.

The rank marks worn with the summer field coat are the same as those worn with the white undress, but all corps and staff devices and buttons are of dull finished bronze to make them less conspicuous.

Winter Field Uniform.— The winter field uniform is made of cloth or serge of the shade known as "forestry green," a grayish olive green, and consists of a coat made in the same general style as the summer field coat except that the lower pockets are larger and are of the "bellows" type, breeches (trousers are worn sometimes), the field hat or winter field cap, tan leather strap puttee leggings, tan shoes, sword suspended from tan leather belt and slings, the belt being worn outside of the coat. Mounted officers may wear tan leather boots.

The insignia indicating rank, corps and staff department and the buttons are the same as those worn on the summer field uniform.

In the field or at drills when it is considered appropriate the coat of the field uniform is not worn, in which case the flannel shirt, of the same color as the field uniform, is worn with the insignia of rank on the collar on each side of the front opening.

The *overcoat* for all officers is a double breasted ulster made of cloth of the same "forestry green" color as the winter field uniform extending to about ten inches below the knee, buttoned to the neck with two rows of large size bronze Marine Corps buttons, with a deep rolling collar, and shoulder straps on the shoulders bearing the insignia of rank in bright metal and the insignia indicating the Staff corps and aides-de-camps

Photo by Harris & Ewing, Washington, D. C.

U. S. Marine Corps. Officer, winter field uniform

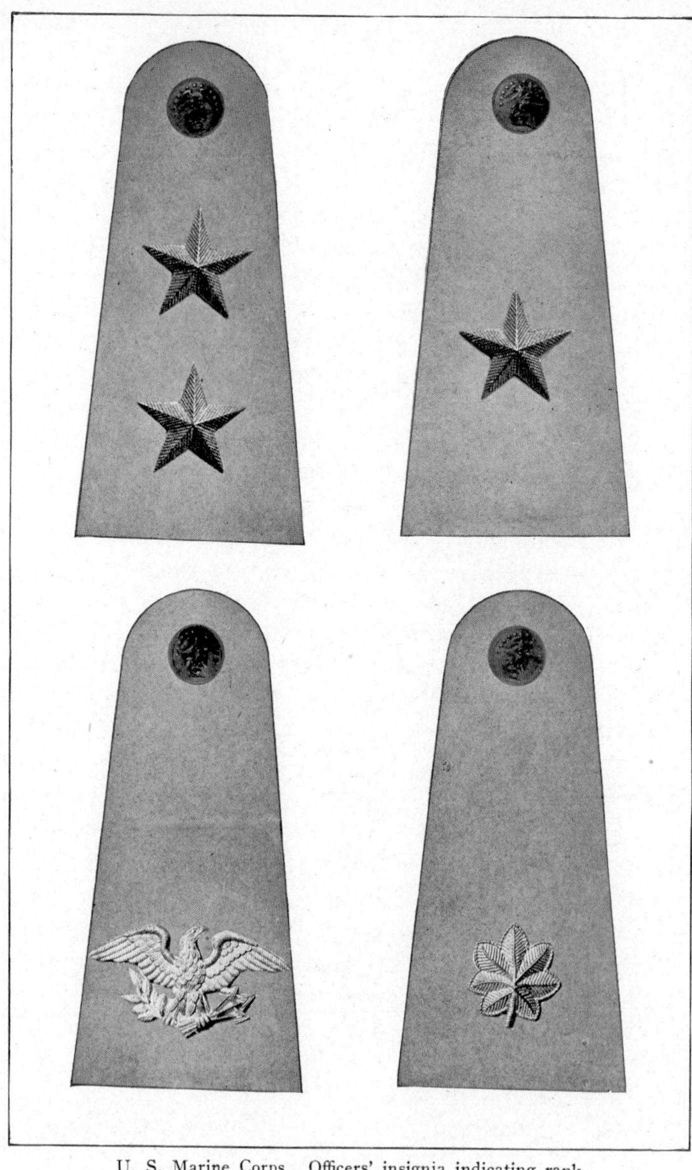

U. S. Marine Corps. Officers' insignia indicating rank

Shoulder straps of blue and white undress coats, summer and winter field coats, white mess jacket and overcoat

1. Major General Commandant
2. Brigadier General
3. Colonel
4. Lieutenant Colonel (Silver Leaf)

in bronze. The sleeves bear ornamentations indicating the rank of the wearer of the same size and design as those for the full dress coat but of the same color as the cloth of the overcoat. There is a double box pleat down the center of the back and straps across the back to button the coat in at the waist. On each side below the waist there is a pocket with a vertical opening.

The *cloak* for all officers is of dark blue cloth lined with scarlet cloth, cut to three-fourths of a circle so as to hang full, and having a rolling collar of black velvet.

For wear in rainy weather each officer is provided with a raincoat and a rain cape of waterproof material, of the same color as the winter field uniform, and extending to about eight inches below the knee.

Shirts and collars for wear with special full dress, full dress, undress and mess dress uniforms are of plain white linen, and those for wear with field uniforms are of flannel of the color of the field uniform.

Warrant officers (Marine Gunners and Quartermaster Clerks) are not required to have special full dress, full dress or mess uniforms.

INSIGNIA OF RANK, CORPS AND STAFF DEPARTMENTS

The rank of officers of the Marine Corps is indicated in three ways: first, by rank insignia worn upon the shoulder straps of the blue and white undress coats and summer and winter field coats; second, by rank insignia worn upon the tops of the epaulets and shoulder knots worn with special full dress, full dress and mess dress coats, and third, by the ornamentations worn upon the sleeves of the full dress coat, mess jacket and overcoat.

The insignia of rank, indicating the rank of the wearer, are practically the same as those for the corresponding ranks of the Army and Navy, and are as follows:

Major General Commandant — two silver stars.
Brigadier General — one silver star.
Colonel — a silver spread eagle.
Lieutenant Colonel — a silver oak leaf.
Major — a gold oak leaf.
Captain — two silver bars.
First Lieutenant — one silver bar.
Second Lieutenant — one gold bar.
Marine Gunner and Quartermaster Clerk } no insignia of rank, the shoulder strap being plain.

The insignia of rank worn on the shoulder straps of the blue undress coat and the winter field coat are embroidered in silver thread, with the exception of the Major's gold leaf which is embroidered in gold thread, and those worn on the white undress coat, summer field coat, white mess jacket and overcoat are of metal, silver for all except the major's leaf and second lieutenant's bar which are of gold.

The insignia of rank worn on the tops of the epaulets and shoulder knots are of the same size but are embroidered upon scarlet cloth to show one-sixteenth of an inch all around.

The sleeve ornamentations indicating the rank of officers of the Marine Corps are as shown in the illustrations. On the full dress coat and mess jacket for the Major General Commandant and the Brigadier Generals they are embroidered in gold upon cuffs of dark blue velvet and on the overcoat they are embroidered in thread of the same color as the overcoat. For Line officers below the rank of Brigadier General they are made of gold lace braid on a backing of scarlet cloth on the full dress coat and mess jacket while for officers of the

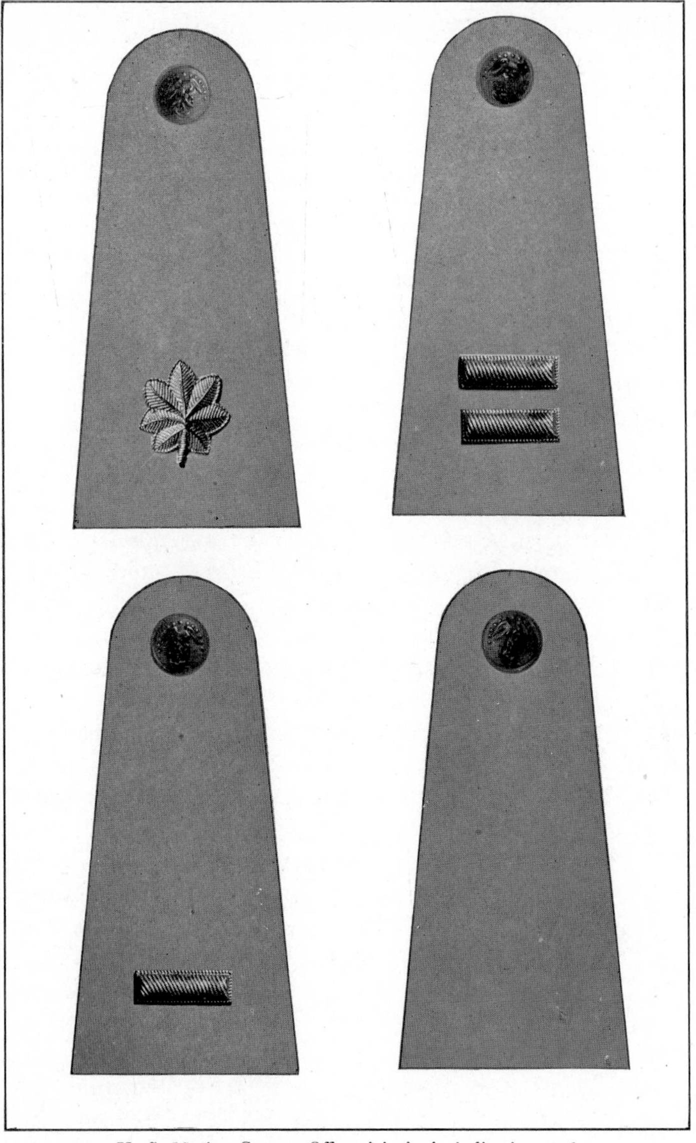

U. S. Marine Corps. Officers' insignia indicating rank
Shoulder straps of blue and white undress coats, summer and winter field coats, white mess jacket and overcoat

1. Major (Gold leaf)
2. Captain
3. First Lieutenant (Silver bar), Second Lieutenant (Gold bar)
4. Warrant officer

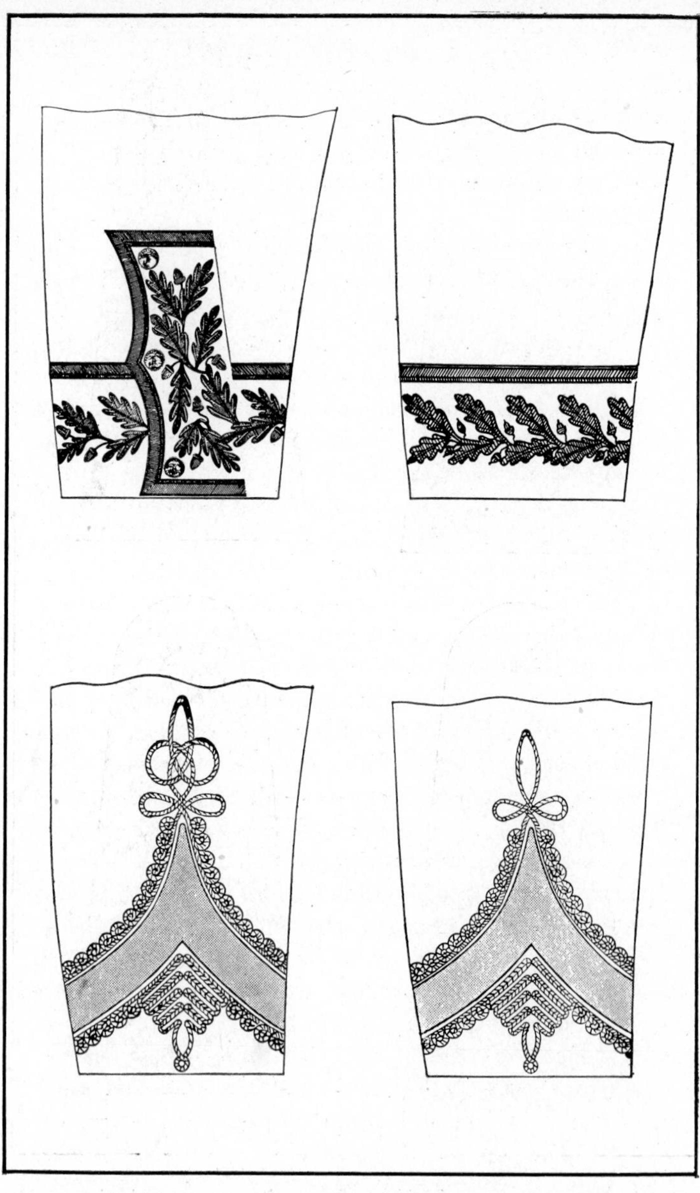

U. S. Marine Corps. Officers' decorations on sleeves indicating rank. In gold braid and embroidery on sleeves of full dress coat and blue mess jacket. In forestry green braid and embroidery on sleeves of overcoat.

1. Major General Commandant
2. Brigadier General
3. Colonel
4. Lieutenant Colonel

Staff the scarlet cloth backing is omitted. On the overcoats for all officers below the rank of Brigadier General they are made of mohair braid of the same color as the overcoat.

It may be noted that the design of the sleeve ornaments for Field officers (Colonels, Lieutenant Colonels and Majors) is in the form of a chevron, while that for company officers (Captains, and First and Second Lieutenants) is a knot known to seamen as a "carrick bend," to artillerymen as a "prolong knot"; and to the civilian as the "True love knot" representing faithfulness on account of the fact that it does not readily slip or pull apart. It was on this account that this particular form of knot was first used as a military emblem to denote faithfulness or loyalty.

The fact that an officer belongs to the Marine Corps is shown by the Marine Corps device or insignia worn upon the front of all caps and field hats, upon the right side of the chapeau, on the top of epaulets and shoulder knots, and upon the collars of the blue and white undress coats, summer and winter field coats and mess jackets.

The Marine Corps device for full dress and undress caps is a fretted silver Western Hemisphere with chased parallels and the continents of North and South America in gold, resting upon a foul anchor in gold, and surmounted by a spread eagle of silver. The shank of the anchor is set at an angle of thirty degrees from the horizontal. The dimensions are, diameter of hemisphere seven-eighths of an inch, height of eagle one-half of an inch, length of anchor one and three-quarter inches. The Corps device worn on epaulets and shoulder knots is of the same size and design but is made entirely of silver. The Marine Corps devices worn on the field hat and on the summer field and winter field caps are of the same design and size as those worn on the undress caps but are made entirely of bronze metal.

The Corps devices worn on the collars of the blue undress coat, white undress coat and white mess jacket are of silver and gold and of the same design as those worn on caps but of only three-fourths the size. Those worn on the collars of the summer field and winter field coats are of the same design and size as those worn on the undress coats but are made entirely of dull finish bronze metal.

The aides-de-camp on the personal staff of a General officer wear a distinctive device consisting of a shield of the United States three-quarters of an inch high surmounted by an eagle one-half of an inch high. This device is worn in the center of the sleeve ornament of the full dress coat and mess jacket and on the collars of the undress and field coats and white mess jackets in rear of the corps devices, and on the shoulder straps of the overcoat. For the full dress, undress and mess dress uniforms the device has the shield in enamel of proper colors, stripes of red and white, field blue with gold stars indicating the rank of the general officer on whose staff the aide-de-camp is serving, two stars for Major General and one star for Brigadier General. For the field coats and the overcoat the device is of the same design but made of dull finish bronze metal.

In order to designate the different departments to which the officers of the Staff of the Marine Corps belong distinctive Departmental Devices are provided to be worn with all uniforms.

Adjutant and Inspector's Department.— The distinctive device for this department consists of a miniature Marine Corps sword and fasces crossed in gold surmounted by a wreath in silver, in the center of which

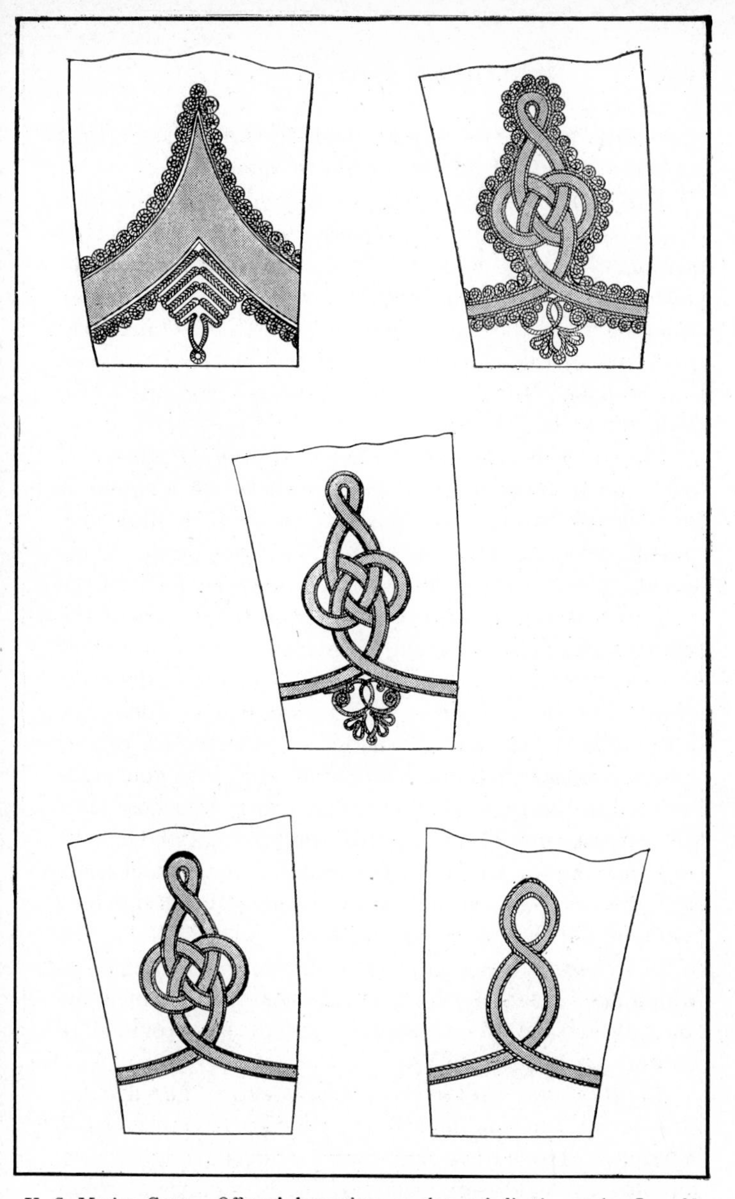

U. S. Marine Corps. Officers' decorations on sleeves indicating rank. In gold braid and embroidery on sleeves of full dress coat and blue mess jacket. In forestry green braid and embroidery on sleeves of overcoat.

1. Major
2. Captain
3. First Lieutenant
4. Second Lieutenant
5. Warrant Officer

U. S. Marine Corps

1. Corps insignia worn on caps and hats
2. Corps insignia worn on coat collars
3. Distinctive mark for Aide-de-camp
4. Departmental insignia, Adjutant and Inspector's Department
5. Departmental insignia, Quartermaster's Department
6. Departmental insignia, Paymaster's Department
7. Marine Corps button

is a shield of thirteen bars of red and white enamel with the field in blue enamel containing one large and twelve small gold stars; the dimensions being, length of sword and fasces one and three-eighths inches, diameter of wreath three-quarters of an inch.

Quartermaster's Department.— The distinctive device of this department consists of a miniature Marine Corps sword and a key crossed in gold surmounted by a gold wheel with a blue enamel rim set with thirteen gold stars, the dimensions being, length of sword and key one and three-eighths inches, diameter of wheel three-quarters of an inch.

Paymaster's Department.— The distinctive device for this department consists of a miniature Marine Corps sword and a quill pen crossed in gold surmounted by an oak leaf and two acorns in silver, the dimensions being, length of sword and quill one and three-eighths inches, length of leaf one and one-eighth inches.

With special full dress, full dress and blue mess dress uniforms these distinctive devices of the Staff Departments are worn on the top of the shoulder knot at the center; with white mess dress, blue undress, white undress, summer field and winter field uniforms they are worn on each side of the collar in rear of the corps device; and with the overcoat they are worn on the shoulder straps above the insignia of rank.

For wear with the summer field and winter field uniforms and with the overcoat the Departmental devices are of the same size and design as for the other uniforms above described but are made of dull finish bronze metal.

Aiguilettes consisting of loops of plaited round gold cord terminating in gilded pencil ornaments are worn with special full dress, full dress, and mess dress by officers of the Staff Departments, and with special full dress, full dress, mess dress, blue undress and white undress uniforms by Aides-de-camp to General officers and Aids on the personal staff of a Flag Officer of the Navy.

Warrant Officers' Distinctive Insignia.— Marine Gunners wear as a distinctive device a bursting spherical shell three-quarters of an inch in diameter with a flame five-eighths of an inch high made of silver for the blue undress and white undress coats and of dull finish bronze metal for the summer field and winter field coats and the overcoat.

Quartermaster Clerks wear the distinctive device of the Quartermaster's Department, in gold and enamel for the blue and white undress coats and in dull finish bronze for the summer field and winter field coats and the overcoat.

These devices are worn on both sides of the collar of the undress and field coats and on the shoulder straps of the overcoat.

Marine Corps Sword.— The sword carried by all officers of the Marine Corps has a steel blade, slightly curved, from twenty-eight to thirty-two inches in length, with a scroll on each side bearing the words "United States Marines." The grip is of the Mameluke type and is made of white ivory and the guard is a straight bar of gilded metal, the ends terminating in acorn designs. The scabbard is of polished silver with two gilded bands and rings for attaching it to the belt slings and a gilded ferrule at the lower end.

The Belt Plate for officers' full dress belts is of gilt metal, oblong in shape, two and one-eighth inches high by three and one-eighth inches wide, decorated with a silver wreath encircling the Arms of the United States in silver.

The Sword Knot worn on the hilt of the Marine

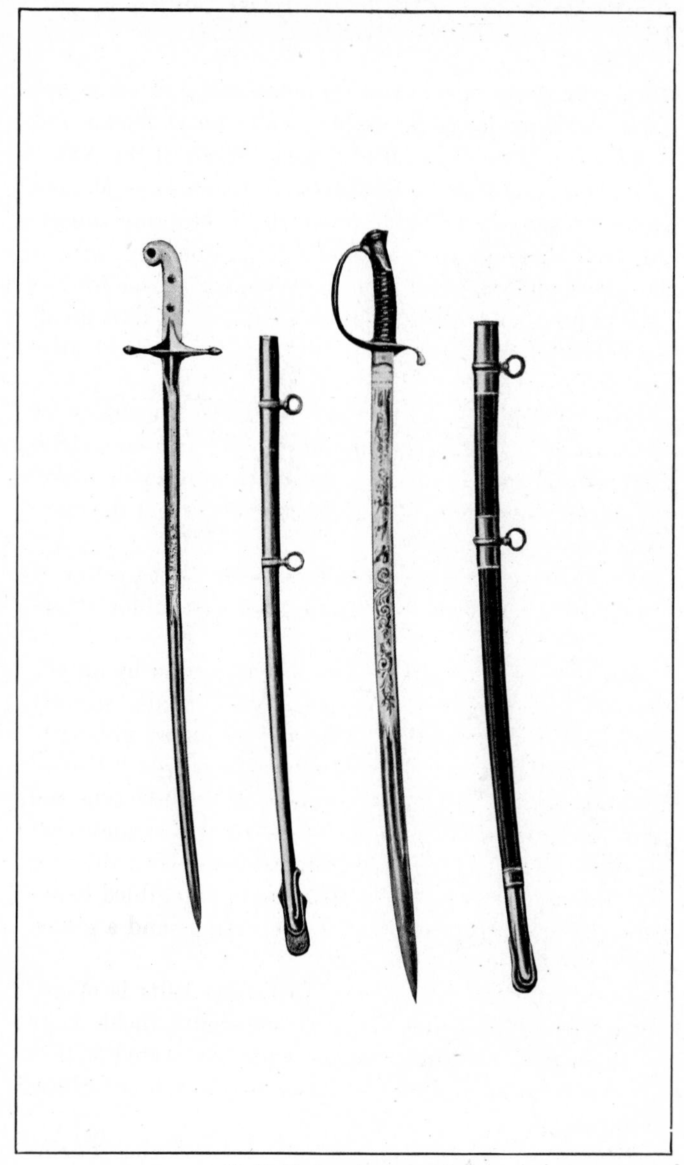

U. S. Marine Corps swords

1. Commissioned officers 2. Non-commissioned officers

Photo by Harris & Ewing, Washington, D. C.

U. S. Marine Corps
Enlisted men in dress uniform
Private First Sergeant

Officers' sword is a loop of round cord ending in a tassel, made of gold and scarlet for full dress and of plaited leather for other uniforms.

Buttons.— The Marine Corps buttons bear a design consisting of a foul anchor placed diagonally with an American eagle above it, surrounded by thirteen stars and a narrow circular band. The buttons for blue and white uniforms are of gilded metal and those for the field uniforms and the overcoat are of dull bronze metal.

Spurs are worn by all officers when mounted.

The uniform for the officers of the Marine Corps Branch of the Naval Militia of the several states and territories is the same as that for the officers of the regular service with the addition of a distinctive mark showing the state or territory to which they belong. This distinctive mark is the authorized abbreviation for the state or territory in metal block letters one-half of an inch high and is worn in rear of the Marine Corps device on each side of the collar of the blue undress, white undress, summer field and winter field coats, on the shoulder straps of the overcoat and on the front of the field hat, gold for the undress coats and bronze for the field coats, overcoat and field hat.

When sworn into the service of the United States the Naval Militia becomes a part of the National Naval Volunteers and the officers wear a metal letter V in place of the state or territory letters described above.

Officers of the Marine Corps Reserve wear the same uniforms as the officers of the regular service with the addition of a letter R worn as prescribed for the state letters of the Marine officers of the Naval Militia organizations.

UNIFORMS OF THE ENLISTED MEN OF THE MARINE CORPS

The enlisted men of the Marine Corps are required to have complete outfits of dress uniform, summer field uniform, winter field uniform and an overcoat.

The occasions upon which the different uniforms are worn is as stated in the table of occasions for the uniforms of enlisted men of the Navy and Marine Corps on page 133.

The different uniforms are as follows:

Dress Uniform.— A single breasted coat of dark blue cloth extending to about ten inches below the waist, with a standing collar, buttoned down the front with a single row of seven Marine Corps gilt buttons, shoulder straps sewn down on the shoulders with a gilt button at the collar end, and a three pointed strap with three gilt buttons on each sleeve cuff. The top and bottom edges of the collar, the front and bottom edges of the coat and the edges of the shoulder straps are trimmed with a piping of scarlet cloth one-eighth of an inch wide. Sky-blue trousers, those for noncommissioned officers having a one inch scarlet stripe down the outer leg seams and those for the other men being plain. A dark blue bell crowned cap with a sloping visor of black patent leather, the top and bottom welts of the band being trimmed with a piping of scarlet cloth one-eighth of an inch wide. Just above the visor there is a chin strap of black patent leather one-half of an inch wide, attached by a small Marine Corps gilt button at each end of the visor. White trousers may be prescribed for wear with this uniform, in which case a white cover is worn fitting tightly over the crown of the cap. The Marine Corps device in bright gilt metal is worn on the front of the

Photo by Harris & Ewing, Washington, D C.

U. S. Marine Corps

Enlisted men in winter field uniform

Private Sergeant

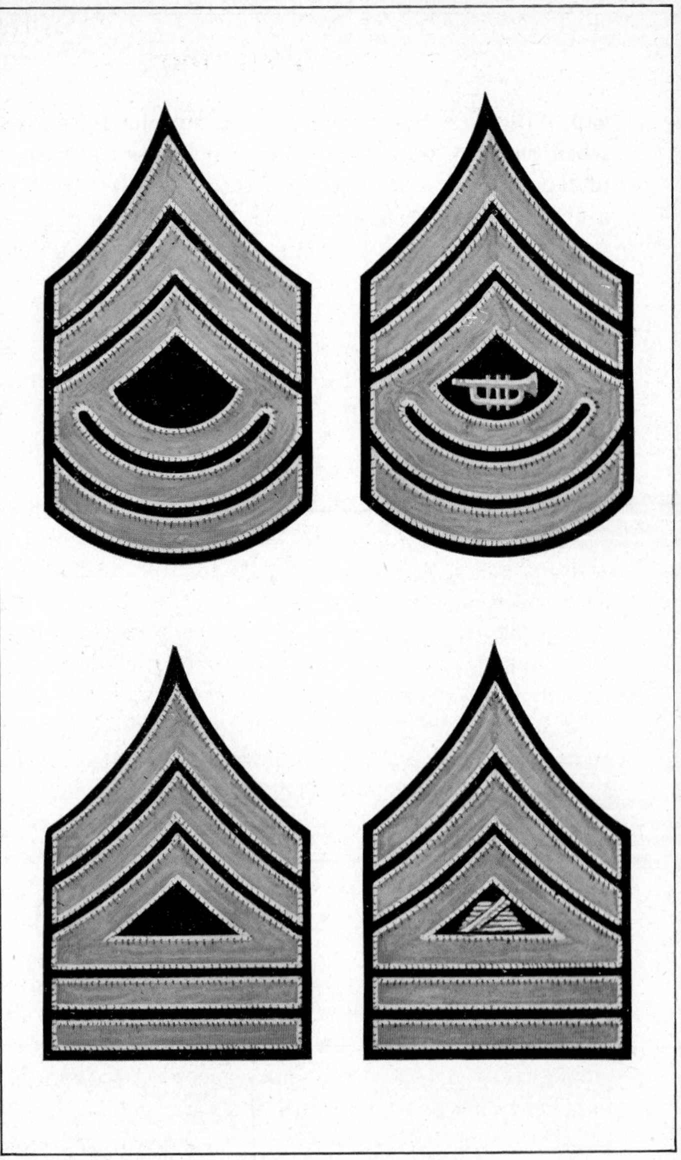

U. S. Marine Corps. Non-commissioned officers' chevrons

1. Sergeant Major
2. Second Leader of Band
3. Quartermaster Sergeant
4. Quartermaster Sergeant, Pay Department

cap. Black shoes are worn with this uniform except when the men wear leggings in which case the shoes are of tan leather. A white leather dress belt closed with a flat polished gilt belt plate is worn when on duty, and white gloves are worn when under arms. For active duty the tan leather belt and cartridge box may be worn.

Summer Field Uniform.— A single breasted coat made of khaki colored cotton material, extending to about ten inches below the waist, with standing collar, buttoned with one row of seven bronze metal Marine Corps buttons, with a patch pocket and buttoned flap on each breast and a strap on each shoulder buttoned down at the collar end by a small bronze button; khaki colored trousers of the same material as the coat; tan shoes; khaki colored canvas leggings; and the field hat of the shape worn by officers, or a khaki colored cover fitting tightly over the dress cap may be worn aboard ship or on other appropriate occasions. The Marine Corps device in dull finish bronze metal is worn on the front of the field hat and cap, and in addition the number of the company in bronze metal letters is worn on the field hat below the Marine Corps device. Tan leather shoes are always worn with this uniform. The tan leather belt or the cartridge belt of webbing is worn with field uniform. In the field or at drills afloat or ashore the coat is sometimes dispensed with and the khaki colored flannel shirt is worn.

Winter Field Uniform.— This uniform is made of the same "forestry green" colored cloth as that worn by officers for winter field uniforms and consists of a single breasted coat of the same general style as the summer field khaki coat but with the addition of an outside pocket on each side below the waist; trousers or breeches of the same material as the coat, khaki colored leggings, tan shoes, woolen gloves of the same color as the coat when needed, the field hat or a cap of the same material as the coat and the same design as the dress cap but with a dark tan leather visor and bronze buttons and corps device. The buttons on the coat of this uniform are also of bronze. At drills and on field duty the coat may be dispensed with and in that case the flannel shirt is worn. The tan leather belt or the webbing cartridge belt is worn with this uniform.

The Overcoat for enlisted men of the Marine Corps is of the same style and design as the overcoat for officers with a pointed cuff instead of the officers' sleeve ornaments.

Rain Clothes for enlisted men consist of a rubber coat, hat and boots, or the khaki colored rubber poncho may be worn in the fashion of a cape.

For wear in very cold climates a turn-down cap of dark brown fur is provided.

Dungarees are provided for artisans and men requiring them.

Pajamas are provided for all enlisted men.

The rank of the Noncommissioned officers is indicated by chevrons worn with the point up upon the sleeves of all coats and the flannel shirt midway between the shoulder and the elbow.

The chevrons for the dress coat are made of stripes of yellow silk braid one half of an inch wide on a backing of scarlet cloth, the total width of the chevron being eight inches.

The chevrons for the summer field coat and for the flannel shirt are made of cloth of a darker shade than the coat, the stripes being three-eighths of an inch in width and the whole chevron being three and one-half inches wide.

U. S. Marine Corps. Non-commissioned officers' chevrons

1. Drum Major
2. First Sergeant
3. Gunnery Sergeant
4. Sergeant
5. Corporal

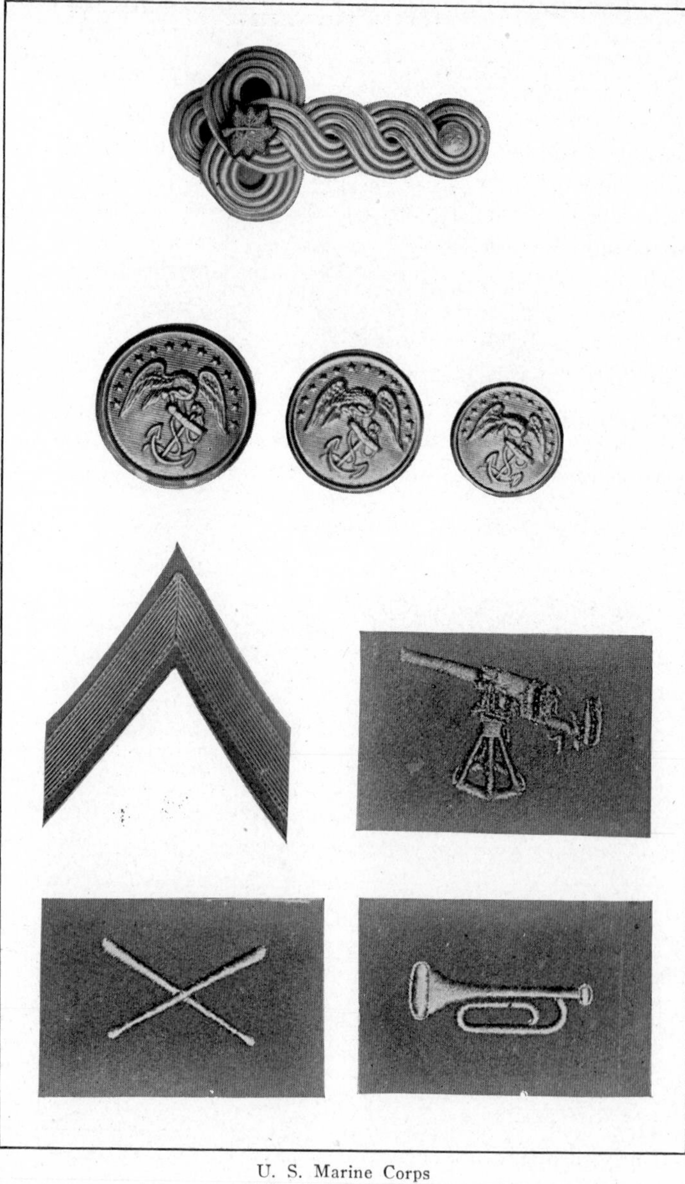

U. S. Marine Corps

1. Officers' shoulder knot
2. Service buttons
3. Chevron for Lance Corporal
4. Gun Pointer's sleeve mark
5. Drummer's sleeve mark
6. Trumpeter's sleeve mark

The chevrons for the winter field coat and for the overcoat are made of the same material as the coat on a backing of scarlet cloth, the dimensions being the same as for those on the summer field coat.

The chevrons for the flannel shirt are the same as those for the summer field coat.

The descriptions of the chevrons indicating the different ranks are, as illustrated, as follows:

Sergeant Major............	Three bars with three arcs of a circle under the bars.
Second Leader of the Band..	Three bars with three arcs and a cornet in the center.
Quartermaster Sergeant.....	Three bars and three straight ties under the bars.
Quartermaster Sergeant of the Paymaster Department	Three bars with three ties and a pile of coins crossed by a quill pen in the center.
Gunnery Sergeant.........	Three bars with a device of a bursting bomb and two crossed rifles in the center.
Drum Major	Three bars with three straight ties under the bars and a five-pointed star in the center.
Sergeant	Three bars.
Corporal	Two bars.
Lance Corporal (Acting corporal)	One bar, on the right sleeve only.

Enlisted men of the Marine Corps who have regularly qualified as gun pointers aboard ships of the Navy wear a design representing a six-pounder gun and mount on the right sleeve midway between the wrist and the elbow, the design to be in scarlet on blue cloth for blue coat and in drab linen thread for the field coats and flannel shirt.

Enlisted men detailed as gun captains aboard ships of

the Navy wear the navy gun captain's mark on the right sleeve midway between the wrist and the elbow.

Enlisted men who have qualified as expert riflemen in the navy rifle target firing course wear a design representing a small arms target about four inches above the bottom of the sleeve of the dress coat, field coats, flannel shirt and overcoat, the design showing a target one inch square with two circles and a bull's-eye inside of it.

Drummers and trumpeters wear their distinctive marks on each sleeve of the dress coat, field coats, overcoat and flannel shirt midway between the shoulder and the elbow; the mark for the drummer being a pair of drum sticks crossed and that for the trumpeter being a trumpet worn horizontal, embroidered in yellow thread on blue coats and in gray thread on the other coats and the shirt.

Service Stripes are worn by all enlisted men who have served faithfully for one or more enlistment terms in any branch of the Government service, one stripe being worn for each enlistment; they are worn on the dress coat, winter field coat and overcoat diagonally across each sleeve between the wrist and the elbow. For the blue dress coat these stripes are of yellow silk braid eight inches long and one-half of an inch wide edged with one-eighth of an inch of scarlet cloth. For the winter field coat and overcoat they are of the same material as the coats, three and three-quarters inches long and three-eighths of an inch wide edged with one-eighth of an inch of scarlet cloth.

Enlisted men of the Marine Corps Branch of the Naval Militia wear the same uniforms as the enlisted men of the regular Marine Corps with the addition of the letters indicating the state or territory to which they belong worn on the collars of the dress coat and field coat, on the shoulder straps of the overcoat and on the front of the field hat, the letters being gilt for the dress coat and bronze for the field coat, overcoat and field hat.

When the Naval Militia is sworn into the service of the United States in time of war it becomes the National Naval Volunteers and the letter V is worn in place of the letters indicating the state or territory.

Enlisted men of the Marine Corps Reserve wear the letter R on the dress cap beneath the Marine Corps device and on the field hat below the right edge of the Marine Corps device, the company numeral being worn in a corresponding position below the left edge of the corps device. These letters are in gilt for the dress cap and in bronze for the field hat.

THE MARINE BAND

The Marine Band, consisting of a Leader, second leader and seventy musicians, is stationed at the Headquarters Barracks of the Corps in Washington, D. C., and one of its principal duties is to furnish music for the official functions at the White House, hence it is popularly known as the "President's Band."

The Leader of the Marine Band wears blue undress, white undress, summer field and winter field uniforms, cloak, sword and overcoat of the same material, colors and design as those worn by commissioned officers of the Line, substituting a lyre one inch high for the insignia of rank, the lyre being of silver for the undress uniforms and of dull finish bronze for the field uniforms. His special full dress uniform is the same as that for a Captain of the Staff, with the addition of seven rows of gold braid across the front each terminating in a double loop at either side, and the substitution of a silver lyre one inch high in place of the insignia of rank. His full dress coat is a single breasted tunic of scarlet cloth trimmed across the front with seven rows of black mohair braid of the same design as for the special full dress coat, and having an ornament consisting of three loops of black braid on each cuff, and a piping of white cloth around the edges of the coat; the gold shoulder knots and aiguilettes are worn with this coat. The trousers worn with this coat are the same as those worn with the special full dress, dark blue cloth with gold lace stripes down the outer leg seams.

The special full dress for the second leader and musicians is a single breasted sack coat of scarlet cloth extending to about ten inches below the waist, with a standing collar, trimmed with piping of white cloth around the edges of the coat, the collar and the straps on the shoulder being of black cloth, the sleeves for the second leader being trimmed with three loops of black mohair braid and the musicians having pointed cuffs of black cloth, trousers of sky-blue cloth trimmed down the outer leg seams with a one-inch stripe of scarlet cloth having a piping of white cloth one-eighth of an inch wide through the center; a cap of the same design as that for other enlisted men but made of scarlet cloth with a black band.

The full dress uniform for the second leader and musicians consists of a coat of scarlet cloth of the same design as the special full dress coat with the addition of seven rows of black mohair braid across the front and shoulder knots and aiguilettes, these being white for musicians and of gold cord for the second leader; trousers and cap the same as for special full dress.

The undress, summer field and winter field uniforms and the overcoat are the same as those worn by other enlisted men of the Marine Corps.

The chevrons for the dress uniforms of the musicians of the band are three and a half inches wide by five inches long and are made of yellow silk with a lyre embroidered in the center in yellow silk. The chevrons for the second leader and the drum major are of the same size and design, but are made of gold lace braid, the second leader having a cornet embroidered in the center and the drum major a star.

The chevrons for the field uniforms and the overcoat are the same as for other noncommissioned officers of the Marine Corps with the addition of the cornet for second leader, the star for drum major and the lyre for musicians.

The chevrons for the special full dress and full dress coats are of the same size and design as for the dress coat but are made of white braid and embroidery.

Identification Tag.— Every officer and enlisted man of the U. S. Marine Corps on active duty is required to wear an identification tag, which consists of a round plate of white metal, one and three-eighths of an inch in diameter, suspended from the neck by a monel metal wire encased in a cotton covering.

These tags are stamped as follows; for officers, full name and rank; enlisted men, full name and date of first enlistment in the Marine Corps. The tags for both officers and men also have the letters "U. S. M. C." plainly stamped upon them.

These tags are for the purpose of identification in case of death or wounds so serious as to produce unconciousness.

SEAL OF THE U. S. COAST GUARD

CHAPTER VII

UNIFORMS AND INSIGNIA OF THE U. S. COAST GUARD

THE uniforms and insignia of the officers and enlisted men of the U. S. Coast Guard are very similar to those of the Navy, and they are made of dark blue cloth for wear in cold or temperate weather and of white duck for wear in the tropics or in hot weather. A variation from this general rule is found in the case of the Keepers and surfmen on duty at the Life Saving Stations who have uniforms of khaki or olive drab cotton duck instead of the white uniforms of the seagoing men of the Coast Guard.

UNIFORMS OF OFFICERS OF THE U. S. COAST GUARD

Commissioned officers of the Coast Guard are required to have complete outfits of full dress, dress, evening dress, blue service dress and white service dress uniforms; the occasions for wearing the various uniforms being as follows:

OCCASION.	UNIFORM
1. State occasions at home and abroad. 2. Receiving or calling officially upon the President of the United States or the president or sovereign or a member of the royal family of any country. 3. At ceremonies and entertainments where it is desired to do special honor to the occasion. 4. At general muster on the first Sunday of each month. 5. When receiving an ex-President of the United States, the Vice President or the Secretary of the Treasury.	Full dress.
6. When receiving an Assistant Secretary of the Treasury. 7. When receiving a member of the President's Cabinet other than the Secretary of the Treasury. 8. When receiving the Chief Justice of the United States, the President of the Senate, the Speaker of the House of Representatives, or a Committee of Congress. 9. When receiving the Governor of an island or group of islands occupied by the United States, or a Governor of one of the States or Territories of the United States, when within the waters of the state or territory or islands of which he is governor. 10. When receiving a Diplomatic Representative of the United States above the rank of Charge d'affaires when within the waters of the country to which he is accredited.	Dress uniform.

OCCASION.	UNIFORM
11. When receiving a military or naval officer of or above the rank of Brigadier General or Commodore. 12. When making the first visit in port to commanding officers and on occasions of ceremony and duty on shore where such uniform would be appropriate. 13. When serving upon Coast Guard service courts. 14. At muster on Sundays other than the first Sunday of each month.	Dress uniform.
15. On all occasions of ordinary duty and service.	Service dress or white service dress.
16. On occasions of ceremony in the evening to which officers are invited in their official capacity, such as public balls, dinners and evening receptions.	Evening dress uniform.

When serving as a part of the Navy during war the uniform prescribed for all ordinary occasions of duty is service dress, blue or white depending upon the temperature and weather.

The Full Dress Uniform consists of a frock coat of dark blue cloth; trousers of dark blue cloth with a stripe of gold lace braid down each outer leg seam, the stripe being one inch wide for all officers above the rank of Third Lieutenant and one-half inch for Third Lieutenant; gold shoulder knots; full dress cap; white gloves; black shoes; and the sword suspended by slings from a full dress belt, the belt and slings being covered with

U. S. Coast Guard. Officers' sleeve braiding indicating rank

Gold braid on full dress, dress, evening dress and blue service coats. Black braid on overcoats, without the shields

1. Captain Commandant
2. Senior Captain
3. Captain
4. First Lieutenant

U. S. Coast Guard. Officers' sleeve braiding indicating rank
Gold braid on full dress, dress, evening dress and blue service coats. Black braid on overcoats, without the shields

1. Second Lieutenant
2. Third Lieutenant
3. Engineer in Chief
4. Lieutenant of Engineers

gold lace braid, the belts for all lieutenants and officers of corresponding rank having four stripes of dark blue silk woven through the gold braid.

The full dress coat extends nearly to the knee, is double breasted with two rows of gilt Coast Guard buttons, nine in each row, has a standing collar trimmed with gold lace braid, the braid being one-half inch wide for officers of the rank of Third Lieutenant and one inch wide for officers above that rank. The sleeves are trimmed with stripes of gold braid as shown in the illustrations, the number of stripes for officers of the Line being as follows:

Captain Commandant.— Four stripes one-half inch wide, the lower stripe two inches above the edge of the cuff, and a gold embroidered shield one inch high above the stripes.

Senior Captain.— Three stripes of one-half inch wide with the gold shield above.

Captain.— Two stripes one-half inch wide with one stripe one-quarter of an inch wide between them and the gold shield above.

First Lieutenant.— Two stripes one-half inch wide with the gold shield above.

Second Lieutenant.— One stripe one-half inch wide with one stripe one-quarter inch wide above it and the gold shield above.

Third Lieutenant.— One stripe one-half inch wide and the gold shield above.

Engineer Officers wear the same stripes as prescribed for officers of the Line of corresponding rank, but not the gold shield.

Constructors and District Superintendents wear the same stripes as officers of the Line of corresponding ranks with the addition of stripes of distinctive color between the gold stripes; these distinctive stripes being of light brown velvet for Constructors and of light green cloth for District Superintendents.

The shoulder knots are made of gold wire cord and consist of a twisted strap terminating in an oval pad. The Corps insignia of the Coast Guard consisting of a silver foul anchor one and five-eighths inches long surcharged with a gold shield and the insignia of rank are embroidered upon the gold lace in the center of the pad.

The full dress cap for commissioned officers is made of dark blue cloth, bell crowned, with a sloping visor of leather covered with dark blue cloth, the visors for Captain Commandant, Senior Captain and Captains being decorated with a design of oak leaves and those for the Engineer in Chief and Captains of Engineers being decorated with a one-half inch gold band around the edge. The Coast Guard insignia are embroidered on the fronts of the caps and consist of a gold spread eagle with a silver shield upon his breast, the talons of the eagle resting upon a silver foul anchor. Across the front of the cap just above the visor is a chin strap of one-half inch gold braid secured by a small gilt button at each end of the visor. The full dress cap for the Captain Commandant only has a narrow welt of gold braid around the upper edge of the crown.

The full dress belt for the Captain Commandant, Senior Captains, Captains and Staff officers of corresponding rank is covered with gold lace braid and that for Lieutenants and Staff officers of corresponding rank is covered with gold lace braid having four narrow stripes of dark blue silk woven through it.

The Dress Uniform.— Is the same as the full dress except that plain trousers of dark blue or white are worn.

U. S. Coast Guard. Officers' shoulder marks indicating rank

Worn on the white service uniform coat and the overcoat. The shields above the stripes indicate Line officers. Gold stripes without the shields indicate Engineer officers. Light brown stripes between the gold stripes, Constructors. Light green stripes between the gold stripes, District Superintendent.

1. Captain Commandant
2. Senior Captain
3. Captain
4. First Lieutenant
5. Second Lieutenant
6. Third Lieutenant
7. Engineer Officers
8. Staff Officers
9. Staff Officers

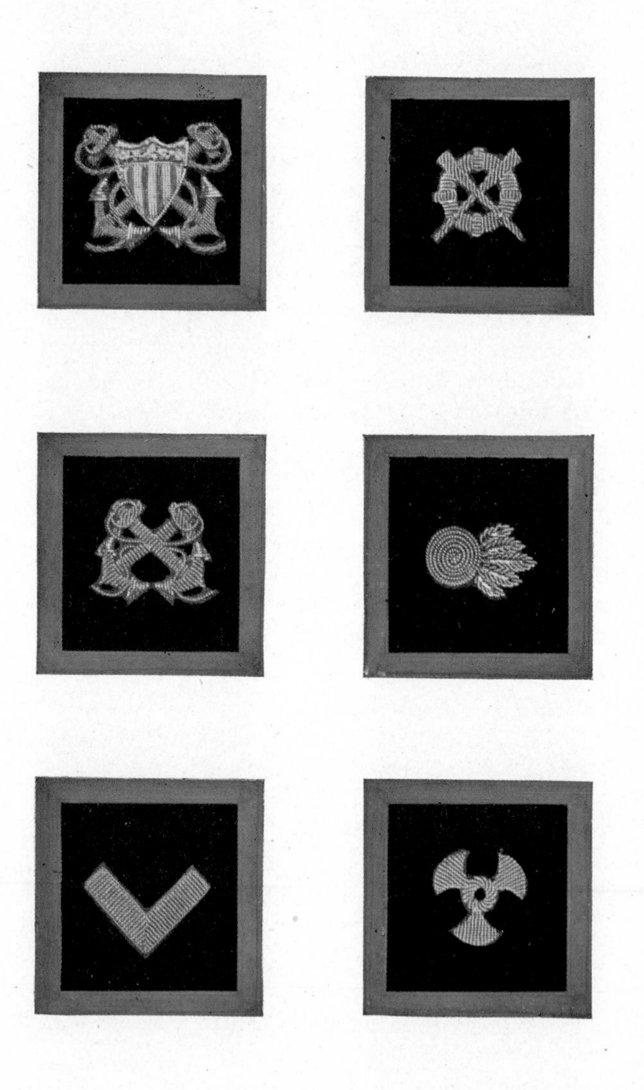

U. S. Coast Guard. Warrant officers' collar insignia

1.	Master's Mate	2.	Keeper
3.	Boatswain	4.	Gunner
5.	Carpenter	6.	Machinist

The Service Dress Uniform consists of the blue or white service coat, plain blue or white trousers and the blue or white service cap, black shoes being worn with the blue uniform and white shoes with the white uniform. When the sword is worn with this uniform it is suspended from a belt of black leather worn under the coat.

The Blue Service Coat is made of dark blue cloth or serge, with a standing collar, single breasted, extending to about ten inches below the waist, trimmed around the collar, down both front edges, around the bottom and up the side seams of the back with black mohair braid one and one-quarter inches wide. The sleeves bear the same gold stripes indicating the rank of the wearer as those on the full dress coat, and on both sides of the collar are embroidered the insignia of rank with the insignia indicating Line or Staff in rear of it.

These insignia for commissioned officers of the Line are as follows:

Captain Commandant.....	A silver spread eagle with a shield upon his breast.
Senior Captain	A silver oak leaf.
Captain	A gold oak leaf.
First Lieutenant	Two silver bars.
Second Lieutenant	One silver bar.
Third Lieutenant	No insignia of rank, the Coast Guard insignia only being worn.

The Coast Guard insignia worn on the collar by commissioned officers of the Line consist of a silver foul anchor surcharged with a gold shield.

Officers of the Staff Corps (Engineers and Constructors) wear the insignia of rank of their corresponding rank in the Line and instead of the Coast Guard insignia worn by the Line officers they wear the insignia of their corps, as follows:

Engineer Officers.— A silver foul anchor surcharged with four gold oak leaves.

Constructors.— A silver foul anchor surcharged with a branch of gold leaves.

The White Service Coat for commissioned officers is a single breasted coat of the same length as the blue service coat, with standing collar, buttoned with a single row of five Coast Guard gilt buttons, and having on each breast a pocket with a flap buttoned by a small gilt button. Shoulder marks indicating the rank and corps of the wearer are worn with this coat.

Shoulder Marks.— The shoulder marks worn on the shoulders of the white service coat and also upon the shoulders of the overcoat to indicate the rank and corps of the wearer are five inches long and two and a quarter inches wide, covered with dark blue cloth, and decorated with gold stripes and corps insignia to indicate the rank and corps of the wearer, these stripes and insignia being the same for the various ranks and corps as those worn on the sleeves of the full dress coat as previously described.

The Blue Service Cap is of the same shape and design as the full dress cap except that the braid around the band is of black mohair and the visor is made of black patent leather, the decorations on the visor for the Captain Commandant, Senior Captains, Captains, Engineer in Chief and Captains of Engineers being of gold embroidery the same as for the full dress cap.

The White Service Cap is of the same shape and description as the blue service cap except that the sides and crown above the band are of white duck.

U. S. Coast Guard. Petty officers' chevrons

1. Master-at-Arms
2. Signal Quartermaster
3. Water Tender
4. Electrician, Third Class

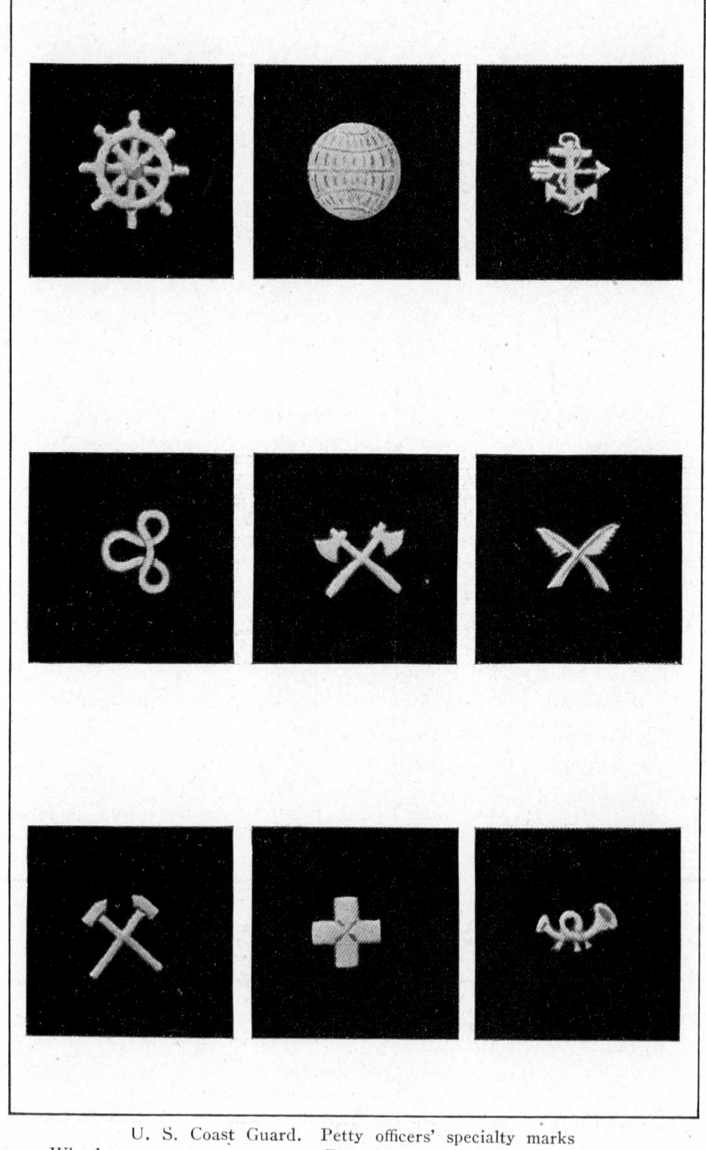

U. S. Coast Guard. Petty officers' specialty marks

1. Wheelman
2. Electrician
3. Coxswain
4. Sailmaker
5. Carpenter, Plumber, Painter
6. Yeoman
7. Blacksmith
8. Bayman
9. Bugler

The Sword and Sword Knot are the same as those for the officers of the U. S. Navy except that the letters "U. S. C. G." are etched upon one side of the blade.

The Overcoat for Commissioned Officers of the Coast Guard is the same as that for officers of the U. S. Navy (see page 116), the rank and corps being indicated by the shoulder knots the same as those worn on the white service coat, and the rank also being indicated by stripes of black braid upon the sleeves, the number and widths of the stripes being the same as for the full dress and blue service coats.

The Cloak for Commissioned Officers is the same as that for officers of the U. S. Navy (see page 117).

The Warrant officers of the U. S. Coast Guard are required to have complete outfits of blue dress, blue service dress, and for all except the Keepers of Life Saving Stations, white service uniforms. The Keepers of Life Saving Stations are required to have an olive drab cotton service uniform in lieu of the white service uniform required for other warrant officers.

The Blue Dress Uniform for Warrant officers is the same as the blue service uniform for commissioned officers except that in place of the gold braid on the sleeves of the coat there is one stripe of black mohair braid one inch in width, and on each side of the collar the insignia of rank are worn, these insignia being for the various ranks as follows:

Master's Mate ...Two gilt foul anchors crossed surcharged with a silver shield.
Keeper ....A gilt life buoy surcharged with two gilt oars crossed.
Boatswain ......Two gilt foul anchors crossed.
Gunner ....A gilt spherical shell bursting into flame.
Carpenter ....A gilt carpenter's square.
Machinist ....A gilt propeller wheel.

The Blue Service Uniform is the same as the blue dress uniform.

The White Service Uniform for Warrant officers is the same as that for the commissioned officers except that the shoulder marks are not worn on the coat, the rank being indicated by metal insignia worn on the collar as described for the blue service coat, and the insignia worn upon the cap being two gilt foul anchors crossed and surmounted by a silver shield.

The Olive Drab Service Uniform worn by the Keepers of Life Saving Stations is of the same design as the white service uniform worn by other warrant officers but the buttons and insignia worn with it are of dull finish bronze metal.

The Overcoat for Warrant Officers is the same as that for commissioned officers except that there are no stripes on the sleeves and the shoulder marks are not worn with it.

The Sword and Belt worn by warrant officers is the same as that worn by commissioned officers with service uniform.

UNIFORMS OF ENLISTED MEN OF THE COAST GUARD

The uniforms of the enlisted men of the Coast Guard are practically the same in style and design as those worn by the enlisted men of the U. S. Navy with minor differences in the buttons and insignia of rank and the rating badges and specialty marks.

The uniforms of the Chief Petty Officers have the buttons of the Coast Guard design on the coats and the insignia on the caps consisting of a vertical gilt foul anchor surmounted by a silver shield.

For Surfmen stationed at Life Saving Stations the summer uniform is made of olive drab cotton duck and the buttons and insignia worn upon the coats and caps are of dull finish bronze metal.

The insignia of rank or rating for Petty Officers are worn upon the right sleeve of the coat or shirt midway between the shoulder seam and the elbow, and consist of a chevron with a spread eagle above it and a specialty mark below the eagle in the upper angle of the chevron.

The chevron is worn with the point down and is made of stripes of cloth three-eighths of an inch wide set one-quarter of an inch apart, these stripes being of scarlet cloth for blue coats and shirts and of blue cloth for white and olive drab coats and shirts.

The eagle and the specialty marks are embroidered in white silk for blue coats and shirts and in blue silk for white and olive drab coats and shirts.

The chevron for Chief Petty Officers consists of three stripes with an arc of a circle connecting the ends of the upper stripe; that for First class petty officers of three stripes, that for Second class petty officers of two stripes and that for Third class petty officers of one stripe, as illustrated.

The Specialty Marks indicating the particular duty or assignment of the petty officers and of certain other men having special duties are, as shown in the illustrations, as follows:

Master-at-Arms.— An upright shield.

No. 1 Surfman.— A circular life buoy surmounted by two oars crossed.

Signal Quartermaster.— Two flags crossed diagonally.

Wheelman.— A ship's steering wheel with eight spokes.

Coxswain.— A vertical anchor crossed by a horizontal arrow.

Electrician.— A hemisphere on a vertical axis.

Electricians, First, Second and Third Class.— A device representing forked lightning, four streaks.

Sailmakers.— A closed clew iron with two eyes.

Blacksmith.— Two sledges crossed diagonally.

Yeoman and Ship's Writer.— Two quill pens crossed diagonally.

Machinist and Oiler.— A ship's propeller with three blades.

Water Tender.— A valve wheel with six spokes.

First and Second Class Carpenters, Plumbers and Painters.— Two axes crossed diagonally.

Bayman (Hospital Nurse).— A red Geneva cross.

Service Stripes.— For each three years service in the Coast Guard or U. S. Navy an enlisted man of the Coast Guard wears one service stripe. These stripes are three-eighths of an inch wide and eight inches long and are worn diagonally across the outer side of the left sleeve of the coat or shirt. They are made of scarlet cloth for blue coats and shirts and of blue cloth for white and olive drab coats and shirts.

Branch Marks.— All enlisted men of the Coast Guard except buglers and mess attendants wear a narrow stripe around the shoulder seam of the right sleeve of the uniform shirts to indicate the branch of the service to which they belong; the stripe being red for the Engineer's force and for all others white on blue shirts and blue on white shirts.

Buttons.— The metal buttons for the Coast Guard have a plain outer rim with an inner rim of rope design enclosing a design in relief, this design consisting of a vertical foul anchor surmounted by an eagle with the wings lifting with a wreath of laurel on one side of the anchor and a wreath of oak leaves on the other side.

The buttons are of bright gilt for blue and white clothes and of dull finish bronze for olive drab clothes.

Enlisted men of the Coast Guard wear a black silk cap ribbon on the blue flat cap, the ribbon for men serving aboard ship having the name of the ship and the letters "C. G.," thus,

U. S. S. ALGONQUIN, C. G.

and the ribbon for men serving at shore stations having the inscription,

U. S. COAST GUARD.

Leggings.— When on landing duty or guard duty ashore officers and enlisted men wear leggings of olive drab similar to those worn in the U. S. Navy.

Gloves of iron gray wool are worn by enlisted men in cold weather.

SEAL OF THE DEPARTMENT OF COMMERCE

CHAPTER VIII

UNIFORMS AND INSIGNIA OF THE U. S. LIGHTHOUSE SERVICE

The United States Lighthouse Service is administered under the Department of Commerce and consists of three divisions; first, the officers and crews of the lighthouse tenders; second, the officers and crews of the lightships; and third, the keepers of the lighthouses and depots on shore.

The lighthouse tenders are steamers which plant and maintain all of the buoys which mark the channels and courses for ships of various sizes in the navigable waters of the United States, including the bays, harbors, lakes and navigable rivers. The lighthouse tenders also carry supplies to the lightships and many of the shore lighthouses.

Lightships are vessels carrying powerful lights anchored in places where it is necessary to have lights to aid in the navigation of seagoing craft but where it would be impossible or impracticable to build lighthouses.

The Depots of the Lighthouse Service are shore establishments where buoys, lights and lightships may be overhauled and repaired and where supplies may be kept in stock.

UNIFORMS OF OFFICERS AND ENLISTED MEN OF LIGHTHOUSE TENDERS

The officers are provided with a blue uniform for cold and temperate weather and a white uniform for hot weather.

The blue uniform consists of a single breasted sack coat of navy blue cloth extending to about ten inches below the waist, with a standing collar, buttoning down the front by buttons concealed under a fly, the collar, front and bottom edges being trimmed with black mohair braid one and one-quarter inches wide; plain trousers of dark blue cloth; and a cap of navy blue cloth with a sloping visor of patent leather, a band of black mohair braid one and one-half inches wide, a chin strap of one-half inch gold braid secured above the visor by means of a small gilt button at each end of the visor. The insignia of the Lighthouse Service, a lighthouse, are embroidered in silver on the front of the cap, surrounded by a wreath embroidered in gold.

The rank of the officer is indicated by stripes of black mohair braid around the sleeves, the number and width of the stripes for the different grades being as follows:

Captain.— Four stripes, the two outer ones one-half inch and the two inner ones one-quarter inch wide.

Chief Engineer.— Three stripes, the two outer ones one-half inch and the inner one one-quarter inch wide.

Master of Tender.— Four stripes one-quarter of an inch wide.

First Officer and Engineer of Tender.— Three stripes one-quarter of an inch wide.

First Officer and First Assistant Engineer of Tender. — Two stripes one-quarter inch wide.

Third Officer and Second Assistant Engineer of Tender.— One stripe one-quarter inch wide.

Insignia indicating the department to which an officer belongs are worn on each side of the collar, a gold anchor for deck officers (corresponding to Line officers in the Navy) and a gold three-bladed propeller for Engineer Officers.

The white uniform is similar in style and design to the blue uniform, the braid being white and the insignia on the coat collar of gilt metal.

The Overcoat for Officers is double breasted, made of dark blue cloth, extending to three inches below the knee, with two rows of black flat buttons down the front, six in each row and a wide rolling collar. It bears no stripes or insignia.

Quartermasters and machinists wear a blue uniform consisting of a double breasted sack coat of dark blue cloth, with five gilt buttons on each side, turn-down collar and lapels, two side pockets with flaps; plain dark blue cloth trousers; and a cap of the same pattern as that worn by officers, but having a black patent leather chin strap, and the letters " U. S. L. H. S." embroidered in gold around the base of the silver lighthouse insignia instead of the gold wreath on the front of the officers' cap.

The insignia indicating the rank, worn on each sleeve midway between the shoulder seam and the elbow, consist

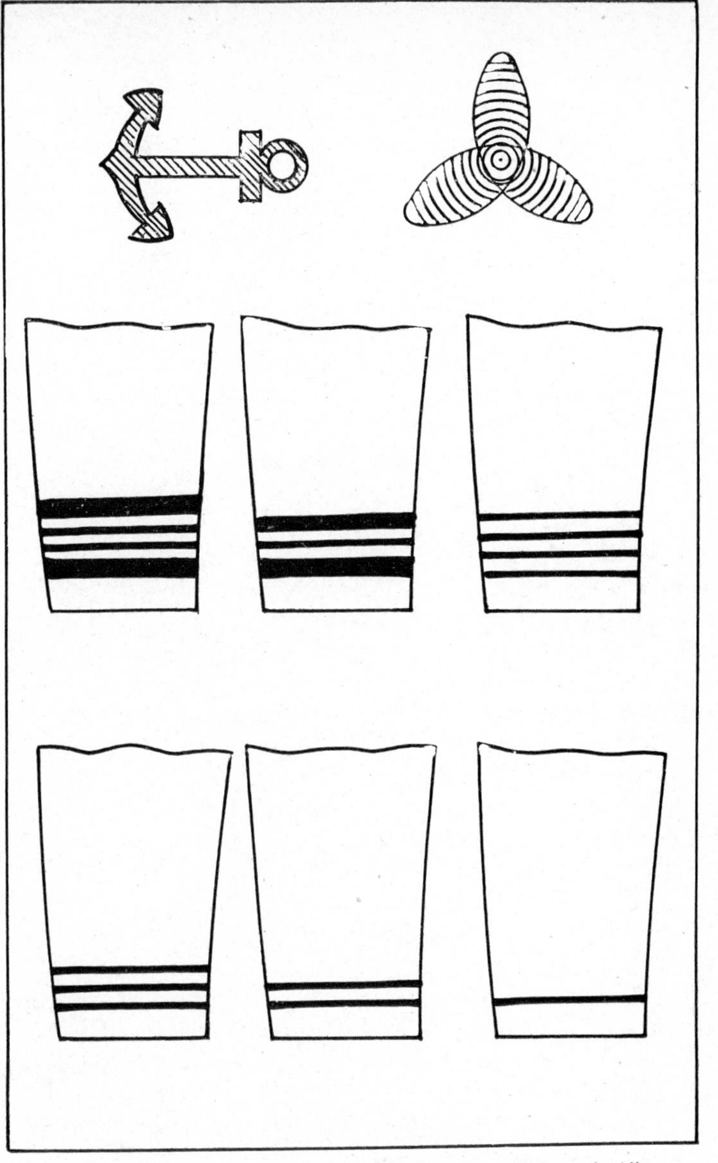

U. S. Lighthouse Service. Officers' collar insignia and sleeve braiding
Collar insignia (Gold embroidery)

1. Deck Officers
2. Engineer Officers

Sleeve braiding (Black mohair braid)

3. Captain
4. Chief Engineer
5. Master of Tender
6. First Officer, Engineer, Master, Lightship
7. Second Officer, First Asst. Engineer, First Mate, Lightship
8. Third Officer Second Asst. Engineer, Second Mate, Lightship

of a ship's steering wheel embroidered in white for quartermaster and a three-bladed propeller embroidered in red for machinist.

For hot weather a uniform of white duck is provided, the design and the insignia being the same as for the blue uniform except that the sleeve stripes are of white braid.

Seamen of the crew wear blue and white uniforms similar to the working uniforms for the enlisted men of the United States Navy, and the firemen wear a blue dungaree uniform of the same pattern.

Stewards, cooks and mess attendants wear a cap similar to the officers' cap but without ornaments or braid; a plain single breasted coat with standing collar and plain trousers. The coats for steward have gilt buttons, the cooks and mess attendants plain buttons.

UNIFORMS AND INSIGNIA FOR OFFICERS AND ENLISTED MEN OF LIGHTSHIPS

The officers wear a uniform of navy blue cloth for winter and of navy blue serge or flannel for summer, consisting of a double breasted sack coat with turn-down collar and lapels, with five gilt buttons on each side; a single breasted waistcoat with a rolling collar and five small gilt buttons; plain trousers; and a cap the same as described for officers of lighthouse tenders.

Insignia are worn on the lapels of the coat, a gold anchor for deck officers and a gold three-bladed propeller for engineer officers.

Stripes of black mohair braid are worn on each sleeve, as follows:

Master.— Three stripes one-quarter inch wide.

First Mate.— Two stripes one-quarter inch wide.

Second Mate.— One stripe one-quarter inch wide.

Engineer.— Two stripes one-quarter inch wide.

Assistant Engineer.— One stripe one-quarter inch wide.

The overcoat is the same as that for officers of Lighthouse Tenders.

The enlisted men of the lightships wear the same uniforms as those described for the enlisted men of the lighthouse tenders.

UNIFORM AND INSIGNIA OF LIGHTHOUSE AND DEPOT KEEPERS

The keepers of lighthouses and depots wear uniforms of the same style, material and color as that described for the Masters of lightships, except that no braid is worn on the sleeves, different insignia are worn on the lapels, and the cap has a chin strap of black leather.

The insignia indicating the rating of the keepers are embroidered in gold on the lapels of the coat, and, as illustrated, consist of a loop with the letter "K" for the keeper and the figure "1," "2," "3" and "4" for the assistant keepers.

Uniforms of white duck of the same description as the blue uniforms may be worn in hot weather.

Watchmen for police duty at the general lighthouse depot wear a navy blue single breasted sack coat, buttoned up to the neck by five regulation gilt buttons, with standing turn-over collar, having the letter "W" embroidered in gold on each side; plain navy blue trousers; and a helmet, blue for winter and light brown for summer, with the silver lighthouse device on the front, the device being surrounded by a gold wreath for the Captain of the Watch.

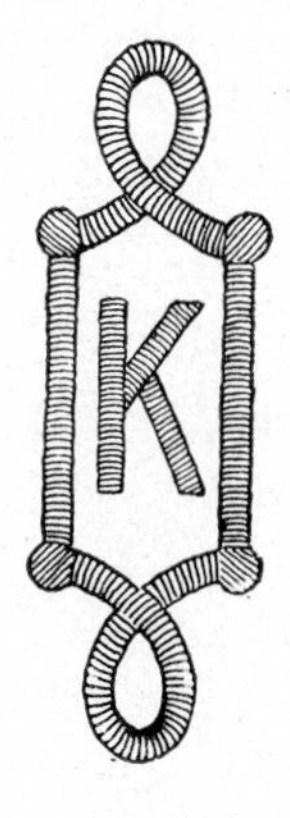

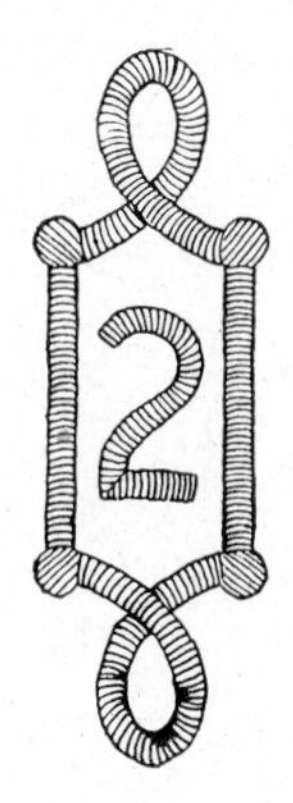

Insignia for Lighthouse Keepers and Watchmen
Light Stations and Depots
Keepers of lighthouses
K for keeper

1 for first assistant keeper
3 for third assistant keeper

2 for second assistant keeper
4 for fourth assistant keeper

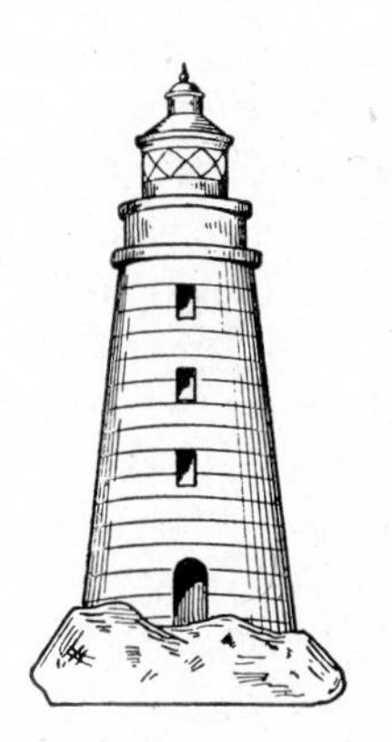

Watchmen at general depot

Shield

Hat ornament

An overcoat of the same style as for officers of Lighthouse Tenders is worn by Watchman.

The shield shown in the illustration is worn on the left breast of the coat and overcoat.

A black leather belt with a loop for the club and a gilt clasp bearing the word " Police " is worn by watchmen when on duty.

The regulation buttons for the Lighthouse service are gilt having a raised design representing a lighthouse rising from the sea, with a circle of rope around the edge.

SEAL OF THE U. S. PUBLIC HEALTH SERVICE

CHAPTER IX

UNIFORMS AND INSIGNIA OF THE U. S. PUBLIC HEALTH SERVICE

The U. S. Public Health Service, operated as a Bureau of the Department of the Treasury, has charge of the enforcement of the quarantine regulations for the prevention of the introduction of contagious and infectious diseases into the United States from abroad or from one state or territory to another; the care of sick and disabled seamen of the merchant marine, and of scientific research at home and abroad regarding diseases of man which may affect the general public health and welfare.

This service was formerly known as the Public Health and Marine Hospital Service, but by an Act of Congress dated August 14, 1912, the name of the service was changed to the Public Health Service and its duties were increased and its powers and responsibilities much enlarged.

The Public Health Service is administered under a Surgeon General stationed at the National Capital, the various duties being assigned to seven divisions.

The Division of Scientific Research, as its name implies, is charged with studies of various diseases such as typhoid, malarial, typhus and yellow fevers, leprosy, tuberculosis, trachoma, pellagra, sanitation and hygiene, water supply and sewage and public health administration in states and cities in cooperation with the local authorities. This division conducts a Hygienic Laboratory at Washington and a number of field laboratories where intensive studies in these subjects are conducted. Through this division the Surgeon General of the Service enforces the laws for the regulation of the sale of viruses and serums and calls annual and special conferences of the health authorities of the several states and territories for the purpose of cooperation in the suppression of preventable diseases and the general improvement of the public health.

The Division of Foreign and Insular Quarantine and Immigration is charged with the execution of the national quarantine laws, this being accomplished at fifty Federal Quarantine Stations in the United States, with additional stations at Panama, Porto Rico, the Virgin Islands, Hawaii and the Philippines. There are also medical officers under this division detailed at various Consular stations of the United States in foreign countries to assist in the prevention of the introduction of contagious or infectious diseases into the United States or its possessions. This division also conducts the physical and mental examinations of all aliens entering the territory of the United States at any of its ports.

The Division of Domestic and Interstate Quarantine has charge of the enforcement of the laws for the prevention of the spread of contagious or infectious diseases from one state or territory to another.

The Division of Sanitary Reports and Statistics has cognizance of the collection and publication of information relative to the diseases which may threaten the public health of the United States and foreign countries.

The Division of Marine Hospitals has charge of twenty-two Marine Hospitals and about one hundred and twenty-five smaller relief stations at the different ports and cities of the country.

At these stations and hospitals the sick and disabled officers and seamen of the Coast Guard and Lighthouse Services, the Mississippi River Commission, the Engineer Corps of the Army at work upon rivers and harbors works, and the registered and licensed ships of the United States merchant marine are given necessary medical and surgical treatment. This division also furnishes the medical officers for the vessels of the Coast Guard.

The Division of Personnel and Accounts has charge of the record of the officers and men of the service and of the expenditures of the moneys appropriated for the service from the public funds.

The Miscellaneous Division issues the various annual reports, public health reports and other publications of the service, including the bulletins of the results of research at the Hygienic Laboratory at Washington.

The officers of the Public Health Service have titles corresponding to their duties and rank assimilated to that of the Army and Navy, the different grades being as follows:

COMMISSIONED OFFICERS

Surgeon General.
Assistant Surgeon General.
Senior Surgeon.
Surgeon.
Professor of Hygienic Laboratory.
Passed Assistant Surgeon.
Assistant Surgeon.
Quarantine Inspector.
Acting Assistant Surgeon.
Chaplain.

WARRANT OFFICERS

Interne.
Pharmacist.
Clerk.

ENLISTED MEN

Station Engineer.
Pilot.
Marine Engineer.
First Cook.
Cooks.
Coachman.
Carpenter.
Yardman.
Messenger.
Laundryman.
Surgical Nurse.
Female Nurse.
Night Watchman.

Ship Keeper.
Boatswain.
Coxswain.
Ordinary Seaman.
Fireman.
Coal Passer.
Boy.

COMMISSIONED OFFICERS' UNIFORMS

The commissioned officers of the service are required to have complete outfits of full-dress, dress, olive drab service, white service and evening dress uniforms.

The Full-Dress Uniform consists of a double breasted frock coat of dark blue cloth with two rows of gilt buttons down the front, and a standing collar trimmed with gold lace braid; dark blue cloth trousers with gold stripes down the outer leg seams, one and three-quarter inches wide for Surgeon-General, one and one-half inches wide for Assistant Surgeon General and one inch wide for other officers; a blue cloth cap with black patent leather visor; black patent leather shoes, white gloves, and full-dress sword belt and sword.

The blue cap has a bell crown, the band being of gold braid one and one-half inches wide with a narrow stripe of maroon silk through the center of it and the chin strap worn across the front just above the visor being of gold braid five-eighths of an inch wide with a narrow stripe of marooon silk through the center. The edge of the visor is decorated with gold embroidery, and on the front and center of the cap the distinctive device of the Public Health Service is embroidered.

The Surgeon General wears gold epaulets on the shoulders of the full-dress coat with the service insignia and the insignia of his rank, one silver star, embroidered on the top, and the other commissioned officers have shoulder straps of maroon colored broadcloth on the shoulders, these straps being trimmed around the edges with a stripe of gold braid three-quarters of an inch wide and having on them at the center the insignia of the Public Health Service and between this and the shoulder end the insignia of rank.

On the sleeves of the full-dress coat are stripes of gold lace braid to indicate the rank of the wearer as follows:

The Surgeon General.— One band two inches wide, gold-thread lace around each sleeve, two inches from lower edge of cuff, with one band one-half inch gold-thread lace one-fourth inch above; the bands being interspaced with maroon broadcloth.

Assistant Surgeon General.— Four bands of gold-thread lace one-half inch wide; distance between bands one-fourth inch; the bands being interspaced with maroon broadcloth.

Senior Surgeon.— Same as for Assistant Surgeon General, omitting uppermost band.

Surgeon.— Two bands of gold-thread lace one-half inch wide, with one band one-fourth inch wide between; distance between bands one-fourth inch; the bands being interspaced with maroon broadcloth.

Passed Assistant Surgeon.— Same as for surgeon, omitting one-fourth inch band; distance between bands to be one-fourth inch.

Assistant Surgeon.— Same as for passed assistant surgeon, substituting one-fourth-inch band for upper band.

The Dress Uniform consists of the blue cap as prescribed for full-dress; dark blue serge trousers with a two-inch welted stripe of the same material down the outer leg seam; black leather shoes; white gloves; and a single breasted sack coat of dark blue serge buttoned down the front by five gun-metal service buttons, with a standing collar. On each shoulder there is a strap of the same material as the coat extending from the shoulder seam to the collar where it is secured by a small service button and on the center of this strap is worn the insignia of rank. There are four patch pockets on the front of the coat each one having a shield shaped flap secured by a small service button, one pocket being on each breast and one on each side below the waist.

The Service Uniform is of the same design as the dress uniform but it is made of olive drab serge or khaki colored cotton drill and tan leather shoes are worn. The cap is of olive-drab serge with a russet leather visor and chin strap, a band of oliver-drab mohair braid and the service insignia of gun metal.

The White Service Uniform is of the same design as the olive-drab service uniform but the material is white linen, and white shoes are worn. The white cap has a black patent leather visor, black mohair band and the same service insignia as worn on the blue cap.

The Blue Evening Dress Uniform is of dark blue cloth, cut after the prevailing style for civilian's evening dress, but having gilt service buttons on the coat and waistcoat, and the same shoulder straps and rank stripes on the sleeves as prescribed for the full dress coat.

The White Evening Uniform consists of a dinner coat, waistcoat and trousers cut after the prevailing style for civilian's clothing, but having gilt buttons on the coat and waistcoat and shoulder straps of the same material as the coat.

The Overcoat for Officers is a single breasted ulster

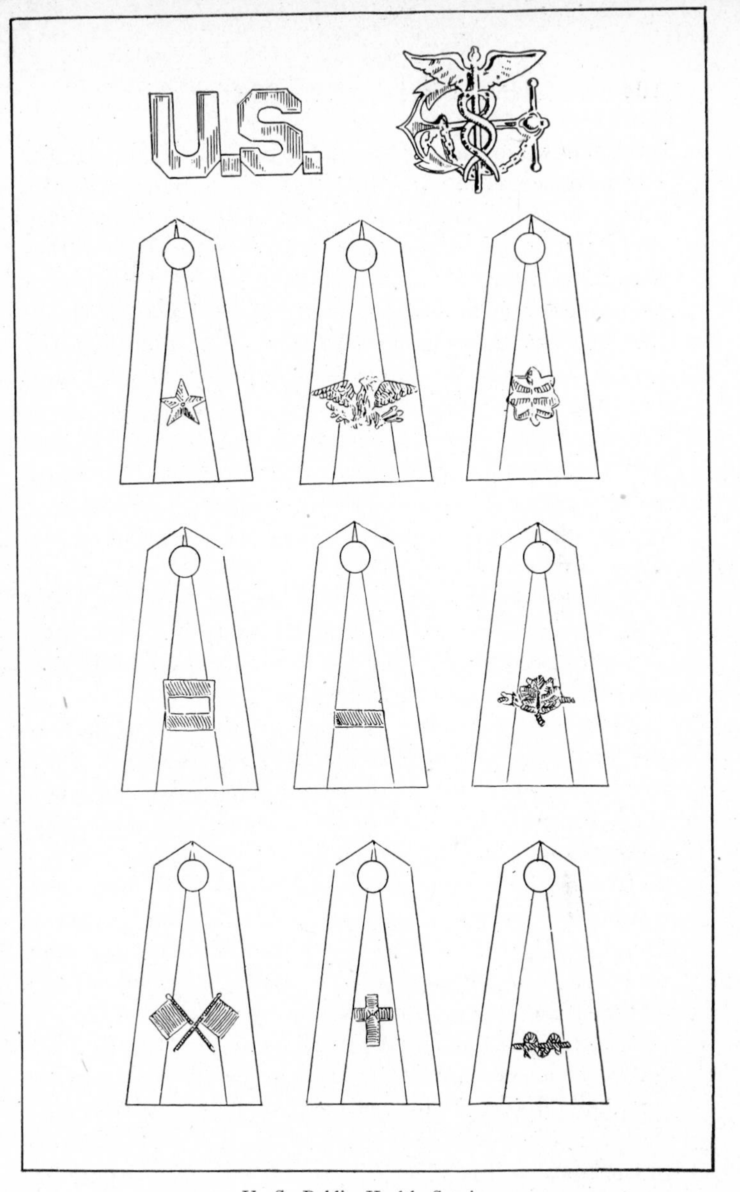

U. S. Public Health Service

1. Letters worn on collar
2. Public Health Service insignia

Shoulder straps of dress and service coats

3. Surgeon General
4. Assistant Surgeon General
5. Senior Surgeon and Surgeon
6. Passed Assistant Surgeon
7. Assistant Surgeon
8. Professor, Hygienic Laboratory
9. Quarantine Inspector
10. Chaplain
11. Interne

of dark blue cloth extending to within twelve inches of the ground, closed down the front by a row of five large flat black buttons, with a standing and falling collar, and having the stripes indicating the rank the same as for the full-dress coat except that they shall be of black mohair braid.

Insignia of Service and Rank.— The insignia of the Public Health Service consist of a foul anchor crossed by a caduceus. The distinctive device worn on the blue cap consists of a gold shield seven-eighths of an inch in height, emblazoned palewise with thirteen pieces with a chief strewn with thirteen stars, surmounted by a gold spread eagle five-eighths of an inch in height and one and five-eighths from tip to tip of wings, the whole being placed upon the service insignia in gold, the staff of the caduceus and the anchor each being one and seven-eighths inches long.

The insignia of rank for commissioned officers are as follows:

The Surgeon General.— One silver star of five rays, of such size that the points of the rays will fill a circle one inch in diameter, to be five-eighths of an inch from one point of the star to the next alternate point. One ray of the star to point toward the collar.

Assistant Surgeon General.— A silver spread eagle, 2¼ inches wide between the tips of wings; distance from tips of wings to center of talon on each side, 1¼ inches; from top of head to bottom of design, 1¼ inches. The insignia for the right side has in the right talon an olive branch and in the left a bundle of arrows. The extreme width from tip of arrowhead to olive branch is 1$^{9}/_{16}$ inches. These insignia are made in pairs, rights and lefts, and the eagle faces to the front on each shoulder.

Senior Surgeon.— A seven-pointed silver oak leaf with stem; 1⅛ inches long from the tip of the stem to the tip of the leaf; 1 1/16 inches wide at the widest point. The top of the leaf points toward the collar.

Surgeon.— A gold oak leaf of the same size and design, and worn in the same manner as for senior surgeon.

Passed Assistant Surgeon.— Two gold bars, each bar 1⅛ inches long and three-eighths inch wide; the bars being parallel, and three-eighths of an inch apart. The bars are worn with the long axis in a line from front to rear.

Assistant Surgeon.— One gold bar of the same size and worn in the same manner as for passed assistant surgeon.

Professor, Hygienic Laboratory.— A gold oak leaf super-imposed upon a silver flaming torch one and one-half inches long.

Quarantine Inspector.— Two crossed flags embroidered in gold, one and one-half inch staff and flags one inch hoist by five-eighths of an inch fly.

Acting Assistant Surgeon.— The same as for Assistant Surgeon except that the rank insignia is silver instead of gold.

Chaplain.— A silver Latin cross one inch high.

The insignia of rank for Warrant Officers are as follows:

Interne.— A rod of Esculapius with a single serpent entwined about it, in silver.

Pharmacist.— No rank insignia on shoulder straps. On the sleeves of the dress and service coats five inches above the edge there is a " cachet " indicating the rank. This consists of a circular piece of maroon broad-cloth one-half inch in diameter surrounded by a circle of gold

U. S. Public Health Service

Chevrons worn on the sleeves by petty officers to indicate rank and duty

1. Station Engineer
2. Marine Engineer
3. Pilot
4. First Cook

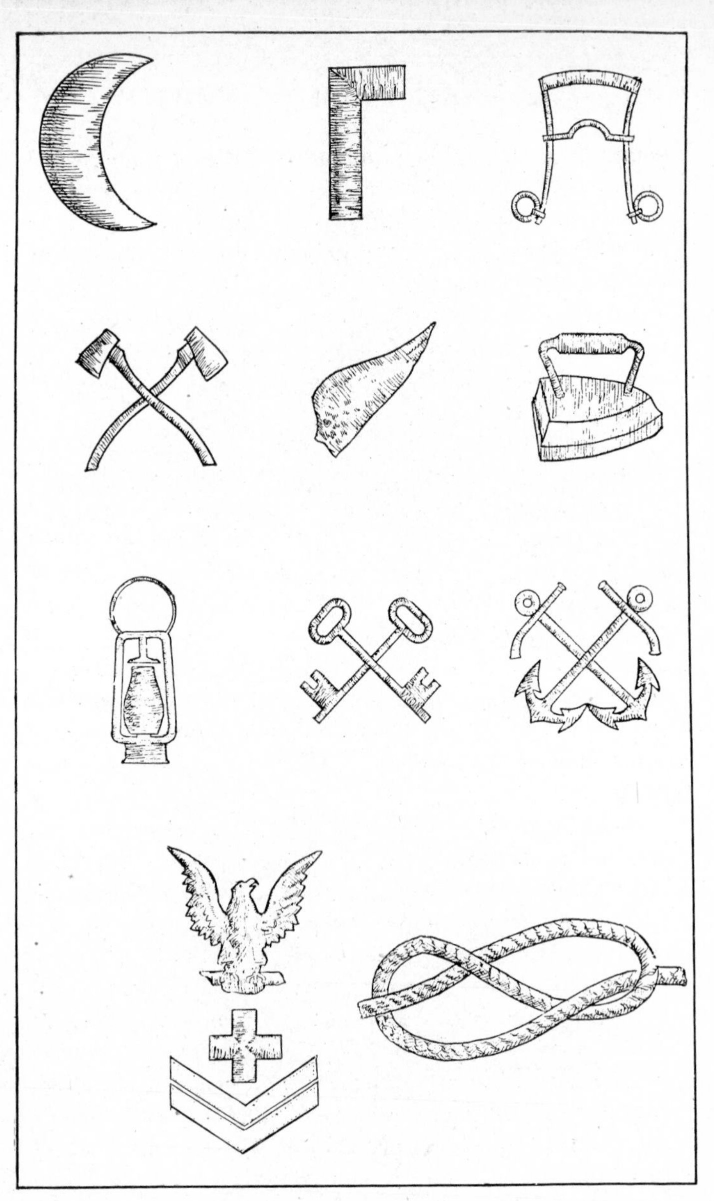

U. S. Public Health Service

Specialty marks worn on the sleeves by petty officers and special detail men to indicate rank or duty

1. Worn by Cooks other than first cooks
2. Carpenter
3. Coachman
4. Yardman
5. Messenger
6. Laundryman
7. Night Watchman
8. Shipkeeper
9. Boatswain
10. Surgical Nurse
11. Coxswain

embroidery one-eighth of an inch wide. For the white service and khaki uniforms the "cachet" is made of enameled metal. Pharmacists of the third class wear one such mark, those of the second class two and those of the first class three.

Clerk.— Two crossed pens one and a quarter inches in length, embroidered in maroon silk on the dress and service coats and made of enameled metal for the white and khaki coats.

Collar Ornaments.— The collar ornaments for the dress and service coats are the letters "U. S." in metal in Gothic design, five-eighths of an inch high, and the service insignia in metal. For the dress and olive-drab and khaki service uniforms these ornaments are of gun-metal and for the white coat they are of gilt metal.

Buttons.— The buttons worn by officers of the Public Health Service are of metal and bear the insignia of the service, a foul anchor crossed by a caduceus, the anchor being horizontal and the staff of the caduceus vertical.

Sword and Belts.— The sword for commissioned officers has a straight blade, of diamond shape, 29 to 32 inches long. Hilt pommel, inverted frustrum of a cone with corps device chased on one side and star on the other. Grip, white sharkskin wrapped with gilt wire. Front guard bears corps device; spring back guard, with trophy device. Black leather scabbard with gilt bands, a five-pointed star on each; upper band to have two rings. Tip to be 5 inches long, with laurel branch engraved on the right side. The belt for full-dress is one and three-quarters inches wide, with two sling straps three-fourths of an inch wide, covered with gold lace braid and closed by a gilt buckle clasp consisting of a wreath of laurel leaves surrounding a design similar to the service button.

The service uniform belt is the same as the full-dress belt but it is made entirely of black grain leather. The sword knot is a strap of one-half inch gold lace twenty-four inches long.

Leggings.— Leggings for wear with olive-drab and khaki service uniforms are of tan-colored pigskin.

WARRANT OFFICERS' UNIFORMS

The uniforms for Warrant Officers are of the same style and design as those prescribed for commissioned officers, omitting the full-dress uniform and the sword.

EMPLOYEES' AND ENLISTED MEN'S UNIFORMS

The employees at the hospitals and stations of the Public Health Service are provided with blue and white uniforms.

The Blue Uniform consists of a double-breasted sack coat of dark blue serge, with notched rolling collar; cut square at the bottom; length one inch below the crotch; with five gun-metal service buttons on each side down the front; trousers of the same material as the coat; black leather shoes; and a blue cap similar to that worn by commissioned officers but having the band of black mohair braid, the visor and chin strap of plain black patent leather and the service insignia in gilt metal on the center of the front.

The White Uniform is of the same pattern as the blue uniform but made of white cotton drill.

The Overcoat is a double-breasted ulster of dark blue cloth, buttoned to the collar by two rows of large size service buttons, with rolling collar.

The uniforms for ordinary seamen, firemen, coal passers, cooks and boys at Quarantine stations is similar in cut and style to that worn by enlisted men of the U. S. Navy, and is of blue cloth for winter and white duck for summer wear. The cap ribbon bears the words "U. S. QUARANTINE" embroidered in gilt thread.

The marks indicating the ratings and duties of the various employees and enlisted men are worn on the sleeves midway between the elbow and the shoulder and are embroidered in maroon colored silk. They are:

(1) *Station Engineer.*— Spread eagle, above two crossed monkey wrenches, and a chevron of three stripes of maroon broadcloth.

(2) *Pilot.*— The same as for station engineer, substituting a steering wheel for the crossed monkey wrenches.

(3) *Marine Engineer.*— The same as for pilot, substituting a propeller for the steering wheel.

(4) *First Cook.*— The same as for pilot, substituting a crescent for the steering wheel, and with a chevron of two stripes.

(5) *Other Cooks.*— The same as for first cook, omitting all marks except the crescent.

(6) *Coachman.*— A curb bit.

(7) *Carpenter.*— A carpenter's square.

(8) *Yardman.*— Two crossed axes.

(9) *Messenger.*— A single wing.

(10) *Laundryman.*— A flatiron.

(11) *Surgical Nurse.*— A spread eagle, Geneva cross, chevron with two bars.

(12) *Night Watchman.*— A lantern.

(13) *Ship Keeper.*— Two crossed keys.

(14) *Boatswain.*— Two crossed anchors.

(15) *Coxswain.*— Figure-of-eight knot, 2 inches long.

UNIFORM FOR FEMALE NURSES

The female nurses at the hospitals wear a uniform consisting of a white organdie nurse's cap, a one-piece dress of white cotton cloth, having a simple waist with plain three quarter length sleeves with reversed cuffs two and one-half inches wide, a flat rolling collar two inches wide with a wide opening at the neck in front; a four-piece skirt from two to two and one-half yards in circumference at the bottom, reaching to within three inches of the floor; top turned in and stitched to the waist with a double-welt seam. The waist and shirt are buttoned down the front with one row of plain 35-ligne white pearl buttons. Upon the left arm midway between the shoulder and the elbow there is a Geneva cross of maroon colored broadcloth. The shoes and stockings are white.

Service Stripes.— All members of the personnel of the service below the grade of Pharmacist wear a service stripe of maroon cloth three-eighths of an inch wide diagonally across the sleeve below the elbow for each period of five years service.

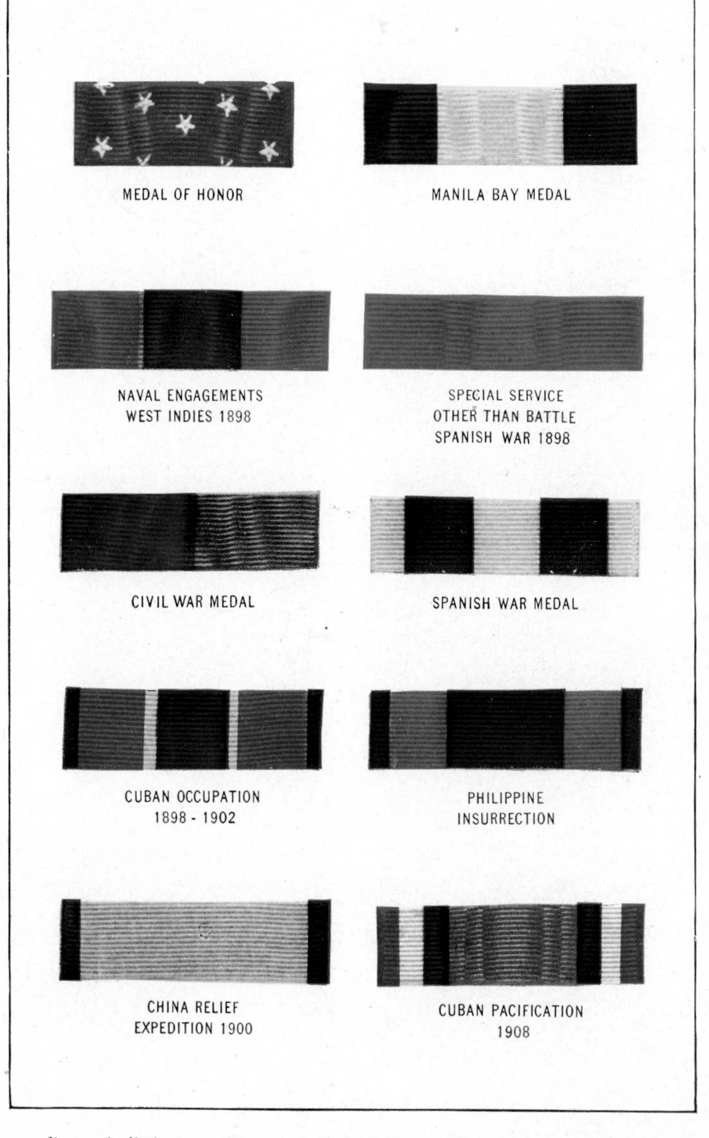

Bars of distinctive ribbons of United States Government medals. Worn by officers and men upon whom the medals have been conferred with dress, undress, service dress and evening dress uniforms.

CHAPTER X

MEDALS, BADGES AND RIBBONS

In all of the nations of the world it is customary to recognize special acts of gallantry upon the field of battle, marked devotion to duty in the service of the country and long and faithful service in the armies and navies by promotion, by granting special honors or orders, or by the conferring of medals and decorations.

In the military and naval service of the United States there are a number of authorized medals and badges presented to the officers and enlisted men in recognition of their gallant services and deeds in the wars in which our country has been engaged.

In addition to the medals conferred for war service there are medals for long and faithful service with the colors and special badges awarded for excellency at target practice both on land and sea.

These medals and badges are proudly worn and highly prized by their recipients and are often handed down to posterity as valued heirlooms.

Medals and badges are usually suspended from a small section of ribbon, the colors of the ribbon being distinctive for each medal.

In accordance with the regulations and orders for the various services medals are to be worn with special full-dress and full-dress uniforms on the left breast in one horizontal line, suspended from a single holding bar, each medal being attached to the bar by the distinctive ribbon authorized for it, and the upper edge of the bar being on a horizontal line one inch below the point of the shoulder, which should bring it between the first and second buttons of the full dress coat for officers.

There is a specified order for the arrangement of the medals upon the holding bar, the medal of the oldest date being worn nearest the center line of the coat and the others in order of precedence, according to the date of the event for which conferred, toward the left shoulder of the wearer.

With undress and service uniforms in lieu of the medals and badges sections of the ribbons from which they are suspended are worn. These ribbons of medals and badges are each equal in length to the full width of the ribbon and three-eighths of an inch wide. Ribbons of medals and badges are worn on the left breast of the coat in the same relative position as the medals and badges which they represent. In case the wearer has received so many that there is not room on the coat to wear them in one row, they are arranged in two rows.

The medals and badges, or the ribbons worn in their stead with undress and service uniforms, show the special military honors which have been conferred upon the wearer and the wars and campaigns in which he has seen active service, and a knowledge of the designs of these bits of metal and of the bright colored strips of silk will often give a fair idea of the services and honors of the man who wears them.

The founders of the United States of America looked askance upon anything that savored of monarchical government and as a result we find that the Constitution provides that,

"No title of nobility shall be granted by the United States;

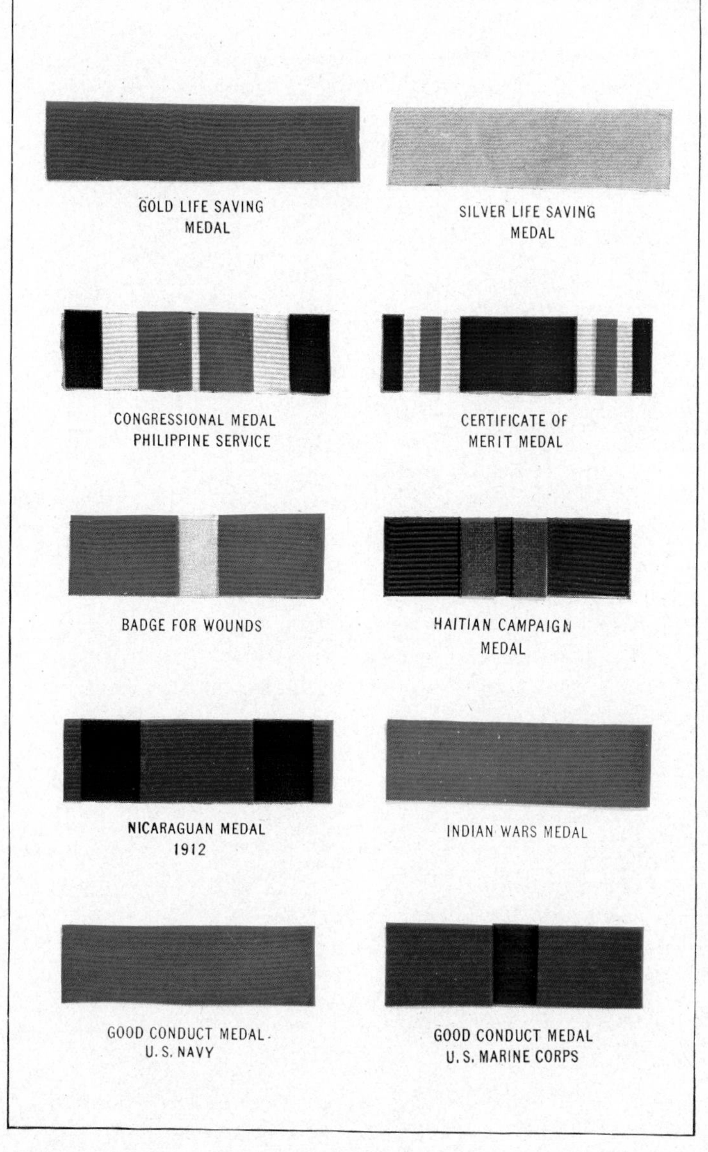

Bars of distinctive ribbons of United States Government medals. Worn by officers and men upon whom the medals have been conferred with dress, undress, service dress and evening dress uniforms.

and no person holding any office of profit or trust under them shall, without the consent of Congress, accept of any present, emolument, office or title of any kind whatever, from any king, prince or foreign state."

Following out this early mandate the regulations of the present day forbid the *wearing* by the officers and enlisted men of the services of the United States of any medal or decoration granted by any foreign state or ruler, although the Congress has in a number of instances authorized officers and enlisted men to *receive* such decorations.

In the early days of the republic Congress on several occasions passed resolutions of thanks to commanders on land and sea whose forces had won notable victories, and these resolutions generally provided for the striking of a medal to commemorate the victory and for a sword of honor to be presented by the government to the victorious commander, but these medals were not intended to be worn with the uniform.

It was not until 1861 that Congress authorized the first medal to be worn as a special badge of honor by soldiers who had especially distinguished themselves in the military service of the country. This decoration was officially styled the "Medal of Honor."

This was followed in later years by the enactment of laws prescribing other decorations and medals and the promulgation of regulations and orders as to the manner in which they should be worn.

The following medals and badges are authorized by Act of Congress or by executive order and in accordance with the regulations of the military and naval services are worn by the officers and enlisted men upon whom they have been conferred.

1. Medal of Honor, U. S. Army.

2. Medal of Honor, U. S. Navy, U. S. Marine Corps, and U. S. Coast Guard.

3. Medal commemorating the Battle of Manila Bay, May 1, 1898.

4. Medal commemorating the Naval Engagements in the West Indies during the War with Spain, 1898.

5. Special Meritorious Medal for Services during the War with Spain, other than in Battle.

6. Certificate of Merit Medal.

7. Civil War Campaign Medal.

8. Indian Campaign Medal.

9. Spanish War Campaign Medal.

10 Congressional Medal for Philippine Service.

11. Philippine Insurrection Campaign Medal.

12. Army of Cuban Occupation Medal, 1898-1902.

13. China Relief Expedition Medal.

14. Gold Life-Saving Medal.

15. Silver Life-Saving Medal.

16. Cuban Pacification Medal.

17. Nicaraguan Campaign Medal.

18. Haitian Campaign Medal, 1915.

19. Good-Conduct Medal, U. S. Navy.

20. Good-Conduct Medal, U. S. Marine Corps.

21. Medals and Badges for Excellence in Gunnery.

22. Medals and Badges for Excellence in small-arms target firing as follows:

(a) Expert Rifleman's Badge, Army and Marine Corps.

(b) Sharpshooter's Medal, Navy and Marine Corps.

(c) Expert Rifleman's Bar Badge, Navy.

(d) Pistol Expert Badge, Army and Marine Corps.

(e) Expert Pistol-shot's Bar Badge, Navy.

(f) Distinguished Marksman's Medal, Marine Corps.

(g) Sharpshooter's Badge, Army and Marine Corps.

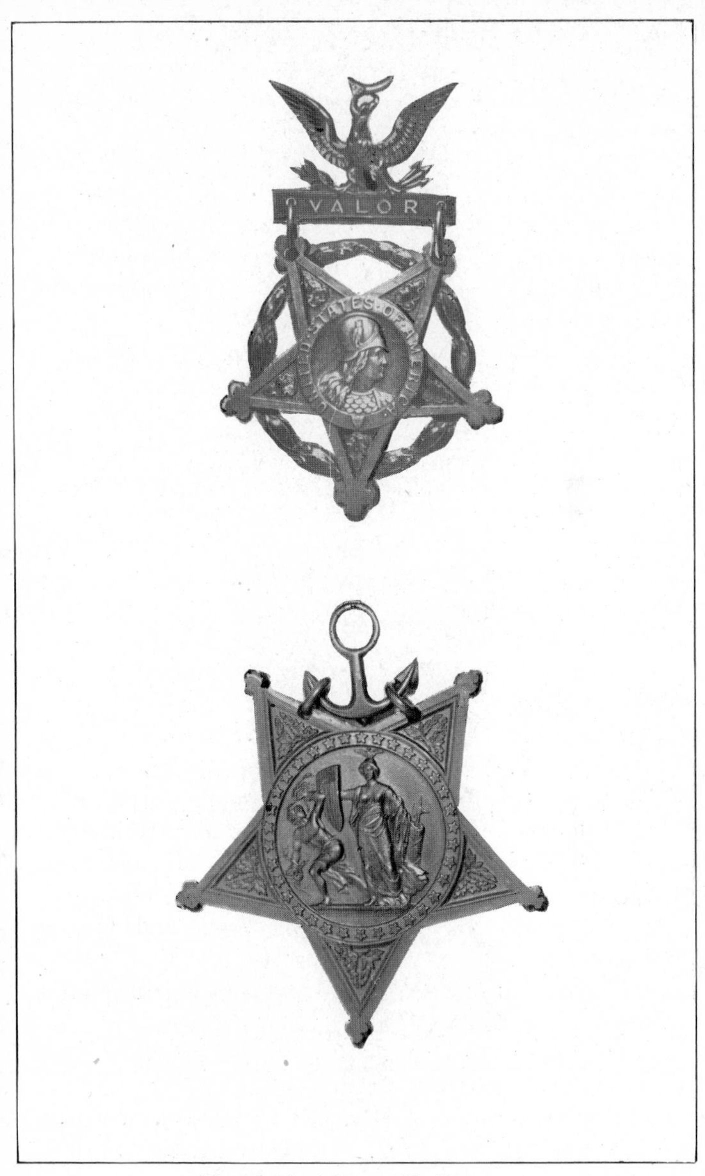

The Medal of Honor, U. S. Army
The Medal of Honor, U. S. Navy

Medal Commemorating the Battle of Manila Bay, May 1, 1898
Medal Commemorating the Naval Engagements in the West Indies during the War with Spain, 1898

(h) Marksman's Badge, Army and Marine Corps.
(i) Division Competition Medal.
(j) Medals given by the National Rifle Association in matches held under its cognizance.

The designs of the various medals and badges and the colors of their distinctive ribbons are shown in the accompanying illustrations.

Laws have been passed authorizing the wearing of the badges of certain societies composed of men who have served in the War of the Revolution, the War of 1812, the Mexican War, the Civil War, the War with Spain, the Philippine Insurrection and the China Relief Expedition, but the regulations prohibit the wearing of these badges while in uniform when medals and badges presented by the government are worn.

The Medal of Honor, U. S. Army.— The Medal of Honor for the Army was first authorized by Act of Congress in 1861 and is awarded to officers and enlisted men of the Army in the name of Congress for particular deeds of most distinguished gallantry in action. In order that an officer or enlisted man may receive a medal of honor he must have performed in action a deed of most distinguished personal bravery or self-sacrifice, above and beyond the call of duty, so conspicuous as to clearly distinguish him for gallantry or intrepidity above his comrades in arms, involving risk of life or the performance of more than ordinarily hazardous service. This medal is of bronze with the wreath in green enamel.

The Medal of Honor, U. S. Navy and Marine Corps. The Medal of Honor for the Navy, including the Marine Corps, was authorized by Act of Congress in 1862, which provided that enlisted men of the Naval Service distinguishing themselves in battle, or by extraordinary heroism in the line of their profession, may be promoted to forward warrant officers, upon the recommendation of their commanding officer, approved by the Flag Officer and the Secretary of the Navy; and that upon such recommendation they shall receive a Medal of Honor and a gratuity of one hundred dollars. This law provided the medal of honor and its accompanying gratuity for enlisted men only, but the Act of Congress of March 3, 1915, extended it to officers by the following proviso: "The President of the United States is hereby empowered to prepare a suitable Medal of Honor to be awarded to any officer of the Navy, Marine Corps, or Coast Guard who shall distinguish himself in battle or display extraordinary heroism in the line of his profession." The Navy Medal of Honor and the anchor from which it is suspended are of bronze.

Medals of Honor for both the Army and the Navy, being the highest decorations awarded by the United States government, are worn suspended from the neck by a ribbon of light blue studded with white stars so that the medal will be at the center of the neck opening of the coat.

The Medal Commemorating the Battle of Manila Bay.— This medal, popularly known as the "Dewey Medal," was the next one authorized by Congress after the Medal of Honor, and was struck in accordance with a joint resolution of the Senate and House of Representatives approved by the President on June 3, 1898, reading as follows:

"*Resolved by the Senate and House of Representatives of the United States of America in Congress assembled,* That the Secretary of the Navy be, and he hereby is, authorized to present a sword of honor to Commodore George Dewey, and to cause to be struck bronze medals commemorating the bat-

1. Medal for Meritorious Service other than in battle, U. S. Navy, 1898
2. Certificate of Merit Medal
3. Civil War Medal, U. S. Army
4. Civil War Medal, U. S. Navy

1. Indian Wars Campaign Medal
2. Cuban Occupation Medal
3. Congressional Medal for Philippine Service, U. S. Army
4. Nicaraguan Campaign Medal, 1912

tle of Manilla Bay, and to distribute such medals to the officers and men of the ships of the Asiatic Squadron of the United States under command of Commodore George Dewey on May first, eighteen hundred and ninety-eight."

The front or " obverse " of this medal bears the bust of Admiral Dewey in low bas-relief and the legend, " The gift of the People of the United States to the Officers and Men of the Asiatic Squadron under command of Commodore George Dewey," while the back, or " reverse," bears the figure of a sailor and a great gun with the inscription, " In Memory of the Victory of Manila Bay, May 1, 1898," and the name of the ship in which the recipient served during the battle. The medal is suspended from a bronze bar by three links of chain and is backed by its distinctive ribbon, blue, yellow, blue.

The Medal Commemorating the Naval Engagements in the West Indies during the War with Spain.— This medal, usually known to the service as the " Sampson Medal," was struck in accordance with a joint resolution of Congress approved by the President on March 3, 1901, reading as follows:

" *Resolved by the Senate and House of Representatives of the United States of America in Congress assembled,* That the Secretary of the Navy be, and he is hereby, authorized to cause to be struck medals commemorative of the naval and other engagements in the waters of the West Indies and on the shores of Cuba during the War with Spain, and to distribute the same to the officers and men of the Navy and Marine Corps who participated in any of said engagements deemed by him of sufficient importance to desire commemoration; *Provided,* That officers and men of the Navy or Marine Corps who rendered specially meritorious service, otherwise than in battle, may be rewarded in a like manner."

The medal commemorating the Naval engagements in the West Indies is of bronze, the obverse bears the bust of Rear Admiral Sampson in low bas-relief and the inscription " U. S. Naval Campaign West Indies 1898. William T. Sampson Commander in Chief," and the reverse bears a representation of a gun's crew in bas-relief; the medal is suspended by its distinctive ribbon, red, blue, red, from a bronze bar bearing the name of the engagement in which the recipient participated. In case the recipient took part in more than one engagement an additional bar is added for each engagement.

Special Meritorious Medal for Services in the War with Spain Other than in Battle.— This medal was struck in accordance with the joint resolution of Congress of March 3, 1901, quoted above, the portion of that resolution authorizing it being as follows:

> "*Provided,* That officers and men of the Navy or Marine Corps who rendered specially meritorious service, otherwise than in battle, may be rewarded in like manner."

This medal is of bronze in the form of a maltese cross with a medallion centerpiece. The centerpiece bears a foul anchor surrounded by a laurel wreath and the inscription " U. S. Naval Campaign West Indies," and the arms of the cross bear the words " Specially Meritorious Service 1898," on the obverse side. On the reverse side is engraved the name of the recipient and the act for which the medal was awarded.

The Certificate of Merit Medal.— This medal is conferred upon enlisted men of the Army by executive order of the President in cases where the recipient thereof has distinguished himself in the service of the country and has been recommended therefor by the commander of his regiment or the chief of the corps to which he belongs. The medal is of bronze bearing on its obverse side an American eagle and the inscription "Virtutis et Audaciae Monumentum et Praemium," and on the reverse side a wreath with the inscription "United States Army" surrounding it and the inscription "For Merit" enclosed in it. The medal is suspended by a distinctive ribbon having a narrow white stripe through the center and three stripes, red, white and blue, on either side.

The Civil War Campaign Medal.— By authority of various acts of Congress medals and ribbons have been awarded to officers and enlisted men of the military services who have actively and honorably participated in engagements and campaigns of the wars in which the United States has been engaged. The senior one of this class of medals is the Civil War Campaign Medal. The Civil War medal for the Army bears on its obverse side the head of Lincoln surrounded by the inscription "With malice toward none with charity for all," and on the reverse side a wreath of palms and laurel enclosing the inscription "The Civil War 1861–1865;" while the one for the Navy and Marine Corps bears on its obverse side a representation of the battle between the *Monitor* and *Merrimac* and the legend "The Civil War 1861–1865," and on the reverse side an American eagle above a foul anchor and the inscription "United States Navy — For Service" or "United States Marine Corps — For Service." The distinctive ribbon for the Civil War medal is blue and gray in stripes of equal width.

The other campaign medals for service in the Army bear upon the reverse side an American eagle above a design of guns and flags and the inscription "United States Army — For Service," while those for service in the Navy bear an eagle above a foul anchor and the inscription "United States Navy — For Service," and those for the Marine Corps the same design for those of the Navy with the inscription "United States Marine Corps — For Service."

The Indian Campaign Medal.— This medal was struck for all the officers and men who participated with honor in the actions and campaigns against the hostile Indians during all the long period of our history when the small Army of the United States, aided by a few hardy and adventurous scouts, protected the settler and his family who journeyed toward the setting sun to engage in the "winning of the west." Its obverse bears the figure of an Indian warrior mounted on a charging steed with spear ready to launch and the words "Indian Wars." The color of the distinctive ribbon for this medal is Indian red.

The Spanish War Campaign Medal.— This medal was conferred upon all officers and enlisted men of the Army, Navy and Marine Corps who saw active and honorable service in the War with Spain in 1898 and were engaged in battle afloat or ashore in any part of the world. The engagements thus commemorated embrace the sea battles and engagements of Manila Bay, Santiago, San Juan, Manzanillo, Cardenas and Matanzas, and the land battles and engagements in Cuba, Porto Rico and the Philippines. This medal bears on its obverse side a representation of the Morro Castle at Havana surrounded by the inscription "Spanish Campaign 1898." A medal of the same design bearing the inscription "West Indies Campaign 1898" was presented to the officers and men of the Navy and Marine Corps who participated in the operations and engagements in the West Indies during the War with Spain. The Spanish War medal is suspended by a dis-

1. Spanish War Campaign Medal, 1898
2. West Indies Campaign Medal, 1898
3. Philippine Campaign Medal, 1899–1903
4. China Relief Expedition Medal, 1900

1. Gold Life Saving Medal (obverse)
2. Gold Life Saving Medal (reverse)
3. Silver Life Saving Medal (obverse)
4. Silver Life Saving Medal (reverse)

tinctive ribbon of blue, yellow, blue, with narrow yellow edges.

Congressional Medal for Philippine Service.— This medal was authorized by Act of Congress in 1899 to be conferred upon officers and men of the Army and Marine Corps who should distinguish themselves in action during the Philippine insurrection. Its obverse bears a representation of three soldiers marching under arms, the central figure carrying the National Colors, surrounded by the inscription "Philippine Insurrection 1899;" and the reverse bears a wreath of palms and laurel surrounding the inscription "For Patriotism, Fortitude and Loyalty." The distinctive ribbon has a blue central stripe with narrower stripes of white, red and white at each side, and narrow edges of blue.

Philippine Insurrection Campaign Medal.— This medal was presented to all officers and men of the military and naval services of the United States who saw active service afloat or ashore in the campaigns incident to the operations against the Philippine Insurrectionists following the War with Spain and lasting until July 4, 1903. The obverse of the medal bears a representation of the Santiago gateway into the walled city of Manila surrounded by the words "Philippine Campaign 1899–1903." It is suspended by a distinctive ribbon of crimson, blue, crimson, with narrow blue edges.

The Army of Cuban Occupation Medal.— This medal was given to all officers and men who had honorable service in the Army of Cuban Occupation, which occupied Cuba while the island was under Military Government between the close of the War with Spain in 1898 and the establishment of the Republic by Cuba in 1902. The obverse side of the medal bears the coat of arms of the Republic of Cuba surrounded by the inscription "Army of Occupation Military Government of Cuba 1898–1902." The distinctive ribbon for the medal is red, blue, red with narrow blue edges, the central blue stripe having narrow edges of yellow.

The China Relief Expedition Medal.—This medal was struck to commemorate the defense of the foreign legations at Peking and their relief by the International Relief Expedition during the Boxer Rebellion in China in 1900, and was presented to all of the officers and men of the United States Army, Navy and Marine Corps who participated in the defense of the legations or fought in the relief column. On its obverse side is a representation of the Chienmen, the main gateway to the walled city of Peking, above a typical "five-toed" Chinese dragon, surrounded by the inscription "China Relief Expedition 1900." It is suspended by a ribbon of yellow with narrow blue edges.

The Gold Life Saving Medal.— The gold life saving medal, established by Act of Congress on June 20, 1874, is awarded to "those only who by extreme and heroic daring have endangered their lives in saving or endeavoring to save lives from the perils of the sea." The medal is made of solid gold and the obverse side bears a design representing a boat's crew rescuing a man from a stormy sea, the design being surrounded by the inscription "United States of America. Act of Congress, June 20, 1874." The reverse side bears a scroll upon which is engraved the name of the recipient, the deed for which the medal is awarded and the date, the scroll being surmounted by a spread eagle and having on one side of it the figure of a woman and on the other side an anchor and the sails of a ship, the design being surrounded by the inscription "In testimony of heroic

1. Reverse of Campaign Medals, U. S. Navy
2. Cuban Pacification Medal
3. Good Conduct Medal, U. S. Navy
4. Good Conduct Medal, U. S. Marine Corps

Medals and Badges for excellence in small arms firing

deeds in saving life from the perils of the sea." The medal is suspended from a clasp of gold representing the head of an eagle, the clasp being suspended by a scarlet silk ribbon two inches in width.

The Silver Life Saving Medal.— The silver life saving medal, established by the same Act of Congress as the gold life saving medal, is awarded to "those who have endangered their lives in saving lives from the perils of the sea or in succoring the shipwrecked." The medal is made of solid silver and the obverse side bears an allegorical figure of a woman rescuing another from the sea, the design being surrounded by the inscription "United States of America. Act of Congress, June 20, 1874." The reverse side bears a wreath surrounded by the inscription "In testimony of heroic deeds in saving life from the perils of the sea." The name of the recipient and the deed for which the medal was granted is engraved within the wreath. The medal is suspended from a silver clasp representing the head of an eagle, the clasp being suspended by a light blue silk ribbon two inches in width.

The Cuban Pacification Medal.— This medal was issued to all officers and men of the Army, Navy and Marine Corps who served in the Army of Cuban Pacification, which was engaged in the pacification and occupation of the Island of Cuba during what is known as "the second intervention" of that country for the reestablishment of stable government after a revolution that threatened its existence. This medal is of bronze and bears on its obverse side an allegorical representation of "Columbia" holding the olive branch of peace over "Cuba." It is suspended from a distinctive ribbon of olive drab edged with three stripes, red, white and blue.

The Nicaraguan Campaign Medal.— This medal was issued to the officers and men of the Navy and Marine Corps who took part in the Nicaraguan Expedition of 1912, which landed at Corinto, and, marching across the country, occupied the capital city of Managua and intervened between two local warring factions for the purpose of putting the country on a prosperous peace basis. The medal is of bronze and it is suspended from a distinctive ribbon of blue, crimson, blue, with narrow crimson edges.

HAITIAN CAMPAIGN MEDAL

The Haitian Campaign Medal.—This medal was given to the officers and enlisted men of the Navy and Marine Corps who participated in the operations in Haiti between July 9, 1915, and December 6, 1915, which resulted in the defeat of the revolutionists, who sought to overthrow the government, and the establishment of a peaceful régime. The obverse of the medal bears a design representing a portion of the coast line of the island with the sea in the foreground and the mountains in the background. At the left of this design is a palm tree and above the design around the edge of the medal is the inscription "Haitian Campaign" while below the design is the date, 1915. The medal is suspended from a distinctive ribbon of blue with two narrow red stripes through the center.

The Good Conduct Medal, U. S. Navy.— The good conduct medal is bestowed upon enlisted men of the Navy who have served a complete enlistment of four years with such constant and especially meritorious attention to duty and efficiency as to win the recommendations of their commanding officers for "Good Conduct." The medal is of bronze, its obverse side showing an anchor surmounted by a central medallion bearing a representation of the U. S. S. *Constitution* and surrounded by an anchor chain and the words "United States Navy." It is suspended by a ribbon of crimson.

The Good Conduct Medal, U. S. Marine Corps.— The good conduct medal for the Marine Corps is bestowed upon enlisted men of that service under similar conditions to those prescribed for the Navy. The medal is of bronze and its obverse side bears an anchor surmounted by a central medallion showing a marine at the breech of a rapid fire gun and surrounded by an anchor chain and the words "United States Marine Corps," with the motto of the Marine Corps, "Semper Fidelis," on a scroll between the flukes of the anchor. It is suspended by a miniature rifle from a bar by the distinctive ribbon of red, blue, red; the bar bearing the inscription "U. S. Marine Corps."

Ribbon Badge for Wounds in Battle.— A ribbon badge has been designed to decorate officers and men who have been wounded in battle. It consists of a ribbon bar of the same dimensions as the ribbon bars for the prescribed medals, the distinctive colors being red with a narrow stripe of white through the center.

CHAPTER XI

UNIFORMS AND INSIGNIA OF FOREIGN ARMIES AND NAVIES

THE uniforms and insignia of the armies and navies of foreign powers present such a great variety in design, style and color as to preclude the possibility of giving a detailed description of them within the limits of this book.

However, in order that the rank of the officers and enlisted men of these foreign services may be readily recognizable under the conditions that ordinarily prevail on active service ashore or afloat, there is included in this chapter a short description of the service uniforms and insignia worn by the officers and enlisted men of the armies and navies of Great Britain, France, Italy, Belgium, Japan, Russia, Germany and Austria-Hungary.

It will be noted that the uniforms of the navies of the world bear more similarity to each other than do those of the armies, thus the rank of naval officers of all the great powers is indicated by stripes of braid worn on the sleeves between the elbow and the lower edge of the cuff, and in most cases by similar stripes or other insignia worn upon straps placed on the shoulders between the base of the collar and the sleeve at the shoulder seam.

In the different armies there is much more diversity in design and color as well as in the method of indicating rank and corps; stripes and various designs upon the cuffs, insignia and stripes upon shoulder straps and insignia of many different designs upon the collar being the most common means.

In one respect all of the naval and military services of the world follow the same custom, medals and decorations awarded for especial deeds of gallantry, for long and faithful service or to commemorate some special event in war or peace are worn upon the left breast with dress uniforms, almost always suspended from a ribbon of distinctive color design, while a small section of this distinctive ribbon is worn with undress uniform and service uniforms. As a special mark of distinction the medals considered the highest in rank are frequently worn on the right breast or suspended from a ribbon or chain around the neck.

A marked tendency toward simplification in design both of uniform and insignia and toward the use of neutral or dull colors is also evident in recent years. This is largely due to the necessity of making the soldier as inconspicuous as possible when on the firing line, but also to the great expense incurred in fitting out very large forces of men in elaborate dress uniforms for which there is no use in the field.

Nevertheless it may be expected that when the world returns to a basis of general peace time conditions the dress uniforms and bright insignia and buttons that add so much to the brilliancy of military gatherings will again be in evidence; especially since there is so much of the tradition of the past associated with these uniforms and badges of rank and corps.

Attractive uniforms induce a corresponding pride in the smartness and neatness of the soldier or sailor and the distinctive badges of regiments and corps with long histories of creditable achievement go far to establish the *esprit de corps* which so surely makes for efficiency and contentment.

UNIFORMS OF THE BRITISH NAVY

In Great Britain the Navy is known as " The Senior Service " as it was organized as a regular service prior to the organization of a regular national Army.

In general the uniforms of the British Navy correspond quite closely to those of the United State Navy in composition and design and are worn upon similar occasions, although they are somewhat more elaborate, but the insignia are of different design.

Commissioned officers must provide themselves with full dress, ball dress, frock coat dress, blue mess dress, white mess dress, blue undress and white undress.

The full dress is very nearly the same in style and design to the special full dress of the United States naval officer, the ball dress is practically the same as the evening dress of the United States naval officer and the frock coat dress and blue and white mess dress the same as the corresponding United States naval uniforms. The blue undress uniform of the British naval officer differs from the service dress of the United States naval officer in that the coat worn with it is a square cut, double-breasted sack coat with turn down collar and rolling lapels with two rows of four buttons each down the front. The white undress of the British officer is the same as the white service dress of the American officer.

The rank of British naval officers is shown by insignia of rank on the tops of the epaulets with uniforms with which epaulets are worn, but with all of the blue uniforms the rank is also indicated by stripes of gold lace braid around the sleeves of the coat above the cuff. The

British Navy. Officers' sleeve decorations indicating rank

1. Admiral of the Fleet
2. Admiral
3. Vice Admiral
4. Rear Admiral
5. Commodore
6. Captain
7. Commander
8. Lieutenant Commander
9. Lieutenant
10. Sub Lieutenant
11. Chief Gunner and Chief Boatswain
12. Midshipman

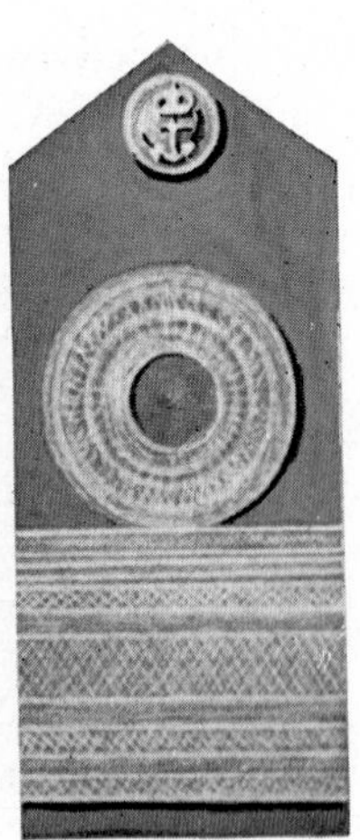

British Navy. Officers' shoulder straps

1. Admiral of the Fleet
2. Admiral
3. Vice Admiral
4. Rear Admiral
5. Commodore, 1st Class
6. Commodore, 2nd Class

number and arrangements of these rank stripes are shown in the accompanying illustration.

With the white mess dress and the white undress the rank is indicated by the stripes of gold braid or by other insignia of rank worn upon the shoulder straps. These shoulder straps are also worn with the great coat. There are no sleeve stripes on the white coats or the great coat.

The insignia of rank used on the shoulder straps of Flag Officers and the stripes indicating rank used on the shoulder straps of officers below the rank of Flag Officer are shown in the accompanying illustrations.

The Corps or Branch of the service to which an officer belongs is shown as follows on the sleeves and shoulder straps:—

Officers of the Line. By the circle or "curl" on the upper stripe of gold lace braid.

Engineer Officers... By the circle or "curl" as above with the addition of stripes of purple cloth between the gold stripes.

Medical Officers.... The circle or "curl" is omitted and there are stripes of scarlet cloth between the gold stripes.

Accountant or Pay Officers .... The circle or "curl" is omitted and there are stripes of white cloth between the gold stripes.

Naval Instructors.. The circle or "curl" is omitted and there are stripes of light blue cloth between the gold stripes.

It will thus be seen that the system of stripes on the sleeves and shoulder straps to indicate rank is practically the same in the British and United States navies, the "curl" in the British navy being used for the same purpose as the gold star in the United States navy, that is, to show that the officer wearing it belongs to the Line, or the command branch of the service.

The officers' overcoat or "great coat" in the British navy is a double breasted coat of ulster style reaching to just below the knees. It has a rolling collar with notched lapels and is closed by two rows of gilt service buttons down the front and has shoulder straps to indicate the rank of the wearer but no stripes on the sleeves. In the back the fulness is held in by a strap secured by two gilt buttons.

The service buttons of the British navy bear a raised design of a vertical foul anchor surmounted by a royal crown, the edge being surrounded by a raised rope design.

The caps and cocked hats of the British Navy are similar to those worn by United States naval officers except that there is more bell to the crown of the British cap. The cap insignia worn by commissioned officers are embroidered on the front of the cap and consist of a vertical foul anchor surrounded by a gilt wreath and surmounted by a royal crown in gilt and scarlet; the anchor being silver in the case of officers of the Line and gilt for officers of the Staff Corps.

The sword worn by British naval officers is much the same in general appearance as that worn by American officers, the differences being in the carved designs upon the hilt and blade of the sword and upon the bands of the scabbard. This is due to the fact that the American sword like the other parts of the American naval uniform was originally adopted from the British Navy.

The officers of the British Naval Air Service wear as a distinguishing mark of their service a gilt spread eagle

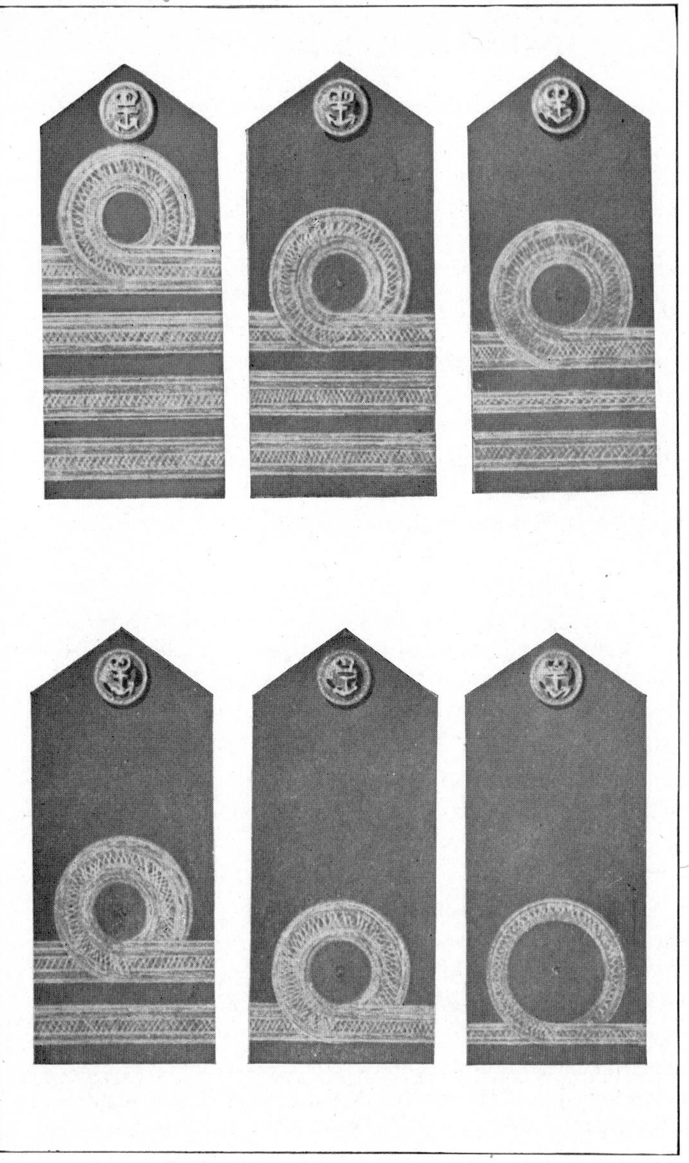

British Navy. Officers' shoulder straps

1. **Captain**
2. Commander
3. Lieutenant Commander
4. Lieutenant
5. Sub Lieutenant, Chief Gunner and Chief Boatswain
6. Gunner and Boatswain

on each sleeve above the rank stripes and a silver spread eagle in the center of the cap insignia in place of the anchor worn there by other officers. Their service buttons also have the spread eagle in place of the anchor for other officers.

Officers of the Royal Naval Division detailed for duty on shore wear a uniform of khaki colored cloth similar in design to the service uniform of British Army officers; their sleeves bearing the rank stripes of the same widths, number and arrangement as for other naval officers but made of braid of a slightly different shade than the material of the coat, and their shoulder straps bearing the same insignia of rank as that worn by the corresponding grades in the army.

Officers of the British Royal Naval Reserve wear the same uniforms as those prescribed for officers of the regular service, except that the stripes on the cuffs and on the shoulder straps while of the same number for the different grades are of a different design. The design of these stripes represents a rope twisted of two strands and in place of the "curl" above the upper stripe to indicate officers of the line there is a star shaped design made up of two interlocked triangles of narrow gold braid. The corps or branch of Staff officers of the Royal Naval Reserve is indicated by stripes of cloth between the twisted strand stripes, the distinctive colors for the different corps or branches being the same for Staff officers of the regular navy.

Officers of the British Naval Volunteer Reserve wear the same uniforms as those prescribed for the officers of the regular naval establishment, except that the stripes on the sleeves and shoulder straps to indicate rank, while being of the same number and arrangement for the different grades, are laid on in waving lines instead of in straight lines as in the case of the regular officers. The distinctive color stripes to indicate the various corps or branches for Staff Officers of the Royal Naval Volunteer Reserve are the same as for the regular service.

Officers of the Royal Naval Reserve and of the Royal Naval Volunteer Reserve attached to the Royal Naval Air Service wear their respective uniforms with the addition of the spread eagle design above the rank stripes on the sleeves and shoulder straps.

Officers of the British Colonial Naval Establishments maintained by the greater colonial divisions of the British Empire wear distinctive marks to indicate their especial service. These naval establishments comprise the Royal Indian Marine, the Australian Navy and the Canadian.

The enlisted men of the British Navy wear uniforms very similar in general design to those worn in the United States Navy with minor differences in the dimensions and cut of the various garments. The Chief Petty Officers wear uniforms of blue or white consisting of a bell-crowned cap with a black mohair band, a black patent leather visor and insignia consisting of two concentric circles surrounding a vertical foul anchor surmounted by a British crown; a double breasted sack coat with two rows of gilt service buttons; and plain trousers. Other petty officers and seamen wear the sailor cap, wide collared shirt and bell mouthed trousers common to the American service, the collar having three rows of narrow white braid around the edges with a black neckerchief knotted beneath it. The three rows of braid commemorate Nelson's three great victories—Copenhagen, the Nile and Trafalgar—and the black neckerchief was first worn as a badge of mourning for this great sea fighter. The cap has a black silk ribbon around the band upon which is the name of the ship in gilt block letters, thus,

H. M. S. DREADNOUGHT

the letters H.M.S. being the abbreviation of "His Majesty's Ship."

Rating badges to indicate the rank or rating of petty officers and men on special duties are worn on the sleeves between the shoulder seam and the elbow and are very numerous and complex, some of the principal ones being, in red,

Petty officer first class.......Two crossed foul anchors with a crown above and three chevrons, points down, below.

Petty officer second class....One vertical foul anchor with a crown above and two chevrons, points down.

Petty officer third class......The same, omitting the crown and with but one chevron.

Gunner's Mate and Gunlayer first class ....Two crossed cannon with one star below and a star and a crown above.

Gunner's Mate ....The same, omitting the lower star.

Gunlayer first class..........Two crossed cannon with a star above and a star below.

Gunlayer second class........The same omitting the lower star.

Gunlayer third class........The same omitting the stars.

Seaman Gunner ....A horizontal cannon with a star above.

Torpedo Gunner's Mate Higher Grade ....Two crossed torpedoes with a star and a crown above and a star below.

Torpedo Gunner's Mate ......The same omitting the lower star.

Torpedo Coxswain ....Two crossed torpedoes with a steering wheel above.

Leading Torpedoman ....Two crossed torpedoes with a star above.

Seaman Torpedoman ....A horizontal torpedo with a star above and a star below.

Chief Signal Yeoman.......Two crossed flags with a star and a crown above and two stars below.

Signal Yeoman.............The same omitting the crown.

Leading Signalman ....The same omitting one of the lower stars.

Signalman ....The same omitting the lower stars.

Ordinary signalman.........Two crossed flags.

Mechanician ....A propeller with one star and a crown above and a star below.

Chief Stoker ....A propeller with a crown above and a star below.

Stoker petty officer..........A propeller with a star above and a star below.

Leading stoker.............The same omitting the lower star.

Stoker ....A propeller.

Chief Telegraphist..........A bar of forked lightning with wings on each side and a crown below.

Leading Telegraphist........The same design but with a star above in place of the crown and a star below.

Telegraphist ....The same omitting the lower star.

Ordinary telegraphist ....The same design omitting stars.

Blacksmith, Plumber, and
Painter, first class.........An axe and a hammer crossed with a star above.

Other Artisans ....The same design omitting the star.

Physical training instructor, first class ....Two crossed Indian clubs with star and a crown above and a star below.

Physical training instructor, second class ....The same design omitting the lower star.

Sick Bay attendants ....A Geneva cross surrounded by a circle.

Bugler ....A bugle horizontal.

Markmanship badge, first class ....Two crossed rifles with a star above.

Marskmanship badge, second class ....The same without the star.

Markmanship badge, third class ....A rifle horizontal.

Badges of other colors are:

Cook ....A white star.

Schoolmaster ....A yellow star.

Steward ....A yellow star.

Good shooting badge, third class ....A yellow rifle horizontal.

Uniforms of the British Royal Marines

The Royal Marines perform duties similar to those performed by the United States Marines both afloat and ashore and hold a high record for efficiency and loyalty. They are divided into two branches, the Royal Marine Artillery and the Royal Marine Light Infantry, the former being popularly known as the "Blue Marines" on account of the fact that their dress coats are of blue cloth and the latter as the "Red Marines" since their dress coats are of red cloth.

Both branches are also provided with khaki colored uniforms for field service ashore.

The rank of the officers is indicated by insignia of rank worn on the shoulder straps, these insignia being the same for the various ranks as those worn by officers of the British Army.

The titles for the different grades of rank of the officers are the same as those for the British Army, namely, General, Lieutenant General, Major General, Brigadier General, Colonel, Major, Captain, Lieutenant and Second Lieutenant.

The ranks of the enlisted men are indicated by badges or chevrons worn upon the sleeves between the shoulder seam and the elbow, as follows:

Sergeant Major............The coat of arms of Great Britain in gold, red and white embroidery.

Quartermaster Sergeant of Infantry ....A British crown in gold and red embroidery.

Quartermaster Sergeant of Artillery ....Two crossed cannon in gold with a British crown above them embroidered in gold and red.

Quartermaster Sergeant, Musketry Instructor ....Two crossed rifles in gold with the crown in gold and red above them.

Sergeant ....A chevron of three stripes worn with the points down.

Corporal ....A chevron of two stripes worn with the points down.

Lance Corporal ....A chevron of one stripe worn with the point down.

Private ....No distinctive badge.

The Corps insignia of the Royal Marines are the eastern hemisphere in silver surrounded by a gold laurel wreath, the insignia being surmounted by two gold cannon crossed for the Marine Artillery and by gold bugle trumpet for the Marine Light Infantry. These insignia are commonly referred to in the British service as " The Globe and Laurel."

Uniforms of the British Army

At the beginning of the present world war the Land Forces of the British Empire embraced the regular troops commonly known as the " Home Army " and the troops of her far-flung colonial possessions and dependencies, such as the Indian Army, the Australian Army, the Canadian Army, the South African Forces, the West Indian regiments, the New Zealand troops, and the Police and Constabulary troops of many minor colonies and possessions.

In the " Home Army " there were many varieties and colors in the uniforms and when we add to this the distinctive uniforms of the various Colonial Forces and the picturesque native uniforms of the Indian forces the resultant assemblage is one which would require many volumes to adequately describe.

In one respect however the clothing of the various units collected from all over the vast British Empire to make up the great " New Army " of Great Britain is practically the same,— the service or field uniform of all is cut on the same lines and the insignia of rank worn with this uniform are the same for all, the variations being in the corps and regimental badges which indicate the portion of the empire from which the regiments come and the arm of the service in which they are serving.

The British were the first to adopt the neutral brown shade known as "khaki" for their field or service uniforms and its practicability and serviceability became so evident to them that its use was extended to all of their armed land forces, with the result that they now have a uniform and equipment which for serviceability, efficiency, comfort and smartness of appearance is excelled by no other nation.

The British Army officers' uniform is made of a standard dark khaki colored cloth or serge and consists of a single-breasted coat with turn down collar and rolling notched lapels, closed in front by a row of four gilt buttons, cut to fit snugly at the waist, easy across the breast and shoulders and with enough flare to the skirt to make it hang well over the full breeches that are worn with it; breeches which lace below the knee; tan leather strap puttees and shoes or tan leather boots; a bell-crowned cap with a sharply sloping visor; and the "Sam Browne" sword and pistol belt. Wrap puttees of khaki colored cloth are also worn for garrison and field service.

The coat has a pleated patch pocket on each breast closed by a buttoned flap, and a large bellows patch pocket on each side below the waist which is also closed by a buttoned flap, and cloth shoulder straps on each shoulder secured by a small button at the collar end.

The rank of an officer in service uniform is indicated by metal insignia of rank worn upon the shoulder straps and also (for officers below the rank of Brigadier General) by stripes of worsted braid around the sleeves just above the lower edge and by worsted insignia of rank worn on a three-pointed strap which crosses the sleeve stripes on the cuffs. These insignia of rank are shown in the accompanying illustrations and are as follows for the various grades of rank:—

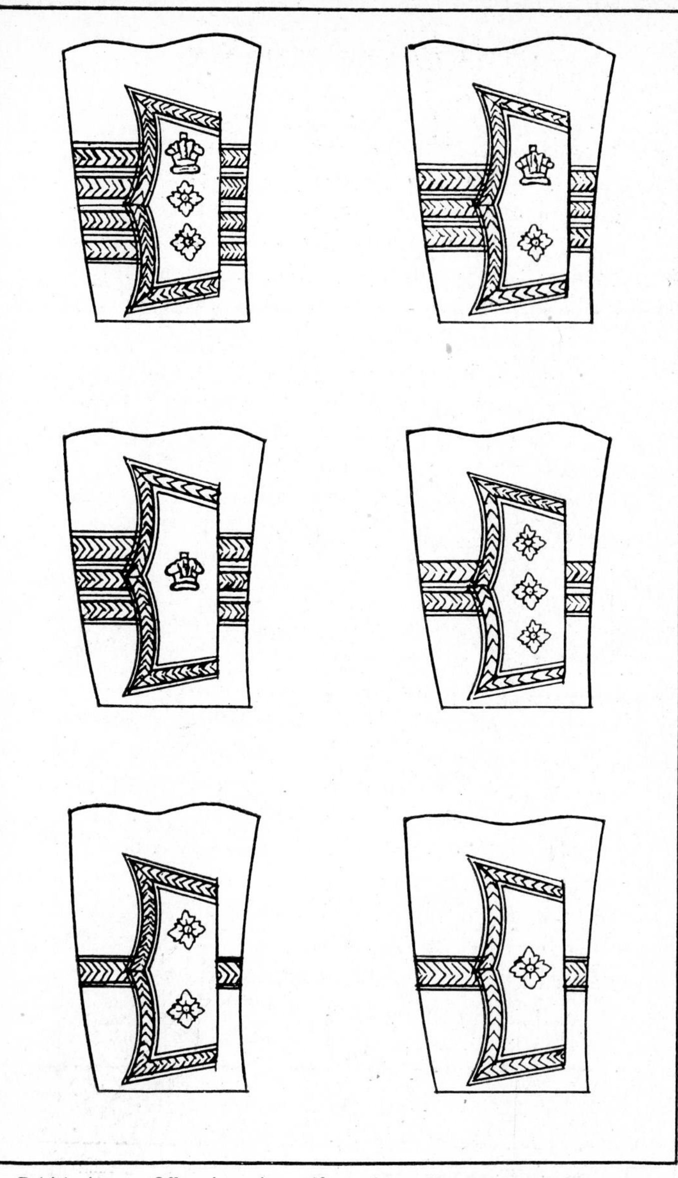

British Army. Officers' service uniform sleeve decorations indicating rank

1. Colonel
2. Lieutenant Colonel
3. Major
4. Captain
5. Lieutenant
6. Second Lieutenant

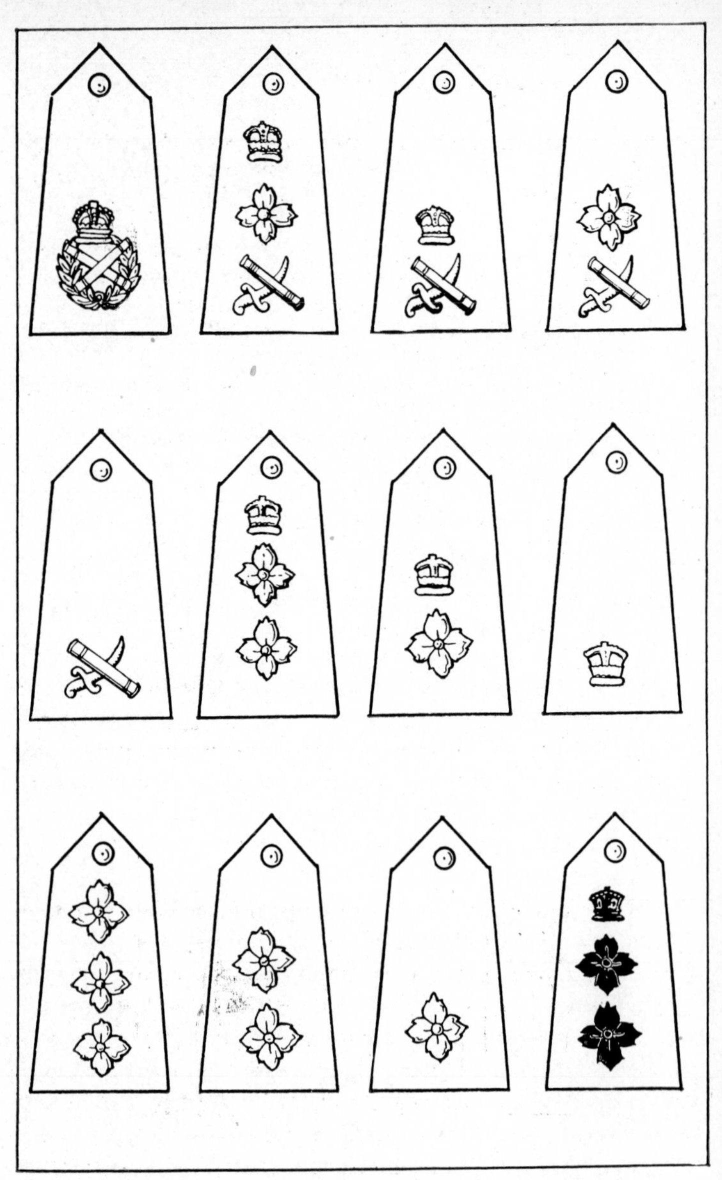

British Army. Officers' shoulder strap insignia indicating rank

1. Field-Marshal
2. General
3. Lieutenant General
4. Major General
5. Brigadier General
6. Colonel
7. Lieutenant Colonel
8. Major
9. Captain
10. Lieutenant
11. Second Lieutenant
12. Chaplain, with rank of Colonel

Field Marshal.....Two crossed batons in red surrounded by a wreath of gold laurel leaves and surmounted by a British crown in gold and red.
General ....A baton and sword crossed with a diamond shaped device above it and a crown above the diamond, all in gold.
Lieutenant General.A baton and sword crossed with a crown above it, all in gold.
Major General.....A baton and a sword crossed with the diamond above, all in gold.
Brigadier General..The same omitting the diamond.
Colonel ....Two diamonds and a crown in a vertical line.
Lieutenant Colonel.The same omitting one of the diamonds.
Major ....A crown.
Captain ....Three diamonds in a vertical line.
Lieutenant ....Two diamonds in a vertical line.
Second Lieutenant.One diamond.

The officers of the Scottish and Highland regiments wear the stripes on the cuffs in a curve from the outer edge of the sleeve to a higher point at the inner edge of the sleeve and the insignia of rank beneath these stripes in a horizontal line instead of in a vertical line as described and illustrated for the other officers.

The wearing of the insignia of rank upon the shoulder straps except by officers of the rank of Brigadier General and higher has been suspended when on actual duty in the field.

The insignia worn upon the front of the cap by a Field Marshal consists of two crossed batons in red surrounded by a gold wreath and surmounted by a gold and red crown above which is a gold British lion; for General officers it is the same except that instead of the two batons there is one baton and a sword crossed; permanent Staff officers wear the crown and lion only on the cap; and a Field Marshal, General officers and permanent Staff officers of field rank or above wear a scarlet band around the cap.

For regimental officers the insignia worn on the front of the cap are the distinctive "Regimental badges" adopted for the regiment. These regimental badges present a great variety in design and often refer to some historic battle in which the regiment has taken part or to some distinctive feature of the county or colony from which the regiment comes.

In many cases the name by which the regiment is commonly known is contained in the design, in others the number of the regiment in its corps is given in the design, and not infrequently the regimental motto has a prominent place.

Thus the regimental badge of the 4th Hussars, a famous cavalry regiment, is a gold circle bearing the inscription "Queen's Own Hussars," surmounted by a gold crown, and having on the center the number of the regiment "IV," and on a scroll beneath the motto "Mente et Manu."

The Irish Rifles have the Irish harp surmounted by a royal crown with a scroll beneath bearing the motto "Quis Separabit," all in green enamel.

The 17th Lancers have as their insignia a skull and cross bones with the words "or Glory" on a scroll beneath, the motto of the regiment being "Death or Glory."

The 12th Canadian Infantry has a gold maple leaf bearing the number of the regiment in silver and the word "Canada" also in silver.

The Grenadier Guards regiments have a gold spherical bursting shell.

Chaplains wear a Maltese cross surmounted by a crown in black enamel.

Officers of the Army Pay Corps wear the monogram "A.P.C." surmounted by a crown.

The insignia of the Royal Army Medical Corps consist of the rod of Esculapius with a single serpent entwined about it surrounded by a wreath and surmounted by a crown with the scroll beneath bearing the inscription "Royal Army Medical Corps," all in gold.

Both officers and enlisted men in the British Army habitually wear gilt buttons and insignia on their service khaki-colored uniforms, although when in the field these buttons and insignia are allowed to tarnish or bronze, and in many cases leather buttons are used on field service in place of the gilt buttons.

The overcoat, or great coat, worn by the officers of the British Army is a double breasted ulster quite similar in design to that worn by officers of the United States Army, but having a lapel collar and reaching only to the knee. It is made of cloth of the same color as the service uniform and has shoulder straps upon which the insignia of rank are worn.

The service uniform of the enlisted men of the British Army is of the same khaki colored cloth as the officers' uniform and consists of a cap similar to that worn by officers with a visor of tan leather or of khaki colored cloth upon the front of which the regimental or corps insignia are worn; a single breasted sack coat buttoning to the neck with a standing turn-over collar, a patch pocket on each breast and a bellows patch pocket on each side below the waist, and shoulder straps upon which are worn, near the arm seam, the regimental badges; breeches of the same color as the coat; wrap khaki-colored cloth puttees; and heavy tan leather laced shoes.

The overcoat is a short double breasted coat with rolling collar and back straps.

In hot weather khaki cotton drill uniforms of the same design are worn.

As variations of this general uniform, the Scottish and Highland troops still wear the kilts as their winter uniform, although in hot weather they also wear the full khaki summer uniform, the troops from Australia and Canada to a great extent wear the wide brimmed felt hat common in the American service, and the Indian troops wear their native turbans and trousers although these are of the standard khaki color.

The rank of the noncommissioned officers is indicated in the British Armies by badges worn upon the sleeves between the elbow and the shoulder, as in the United States Army, many of these insignia being nearly the same for the various grades, doubtless due to the fact that the American insignia were originally taken from the British during the revolutionary period.

The principal insignia of rank worn on the sleeves of noncommissioned officers and enlisted men holding special assignments of duty are as follows:

Staff Sergeant Major, Army Service Corps............. A crown surrounded by a wreath.

Master Gunner 1st and 2nd class, Field Artillery...... A field gun with a crown above it.

Master Gunner 3rd class, Field Artillery .... The same without the crown.

Sergeant Major .... A crown.

Bandmaster .... A lyre with leaves at the base and a crown above it.

Cavalry Squadron Corporal
Major .... A chevron of four stripes worn point up with a crown above it.

Regimental Quartermaster
Sergeant .... A chevron of four stripes worn point up with a twelve pointed star above it.

Quartermaster Sergeant..... A chevron of four stripes worn point up.

Company Sergeant Major ... A chevron of three stripes worn point down with a crown above it.

Color Sergeant .... A chevron of three stripes worn point down with crossed flags and a crown above it.

Sergeant .... A chevron of three stripes worn points down.

Corporal .... A chevron of two stripes worn points down.

Lance Corporal .... A chevron of one stripe worn point down.

Infantry Pioneer .... Two axes crossed.

Roughrider of Cavalry....... A spur worn rowel up.

Scout Corporal .... A three pointed lance head with a cross below it.

Squadron Scout, Cavalry.... A three pointed lance head.

Bugler .... A horn bugle with cords.

Bugler of Rifle Regiments... Two such bugles.

Sergeant Trumpeter......... Two straight trumpets crossed with a three pointed lance head vertical in the center.

Drummer .... A snare drum.

Machine Gunner .... The letters "M. G." surrounded by a wreath.

Horseshoer .... A horseshoe worn toe up.

Saddler .... A horse's bridle curb bit.

Wheelwright and Carpenter.. A wagon wheel.

Flight Sergeant of Royal Flying Corps .... Chevrons as for other sergeants with a four-bladed propeller and a crown above it.

Sergeant of Royal Flying Corps .... The same without the crown.

Flying Corps Badge .... The words "Royal Flying Corps" on a blue ground.

Qualified Pilot, Flying Corps. Two horizontally spread wings with a crown above and the initials "R. F. C." in the center.

Engineer Noncommissioned Officers .... The same chevrons as other noncommissioned officers with a bursting bomb above.

Royal Army Medical Corps enlisted men .... A scarlet Geneva cross in a yellow circle.

Excellence in target practice with rifles and guns is indicated by special badges worn on the sleeves between the elbow and the shoulder as follows:

Best rifle shot in Regiment.. Two rifles crossed surrounded by a wreath with a crown above it.

Best shooting squadron or company in a Regiment... The same without the wreath.

Best shot in squadron, company or band .... Two rifles crossed with a star above.

First Class Gunner, Artillery. Two cannon crossed with a crown above.

Best swordsman in Regiment, Cavalry .... Two sabers crossed with a crown above.

Best swordsman in Troop, Cavalry .... Two sabers crossed with a star above.

Best swordsman in every twenty men, Cavalry	The same without the star.
First Prize Gunner, Artillery	The letter "G" with a wreath beneath and a crown above.
Second Prize Gunner, Artillery	The same with a star instead of the crown.
Gun Layer, Artillery	The letter "L" with a wreath beneath.

A new type of distinguishing mark adopted during the present war consists of pieces of cloth of various shapes worn in the center of the back between the shoulders to enable officers to distinguish the organization to which a man on the firing line belongs.

Uniforms of the French Army

Up to within a few years the uniform of the troops of the Line of the French Army consisted of a dark blue coat and red trousers, with caps of the *kepi* design and white gaiters or short leggings. This uniform was decorated with gold and silver ornamentation and rank insignia and as a variation in the headdress the cavalry wore helmets with plumes.

At the time of the Boer War in South Africa the question of a less conspicuous uniform was agitated with the result that a coat of mignonette green (or *reseda* as it was called in France) was adopted although the red trousers were retained. With this uniform a helmet of the same color as the coat was adopted. Some of the troops still retained the dark blue coats however and discussion as to the uniform to be finally adopted continued.

In 1912 a single breasted sack coat of a light gray-blue color was tried with the blue and red *kepi*, and red trousers which were worn tight around the calves of the legs. The wrap puttee was also worn to some extent.

Shortly after the beginning of the present war it was demonstrated by service in the field that the red trousers and gold trimmings were too conspicuous for modern field service, and as a result a uniform of the light gray-blue color, known as "horizon blue," was adopted for both officers and enlisted men on field service, but the old dress uniforms were not abolished though not worn during war. In this uniform simplicity was sought and all bright buttons, insignia and trimmings were reduced to a minimum with the object of securing a serviceable and inconspicuous uniform.

The officers' service uniform consists of a single breasted sack coat with a standing turn-down collar, shoulder straps and four outside patch pockets similar to the service coat of United States Army officers; breeches; tan leather strap puttees and shoes, or tan leather boots, and a cap (*kepi*) of the same color as the coat and trousers. The color of this uniform is a light blue-gray. The buttons are of silver-bronze.

The cap, or *kepi,* has a sloping visor of black patent leather with a band covered with gold lace for general officers and of distinctive colored cloth with narrow gold stripes indicating rank for other officers, and the top of the crown is slightly less in diameter than the band. In the case of general officers the visor is ornamented with gold decorations.

In the trenches when under fire a steel helmet is worn as a protection against long range rifle bullets and pieces of shrapnel. This helmet is of the same color as the service uniform and it has a distinctive corps insignia on the front in metal of the same color.

When on duty away from the actual battle front the

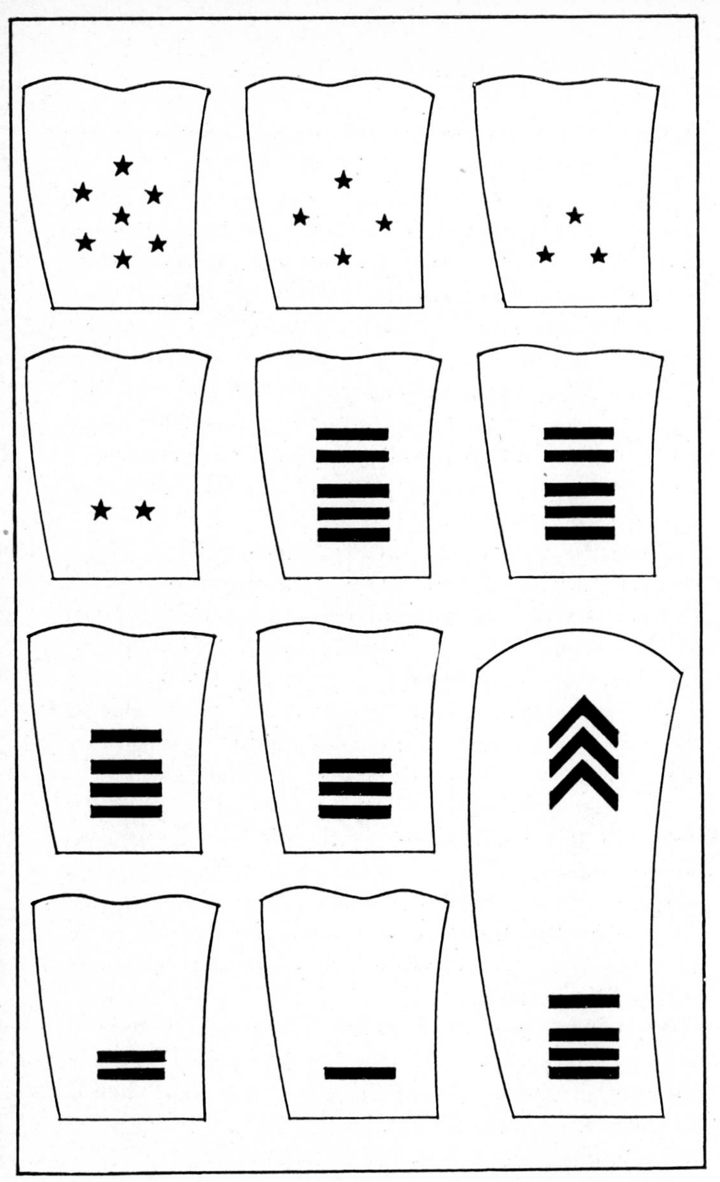

French Army. Officers' sleeve decorations indicating rank and service
All of the stripes are gold, except in the case of Lieutenant Colonel, where the second and fourth are silver

1. Marshal of France
2. General
3. General of Division
4. General of Brigade
5. Colonel
6. Lieutenant Colonel
7. Major
8. Captain
9. First Lieutenant
10. Second Lieutenant
11. War service chevron

dress cap of red or blue (according to the corps) is frequently worn.

The rank of officers in the French Army was formerly indicated by stars on the cuffs for General officers and by gold or silver stripes around the cuffs of the coats for other officers, the widths, number and arrangement of the stripes being practically the same as those worn by officers of the same relative rank in the navy. These stripes proved too conspicuous for field service and a small section of the stripes showing on the front of the sleeve only was adopted for the service coats. These short stripes or *galons* are of dull gold or silver depending on the rank and are as shown in the accompanying illustration.

The insignia for the different grades of rank are as follows:

Marshal of France....Seven stars on each cuff, arranged in three vertical rows, the center row having three stars and the outer rows having two stars each.
General ....Four stars on each cuff, two placed horizontally in the center and one above and one below.
General of Division...Three stars on each cuff arranged in a triangle with the point up.
General of Brigade...Two stars placed on each cuff horizontally.
Colonel ....Five gold stripes, or *galons,* on each cuff.
Lieutenant Colonel ..The same as for Colonel except that the second and fourth stripes are of silver.
Major ....Four gold stripes.
Captain ....Three gold stripes.
Lieutenant ....Two gold stripes.
Second Lieutenant ...One gold stripe.

The corps or branch of the service is indicated in the French Army by distinctive insignia or color patches worn on the collar at the front on both sides of the neck opening.

A distinctive feature of the French Army uniforms for both the officers and enlisted men is the "war service chevrons" worn on the right sleeve between the elbow and the shoulder with the point of the chevron up. A chevron of one stripe shows that the wearer has had one year's active service at the front during the present war and an additional stripe is added to the chevron for each additional period of six months service at the front. These service chevrons are of dull gold.

Officers of the Algerian Corps and of the Colonial Infanterie wear winter service uniforms of khaki-colored cloth and hot weather uniforms of khaki cotton material; the design of the garments being the same as for those of the home troops except that the Algerians wear very loose baggy trousers cut after the "Zouave" style.

Officers in the Aviation service also wear khaki-colored uniforms.

The officers' overcoat is single breasted reaching to about three inches below the knees, closed with a single row of bronze buttons down the center of the front, buttoning to the neck, with a wide falling collar, and a large pocket on each side. Like the enlisted men's overcoat it is fitted to have the fronts of the skirt button back to permit freedom of the legs in marching. The same stripes indicating rank are worn upon the sleeves as upon the service coat.

In the French Army there is a rank called "Adjutant" which corresponds to that of Warrant officer in the United States Navy and Marine Corps but for which there is no corresponding rank in the United

States Army. His service uniform is similar to that worn by commissioned officers; his cap bears no rank stripes, and his rank is indicated by a narrow gold cuff stripe broken with sections of black.

The sword belt for officers is of tan leather with a cross strap over the right shoulder and diagonally to the left side above the hip, very similar to the British "Sam Browne" belt. It is worn by officers at all times when on duty in service uniform.

The enlisted men of the French Army have service uniforms of the same color as those for officers. The uniform consists of a single breasted sack coat, with standing collar and a patch pocket with buttoned flap on each side below the waist, cut to fit easily; breeches cut full above and close fitting below the knees; wrap puttees of cloth of the same color as the coat and breeches; tan leather shoes; and a plain cap of the *kepi* pattern with sloping visor.

The Algerian troops wear uniforms of the same design but of khaki-colored cloth and very loose "Zouave" style breeches.

The Colonial Infantry wear service uniforms of the same design as those for the home troops but of khaki-colored material.

Mounted troops and field artillery wear tan leather boots or tan leather leggings and shoes.

The overcoat for enlisted men is single breasted, reaching a little below the knee, with side pockets, and fitted to have the skirts buttoned back from the front so as not to interfere with the freedom of the legs in marching. The overcoats are of the light blue-gray cloth.

The rank of noncommissioned officers is indicated by short stripes of cloth worn diagonally across the outer side of the coat sleeves between the elbow and the lower edge, as follows:

Sergeant Major....	Three stripes of dull gold braid.
Sergeant	Two stripes of dull gold braid.
Corporal	Two stripes of cloth of the distinctive color of the arm of the service.
First class private..	One stripe of cloth of the distinctive color of the arm of the service.

The arm of the service to which an enlisted man belongs is shown by color patches upon the collar on both sides of the front opening. These patches are of yellow for infantry, blue for cavalry, red for artillery and black for engineers, and have the number of the regiment upon them in black figures for infantry, white for cavalry and artillery, and red for engineers. Aviators wear an insignia consisting of two eagle's wings upon each side of the collar.

The belts, belt suspender straps and cartridge boxes are of tan leather, though webbing is also in use. The water bottle (canteen) is covered with cloth of the same color as the uniform.

The buttons worn by enlisted men upon the service uniform coat and overcoat are plain and of the same color as the material of the coats.

In some special corps of the French service there are variations from the standard uniform above described, thus the Chasseurs Alpin wear a uniform of dark-blue cloth with a dark blue *beret,* a full-crowned visorless hat something after the style of the tam-o-shanter, and the Algerian troops wear a round turban of khaki-colored cloth with a tassel in the center, after the style of the fez.

Uniforms of the French Navy

The uniforms of the officers and men of the French Navy, while following in general the usual naval style present some variations as to the combination of garments, the decorations, the number and arrangements of the rank stripes on the sleeves and the designs of the insignia of rank and corps.

Commissioned officers are provided with five separate uniforms, full dress, No. 1 dress, No. 2 dress, No. 3 dress blue, and No. 3 dress white.

The full dress corresponds to the United States naval officer's special full dress uniform, and consists of a cocked hat, a dark blue double breasted cutaway frock coat, gilt epaulets, dark blue cloth trousers decorated with gold lace stripes down the outer seams.

No. 1 dress corresponds to the United States naval officer's full dress uniform and consists of a cocked hat, blue cap or white cap, a dark blue double breasted frock coat with epaulets, and plain dark blue or white trousers.

No. 2 dress corresponds to the undress uniform of the United States naval officer and consists of the blue or white cap, the dark blue frock coat or the white tunic and dark blue or white trousers.

No. 3 dress, blue, corresponds to the blue service dress of the United States naval officer and consists of the dark blue cap, dark blue frock coat or dark blue tunic (sack coat) and dark blue or white trousers.

No. 3 dress, white, corresponds to the white service dress of the United States naval officer and consists of the white cap, white tunic and white trousers.

Black shoes are worn with all except white uniforms, with which white shoes are worn.

The rank of commissioned officers is shown by means

of insignia on the tops of the epaulets, with uniforms of which epaulets form a part, and by decorations on the cuffs of the sleeves of the frock coat and service sack coat. These sleeve decorations are as shown by the illustrations:—

Admiral of France......	Two batons crossed in gold embroidery.
Vice Admiral	Three silver stars.
Rear Admiral	Two silver stars.
Captain	Five stripes of gold braid.
Commander	Five stripes of braid, the second and fourth being silver and the other three gold.
Lieutenant-Commander ...	Four stripes of gold braid.
Lieutenant	Three stripes of gold braid.
Lieutenant, Junior Grade.	Two stripes of gold braid.
Ensign	One stripe of gold braid.
Midshipman	One stripe of gold braid broken by interwoven stripes of blue silk.

The officers of the Line or Command branch wear the rank insignia on the dark blue cloth of the coat sleeve; while the officers of the Staff Corps have cuffs of distinctive color beneath the stripes, these colors being for:—

Engineer officers	violet velvet.
Medical officers	red velvet.
Constructors and Ordnance officers...	black velvet.
Paymasters	brown velvet.

On the white service tunic or coat the rank is indicated by stripes upon shoulder straps, these stripes being similar to those worn on the sleeves of the blue frock coat and tunic.

French Navy. Officers' sleeve decorations indicating rank
All of the stripes are gold with the exception of those for Commander, in which case the second and fourth stripes are silver

1. Vice Admiral
2. Rear Admiral
3. Captain
4. Commander
5. Lieutenant Commander
6. Lieutenant
7. Lieutenant, Junior Grade
8. Ensign
9. Midshipman

The cap for Flag Officers is of blue cloth with a patent leather visor and a band of gold embroidery, and it has an insignia on the front consisting of a gold anchor with various decorations of leaves for the different grades and corps.

The cap for officers below the rank of Rear Admiral is of the same design, with narrow stripes of gold braid around the band to indicate the rank of the wearer. On ordinary service aboard ship a cap of the same design with a band of black silk ribbon is worn. The device worn on the front of the cap by these officers is a gold foul anchor placed vertical.

Warrant officers wear dress uniforms similar to those worn by commissioned officers; their cap has one narrow gold stripe around the band and a gold anchor on the front, and their sleeves have three narrow stripes, the upper one of gold one-quarter of an inch wide, the middle one a twisted silver rope one-eighth of an inch wide and the lower one of gold of the same rope design.

The enlisted men of the French Navy wear uniforms of dark blue cloth for cold weather and of white for hot weather, those for the chief petty officers consisting of a plain cap with black leather visor, a sack coat with gilt buttons and plain trousers, and those for enlisted men of lower ratings consisting of a flat sailor cap, overshirt and trousers of a design similar to those worn in the British Navy. A prominent feature of their uniform cap is a red pompon in the center of the top of the crown.

The overcoats are of dark blue cloth of the design commonly styled " pea jackets."

The rating or rank of the petty officers is indicated by distinguishing marks worn upon the sleeves; some of the principal ones being:—

Chief Petty Officers.

Seaman Branch.........Two narrow gold stripes on each sleeve above the cuff, and on the cap a gold anchor and a narrow gold stripe around the band.

Commissary Branch.....The same except that the sleeve stripes are silver.

Musicians ....Two twisted gold stripes on the cuff and a gold lyre on each side of the collar.

Petty Officers, First Class.

Seaman Branch ....One gold stripe on each sleeve above the cuff, and a gold anchor on the cap.

Commissary Branch.....The same except that the sleeve stripe is silver.

Buglers and Drummers..One gold stripe on each sleeve, worn diagonally.

Musicians ....One twisted gold stripe on each sleeve and a gold anchor on each side of the collar.

Petty Officers, Second Class.

Seaman Branch.........Two stripes of red cloth on each sleeve between the elbow and the cuff.

Yeoman Branch.........One broken gold stripe on each sleeve between the elbow and the shoulder.

Musicians ....Two stripes of red cloth on each sleeve between the elbow and the cuff.

Stewards ....Two stripes of orange colored cloth on each sleeve between the elbow and the cuff.

Buglers and Drummers..One diagonal gold stripe on each sleeve.

All petty officers of the second class and also seamen

wear two anchors crossed on the upper part of the right sleeve.

There are also a number of specialty marks for such special ratings as cook, tailor, shoemaker and armorer.

The distinctive mark of band musicians is a gold lyre worn on each side of the collar, and that of the hospital corps is the red Geneva cross.

Uniforms of the Italian Army

In the Italian Army the peace time dress uniforms consist, as a rule, of a dark blue braided coat, light gray trousers with stripes of distinctive corps color down the outer seams, and black leather boots for officers and leggings for enlisted men. The head dress varies with the corps and arm of the service, the infantry wearing a dark blue cap trimmed with colored braid, the cavalry a metal trimmed helmet or a fur busby, the field artillery a black shako with bright brass ornaments, and the Bersaglieri a black felt hat with a plume of feathers falling over the left shoulder.

The field service uniform is of gray cloth having a greenish tinge and is practically the same for all arms of the service and for all corps, except that the Bersaglieri wear their regular uniform of dark blue with red facings and their distinctive head dress.

The officers' field uniform consists of a short sack coat with a standing-falling collar and a patch pocket on each breast; breeches or trousers cut to fit the legs tightly below the knee, black boots or tan leather shoes and leggings, and a straight crowned cap with sloping visor of black leather and a band of distinctive corps color. The coat is closed by buttons down the front concealed by a fly or by concealed hooks and eyes. On each side of the collar at the front is a silver star with a circular disc in the center upon which are the insignia indicating the corps or arm of the service to which the officer belongs.

The rank is indicated by the shoulder straps and the insignia worn upon them. The shoulder knots for General officers are covered with silver and bear gold stars to indicate the rank, those for Field officers having a narrow edging of silver braid and silver stars to indicate the rank, and those for company officers having only the silver stars to indicate the rank; as follows:—

General ....Silver covered shoulder straps with three gold stars.
Lieutenant General. Silver covered shoulder straps with two gold stars.
Major General.....Silver covered shoulder straps with one gold star.
Colonel ....Shoulder straps edged with silver braid and with three silver stars.
Lieutenant Colonel. Shoulder straps edged with silver braid and with two silver stars.
Major ....Shoulder straps edged with silver braid and with one silver star.
Captain ....Plain shoulder straps with three silver stars.
First Lieutenant...Plain shoulder straps with two silver stars.
Second Lieutenant. Plain shoulder straps with one silver star.

The rank of officers is also shown by the braid around the cap; the cap for General officers having a red band embroidered in silver with bands of narrow gold braid above it, three for general, two for lieutenant general and one for major general; the cap for Field officers having one wide silver stripe around the band with narrow stripes of silver braid above it, three for colonel, two for lieutenant colonel and one for major; and the cap for company officers having stripes of narrow silver braid around it, three for captain, two for first lieutenant and one for second lieutenant.

The corps of officers is shown by patches of distinctive color upon the collar at each side of the neck opening and also by the insignia upon the center of the silver star worn on each side of the collar.

The enlisted men wear service uniforms of the same color as that of the officers, the coat and trousers being similar to that for officers and the cap being a plain cloth kepi of the same color as the coat with a sloping visor of black leather. The cavalry wear gray helmets, the Bersaglieri wear their own distinctive plumed hat and all men on duty in the trenches wear steel trench helmets similar to those worn by the American, British and French soldiers.

The rank of noncommissioned officers is indicated by chevrons worn points up on the sleeves between the elbow and the bottom edge of the cuff, as follows:—

Sergeant Major ...Chevron of four stripes in silver.
Sergeant ....Chevron of three stripes in white cloth.
Corporal ....Chevron of three stripes in red cloth.

Distinctive badges are also worn on the sleeves to indicate special duties or assignments of enlisted men.

The arms of the service and corps of an enlisted man is indicated on his uniform by patches of the distinctive corps color upon the collar at each side of the front opening, and the regiment is shown by numerals on these color patches.

Uniforms of the Italian Navy

The uniforms for the officers and enlisted men of the Italian Navy are made of dark blue cloth for dress uniforms and for undress uniforms for winter wear and of white cotton duck or linen for wear in hot weather. In general the design of the uniform is similar to those of the British Navy with the exception of the undress coat which is similar to the service coat for officers of the United States Navy.

Commissioned officers are required to have special full dress, full dress, dress, blue undress and white undress uniforms.

The special full dress uniform consists of a cocked hat very similar to that worn by American naval officers, a double breasted cutaway frock coat with turndown collar and notched lapels buttoned down the front with two rows of service gilt buttons; dark blue trousers with gold lace braid stripes down the outer leg seams, and black shoes. Epaulets similar to those worn in the United States Navy and a sword belt covered with gold lace are worn with this uniform, and a blue silk sash is worn from the right shoulder diagonally across the body to the left side where it is knotted and the ends have tassels.

The full dress uniform consists of a double breasted frock coat very similar to that worn in the United States Navy; a bell-crowned cap of dark blue cloth with a sloping visor; plain dark blue trousers, and black shoes. Epaulets and the full dress belt are worn with this uniform.

The dress uniform is the same as the full dress with the exceptions that the epaulets are omitted and the sword belt is of black leather.

The blue undress uniform consists of the blue cap, a single breasted sack coat on the lines of that worn by officers of the United States Navy with black braid trimming around the edges and collar and down the front with which shoulder straps are worn.

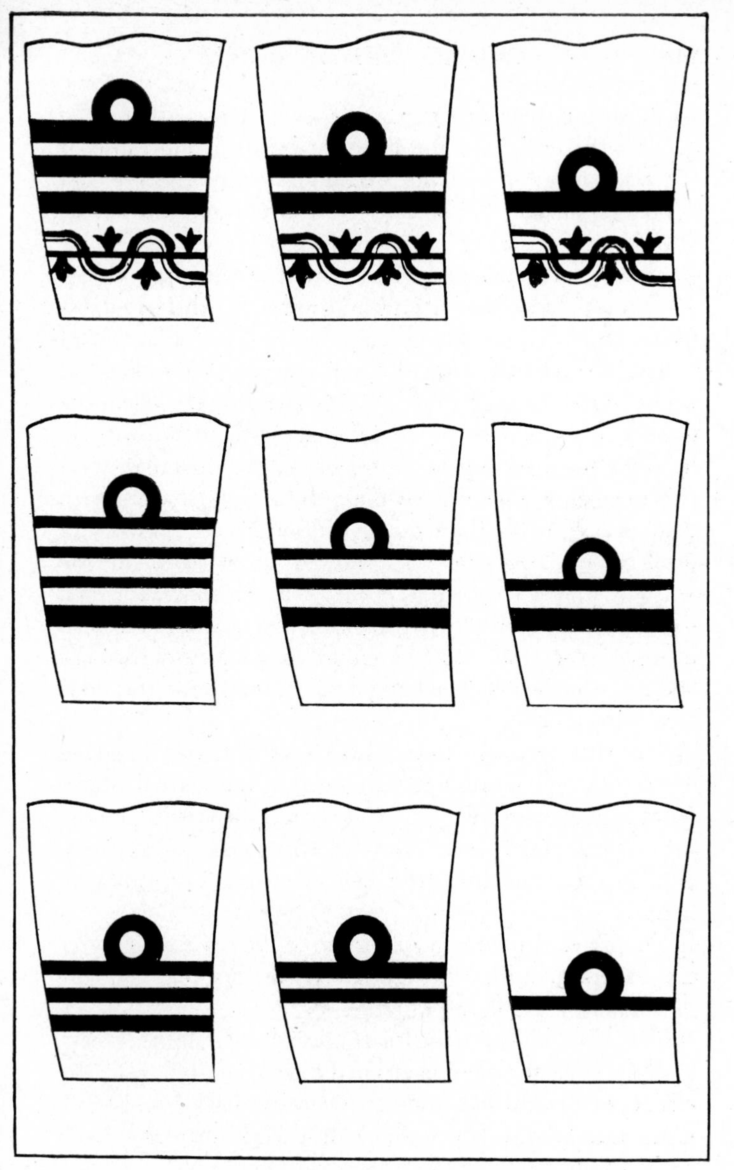

Italian Navy. Officers' sleeve decorations indicating rank

1. Admiral
2. Vice Admiral
3. Rear Admiral
4. Captain
5. Commander
6. Lieutenant Commander
7. Lieutenant
8. Sub Lieutenant
9. Midshipman

The white undress uniform is of the same description as the blue undress except that the material is white cotton or linen duck.

The rank of officers in the Italian Navy is indicated by gold braid stripes around the sleeves above the cuffs as shown in the accompanying illustration.

The corps or branch of the service to which an officer belongs is indicated as follows:—

Line officers	By the "curl" in the upper rank stripe.
Engineer officers...	By stripes of black velvet between the rank stripes.
Naval Constructors.	By stripes of crimson velvet between the rank stripes.
Medical officers....	By stripes of light blue cloth between the rank stripes.
Paymasters	By stripes of red cloth between the rank stripes.

Officers of the Staff Corps do not have the "curl" in the upper rank stripe.

The insignia on the front of the cap consist of an oval medallion surrounded by a gold wreath and surmounted by the Royal Crown of Italy in gold on a blue ground. The medallion in the center shows the corps or branch of the service, Line officers having a gold foul anchor on a light blue ground, Engineer officers a gold three-bladed propeller on a black ground. Medical officers a red Geneva cross on a white ground, Naval Constructors a gold helmet on a red ground, and Paymasters a gold star on a red ground.

The band of the cap is of the distinctive color of the corps or branch of the officer and has sewn upon it gold stripes indicating the rank of the wearer.

On the right side of the cocked hat there is a cockade of red, white and green silk.

Chief Warrant officers wear uniforms similar to the commissioned officers' uniforms with one gold stripe broken by diagonal blocks of blue silk with the corps mark above it on the cuffs. Their cap has a black mohair braid band and insignia on the front like those of commissioned officers except that the Royal crown is omitted.

Warrant officers wear the same uniform as Chief Warrant officers except that the stripe of gold braid on the sleeve is omitted and the corps insignia alone are worn on the sleeves above the elbow.

Enlisted men wear uniforms of dark blue cloth or white duck depending upon the temperature, these uniforms being similar in general design to those of the United States Navy.

The insignia of rank for Petty officers are as follows:—

Chief Petty officers. A gold chevron of one wide stripe and one narrow stripe on each sleeve above the elbow with the branch mark above it. An additional chevron is added after three years' service in the grade.

Petty officers....... A red chevron of one wide stripe and one narrow one on each sleeve above the elbow with the branch mark above it, in red.

Leading Seamen... A chevron of one narrow red stripe with the branch mark above it, in red.

Able Seamen...... The branch mark in red on each sleeve above the elbow.

Ordinary Seamen.. The sleeves are plain.

The specialty or branch marks for the different corps or branches of the enlisted men are as follows:—

The Line or Deck branch. A foul anchor.

Navigating branch ......A steering wheel.
Engineers ....A three-bladed propeller.
Firemen ....A two-bladed propeller.
Torpedo branch ....Two torpedoes crossed with a hammer below.
Gunnery branch ....Two cannon crossed.
Gunlayers ....Two cannon crossed with a bursting bomb in the center.
Electricians ....A device representing three branches of zig-zag lightning with a hammer in the center.
Mining division ....A submarine mine case.
Divers ....A submarine mine case and a hammer.
Carpenters ....Two hatchets crossed.
Plumbers ....Two hatchets crossed with a flame in the center.
Joiners ....A saw.
Musician of the band ...Two anchors crossed with a harp in the center.
Radio operators.........Three branches of zig-zag lightning.
Hospital man ....A gold star with a red Geneva cross on white ground in the center.
Stewards ....A sheaf of wheat.
Buglers ....An anchor crossed by a trumpet.
Signalman ....A triangular pennant with vertical stripes.

Enlisted men who have been promoted for gallantry in war service wear a gold crown on the sleeves above the specialty marks.

Uniforms of the Belgian Army

Before 1914 the uniforms of the Belgian Army for home service were very elaborate and decorated with gold and silver braid and ornaments, although uniforms of cotton khaki were worn in hot weather on foreign service; but the experience of the present war showed the necessity of an inconspicuous dress for field service, and as a result the army is now provided with a field uniform designed after the British Army service uniform and made of dark khaki colored woolen cloth.

The officers' field service uniform consists of a coat similar to that worn by British officers except that it has a standing collar; breeches of the same material and color as the coat; a cap after the British design, and tan leather boots, or tan leather shoes with khaki colored wrap puttees or tan leather strap puttees.

With this uniform the British "Sam Browne" tan leather belt and shoulder strap is worn.

The corps or arm of the service to which an officer belongs is shown by patches of colored cloth on the collar at each side of the neck opening. The rank of officers is indicated by insignia upon these collar patches, as follows:—

Major General ....Three stars arranged to form an equilateral triangle with two vertical bars in front of it and a device made up of the King's monogram, wings, a spear head and bolts of lightning, all in gold embroidery.

Brigadier General..The same as for major general, except there is but one vertical bar.

Colonel ....Three gold stars arranged in the form of an equilateral triangle pointing down with a semicircular gold bar beneath it.

Lieutenant Colonel.The same as for colonel except there are but two stars.

Major ....The same as for lieutenant colonel except there is but one star.

Commandant .....Three gold stars arranged in the form of an equilateral triangle pointing down.
Captain ....The same as for commandant except that the lower star is silver.
First Lieutenant ..Two gold stars.
Second Lieutenant. One gold star.
Adjutant ....One silver star.

The grade of Commandant has no corresponding one in the United States Army; the rank is between those of Major and Captain.

The grade of Adjutant corresponds to that of a Warrant Officer in the United States Navy and Marine Corps.

The service uniform of the enlisted men in the Belgian Army is similar in design and color to that of the British soldier.

The rank of noncommissioned officers is indicated by stripes upon the cuffs as follows:—

Regimental Sergeant Major. Three narrow stripes around the cuff parallel to the lower edge.
Sergeant Major ....Two stripes around the cuff with two diagonal stripes above them.
First Sergeant ....Two stripes around the cuff.
Quartermaster Sergeant ....One stripe around the cuff with one diagonal stripe above it.
Sergeant ....One stripe around the cuff.
Corporal ....One stripe around the cuff, narrower than that worn by a sergeant.

Specialty marks are worn upon the sleeves above the elbow to mark men assigned to special duties.

Engineers ....A plumed helmet.
Aviator ....The King's monogram with an eagle's wing at each side.

Hospital Corps ....A caduceus surrounded by a wreath.
Cycle Corps ....A bicycle wheel.
Grenadiers ....A bursting bomb.
Bandsmen ....A lyre.

The men wear tan leather belts and cartridge pouches.

Uniforms of the Russian Army

The officers and enlisted men of the Russian Army formerly had a great variety in uniforms for the different corps and branches of the service; the infantry of the regular Line wore uniforms of green cloth with red facings; the hussars wore green jackets trimmed across the front with white stripes and loops, red breeches and black high boots; the guards wore green uniforms with yellow facings; the Don Cossacks wore uniforms of dark gray, the coat being long and the breeches very loose and the headdress being a black shako; and the Kuban cossacks wore a uniform of similar design of reddish brown cloth.

During the Russo-Japanese War of 1904–5 an effort was made to standardize the field service uniforms with the result that the present service uniform is of cloth of a gray-brown shade. The Cossacks have to some extent preserved their distinctive dress.

The service uniforms for officers consists of a single-breasted sack coat with a standing collar, a pocket with flap on each breast and closed by a row of gilt buttons down the front; breeches of the same color with stripes down the outer leg seams of varying widths according to rank and of different colors according to the corps or arm of the service; a bell-crowned cap with sloping visor, and black boots.

The rank is indicated by the trimming and ornamentation of flat shoulder straps, those for the various grades

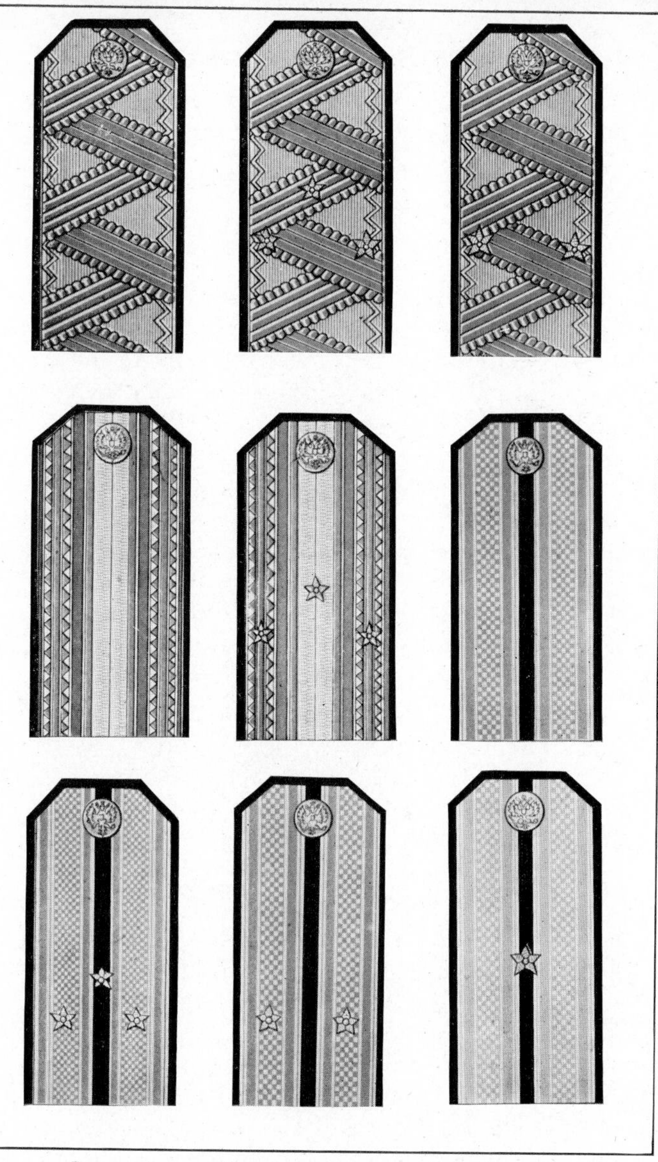

Russian Army. Officers' shoulder straps indicating rank
The straps are of black cloth covered with gold or silver lace, depending upon the rank and corps of the officer. Those for General Officers are of gold lace with silver stars

1. General
2. Lieutenant General
3. Major General
4. Colonel
5. Lieutenant Colonel
6. Senior Captain
7. Junior Captain
8. First Lieutenant
9. Second Lieutenant

of rank being shown in the accompanying illustration. It will be noted that there are no grades of Brigadier General or Major in the Russian Army, but that there are two grades of the rank of Captain, called First and Second or Senior and Junior Captain. The duties of the Senior Captain correspond in a measure to those of Major in the United States services. Line officers of the rank of Colonel and below wear the number of their regiment in the center of the shoulder strap.

The Russian officer's service cap is similar to that worn by officers of the United States Army except that the top of the crown is relatively greater in diameter. The band is of the distinctive color of the corps or arm of the service. A medallion made up of the national colors is worn at the center of the band in front and the visor and chin strap are of brown leather. In some of the regiments gray sheepskin shakos are worn by both officers and men instead of the cap.

The arm of the service or corps is indicated by patches of colored cloth on the front of the collar on each side of the neck opening.

The sword belt is of tan leather with a cross strap from the right shoulder to the left side at the waist although in some corps the sword is suspended from the diagonal cross strap only, the waist belt not being worn by officers.

The uniform of the enlisted men is of similar cut to that of the officers except that the coats are looser and in some corps are closed by a row of buttons down the right side.

The rank of the noncommissioned officers is indicated by stripes and other insignia upon narrow flat shoulder straps worn from the base of the collar to the top of the sleeve shoulder seam.

The Russian Army has an officer of Warrant rank, intermediate between the commissioned officers and enlisted noncommissioned officers. These Warrant officers wear one broad stripe across the shoulder strap near the collar end.

The noncommissioned officers wear narrow stripes on their shoulder straps in the same position; a sergeant major having three such stripes, a sergeant two and a corporal one.

There have been various corps and specialty insignia but as these are now in a process of being changed they cannot be given accurately.

The Russian noncommissioned officers wear swords suspended from tan leather belts and the privates wear a tan leather belt with cartridge boxes of the same material. All of the enlisted men carry their extra clothing in a blanket roll over the right shoulder and diagonally across the body to the left side at the belt.

Uniforms of the Russian Navy

The uniforms of the officers and enlisted men differ in many respects from those which are common to the navies of the other principal powers.

The officers' uniforms are as a rule made of a dark green cloth for dress and winter wear and of white cotton or linen for hot weather.

The prescribed uniforms are full dress, dress, undress and service (working) dress.

The full dress uniform consists of a cocked hat, tunic with standing collar, epaulets, and trousers with gold lace braid on the outer leg seams.

The dress uniform consists of a cap, double breasted frock coat, with epaulets, and plain trousers.

Russian Navy. Officers' sleeve decorations indicating rank

1. Admiral
2. Vice Admiral
3. Rear Admiral
4. Captain
5. Commander
6. Lieutenant Commander
7. Lieutenant
8. Sub Lieutenant
9. Warrant Officer

The undress uniform is the same as the dress uniform without epaulets.

The service or working uniform consists of a cap, a short single breasted tunic of dark blue cloth and plain trousers.

In hot weather a similar uniform of white cotton or linen material is worn.

An overcoat of black cloth and a heavier one of gray cloth with a fur collar are worn by officers.

In May, 1917, the shoulder straps and the insignia of rank formerly worn upon them were abolished and stripes on the sleeves above the cuff to indicate rank with distinctive colors to indicate the Staff corps, were adopted for all uniform coats and the overcoat.

These stripes for the different grades of rank are as shown by the accompanying illustrations.

Officers of the Line and of the Engineer Corps wear gold stripes, and officers of the Medical Corps, Naval Constructor Corps, Judge Advocate's Corps, and Paymasters wear silver stripes, with the stripes edged with cloth of a distinctive color for each corps.

These distinctive colors are:

Medical officers .... White.
Naval Constructors .... Red.
Judges Advocate .... Crimson.

Paymasters wear silver stripes without the "curl" and without edgings of colored cloth.

Officers wear a sword on all occasions of dress and ceremony, but on occasions of ordinary duty they wear a short dirk in place of the sword.

The warrant officers of the Russian Navy wear uniforms similar to those worn by commissioned officers, the distinguishing mark being a narrow gold stripe around the sleeves above the cuff.

Enlisted men wear black cloth trousers, a jersey with blue and white horizontal stripes and a blue jumper.

The caps are similar to those worn by enlisted men of the British Navy.

The name of the ship is given on the cap ribbon as in other navies, this ribbon being tied at the back so that it hangs down in streamers.

White duck uniforms of the same pattern as the blue ones are worn in hot weather.

The ratings of petty officers are indicated by badges worn on the sleeves above the elbow; these badges are at present being revised and hence cannot be accurately given.

All enlisted men are provided with short overcoats of gray cloth.

Uniforms of the Japanese Army

Previous to the Russo-Japanese war of 1904–5 the officers and enlisted men of the Japanese Army wore uniforms of dark blue or red cloth with facings of distinctive colors for the various arms, but this proved so conspicuous on the battlefields of that war that a service uniform of khaki-colored cloth for winter and khaki cotton drill for summer was adopted. The officers, however, retained for their dress uniforms the old dress uniforms of dark blue and red cloth with heavy decorations of gold lace.

The dress uniform of the officers consists of a dark blue double breasted frock coat with standing collar; trousers of dark blue cloth with stripes of the corps color down the outer leg seams for all arms except the cavalry in which the officers wear red breeches; black boots; and a *kepi* style cap decorated with gold lace and having a red and white standing plume at the front, this cap being of red cloth for the cavalry and of blue cloth for the other arms.

The collar of the dress coat is covered with gold lace; the buttons are gilt with a design of chrysanthemums and cherry blossoms; shoulder knots of plaited gold cord and a sash belt of gold and red stripes with heavy tassels at the left side are worn with it, and the rank is indicated by sleeve decorations consisting of a knot made up of narrow stripes of gold braid of the same design as that worn by officers of the United States Army. This sleeve knot is made of one stripe for Second Lieutenant and one additional stripe for each step up in grade through the ranks of First Lieutenant, Captain, Major, Lieutenant Colonel, Colonel, Major General, Lieutenant General and Field Marshal, the latter having a knot of nine stripes.

The distinctive colors for the different arms of the service are red for infantry, green for cavalry, yellow for artillery, crimson for pioneers, gray for the quartermaster corps, and black for the gendarmerie (national police).

The service uniforms for both officers and enlisted men consist of a single breasted sack coat of khaki colored woolen cloth for winter and cotton drill for summer; trousers or breeches of the same materials, and a bell-crowned cap with sloping visor of tan leather and a band of the distinctive color of the arm of the service.

The service coat has a standing collar with a patch of the distinctive color for the arm of the service on each side of the neck opening, a pocket with buttoned flap on each side of the breast and a plain pocket on each side below the waist.

Officers wear breeches and boots when mounted and tan leather leggings or khaki-colored wrap puttees for dismounted service. The shoes worn by both officers and enlisted men with the service uniform are of tan leather.

The rank of the officers is indicated by shoulder straps worn transversely across the shoulders next to the shoulder seams of the sleeves, after the style of the shoulder strap worn by officers of the United States Army with their blue dress coats. These are the only two great armies in which this form of shoulder strap is worn by officers to indicate rank.

These shoulder straps are covered with cloth of the distinctive color of the arm of the service with stripes of gold braid running lengthwise of them on the same scheme as that used on the shoulder straps worn by Japanese naval officers as illustrated, namely, for General officers one wide stripe, for field officers two narrow stripes and for company officers one narrow stripe. On the gold stripes silver stars are worn for the different grades of rank in each class. The number of stripes and stars for each grade is as follows:

General Officers.

General ....Three stars on one wide gold stripe.
Lieutenant General ...Two stars on one wide gold stripe.
Major General ....One star on one wide gold stripe.

Field Officers.

Colonel ....Three stars on two narrow gold stripes.
Lieutenant Colonel ...Two stars on two narrow gold stripes.
Major ....One star on two narrow gold stripes.

Company Officers.

Captain ....Three stars on one narrow gold stripe.
First Lieutenant .....Two stars on one narrow gold stripe.
Second Lieutenant ....One star on one narrow gold stripe.

The rank of noncommissioned officers is shown by narrow stripes around the cuffs, and for all enlisted men the arm of the service is indicated by the color patches on each side of the collar and the regimental number is worn upon these collar patches, Arabic figures being used for the regular service, Roman numerals for the militia and Arabic figures on one side of the collar and Roman on the other for the reserves.

The overcoat for officers is a double breasted ulster similar to that worn by American officers, and that for enlisted men is single breasted and short. The overcoats are of khaki-colored cloth.

The service belts for both officers and men are of tan leather.

Uniforms of the Japanese Navy

When Japan began to build and man her modern navy she derived much early training and experience from the British Navy, which was then as now, the largest of the world's navies.

As a result the uniforms of both the officers and men of the Japanese Navy are similar in most respects to those of the British Navy. The principal difference is that the Japanese naval officers' undress or service uniform coat is a single breasted blouse with standing collar similar to that worn by officers of the United States Navy, the collar and edges being trimmed with black braid.

In the insignia of the Japanese Navy the cherry blossom usually takes the place where the crown appears in the British naval insignia, as may be seen by reference to the illustrations.

The uniforms for both officers and enlisted men are

of dark blue cloth for full dress and dress uniforms, the undress or service uniform being of dark blue cloth for winter wear and of white cotton duck or linen for wear in hot weather.

The rank of officers is indicated by stripes around the sleeves above the cuff on the blue uniforms and by shoulder straps on the white service uniform.

The sleeve stripes are of gold lace braid for full dress and dress coats and of black braid for the blue service coat.

The number, width and arrangement of the sleeve stripes for the different ranks are as shown in the accompanying illustration.

The corps or branch of the service to which an officer belongs is shown by the circular curl above the upper stripe for officers of the Line, and by stripes of colored cloth between the rank stripes for the officers of the Staff Corps, the distinctive colors for the various corps being as follows:—

Engineer Corps ....Purple.
(The officers of the Engineer Corps also wear the curl above the upper rank stripe, officers of the other Staff Corps do not wear the curl.)
Medical Corps ....Red.
Engineer Constructors ....Brown.
Ordnance Constructors ....Maroon.
Paymaster Corps ....White.
Hydrographic Corps ....Light blue.
Chief Carpenter (warrant officers)...Green.
Bandmasters (warrant officers)......Gray.

These distinctive colors for officers of the different Staff Corps are also worn around the bands of the caps.

Japanese Navy. Officers' sleeve decorations indicating rank

1. Admiral 2. Vice Admiral 3. Rear Admiral
4. Captain 5. Commander 6. Lt. Commander
7. Lieutenant 8. Sub Lt., 1st Class 9. Sub Lt., 2nd Class
10. Midshipman 11. Warrant Officer, Line 12. Warrant Officer, Engineers

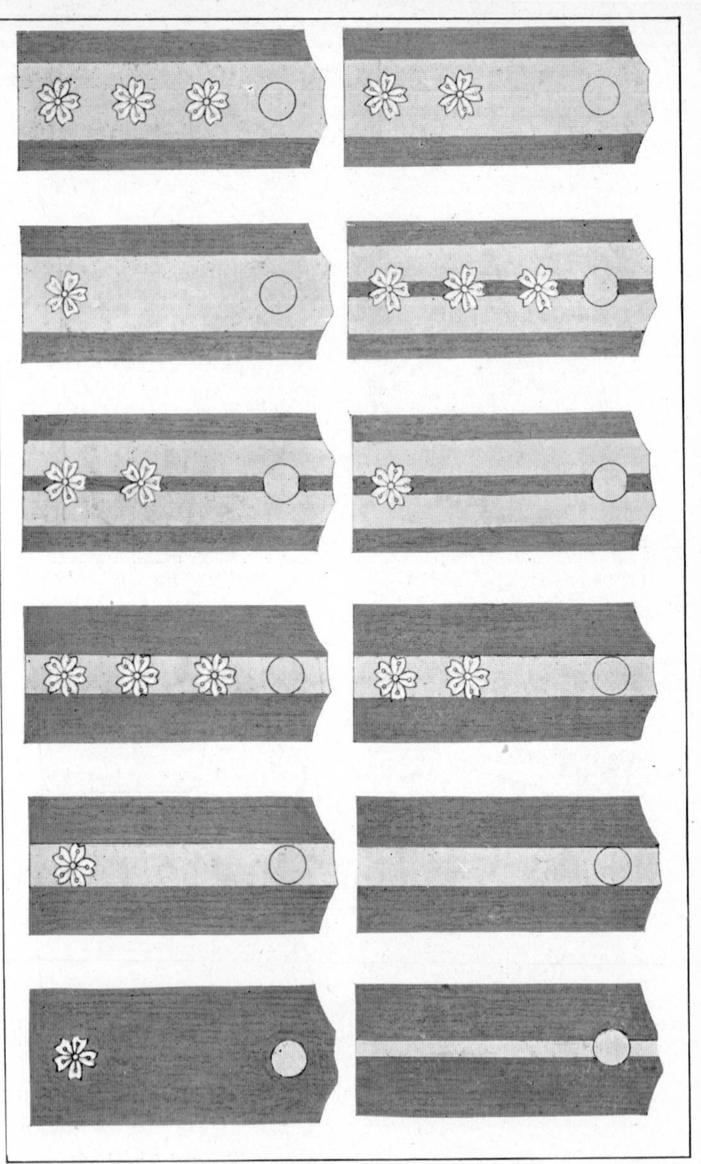

Japanese Navy. Officers' shoulder straps showing rank, summer service uniform

1. Admiral
2. Vice Admiral
3. Rear Admiral
4. Captain
5. Commander
6. Lt. Commander
7. Lieutenant
8. Sub Lt., 1st Class
9. Sub Lt., 2nd Class
10. Chief Warrant Officer
11. Warrant Officer
12. Midshipman

The rank or rating of enlisted men who are petty officers or who are assigned to special duties is shown by distinctive marks worn on the left sleeve of the coat or overshirt; the principal ones being:—

Seaman ....An anchor.
Writers ....A writing brush.
Hospital Corps ....A pair of forceps.
Firemen ....A double pipe spanner.
Carpenter's Mate........An ax.
Stewards ....A key.
Musicians ....A lyre.

Uniforms of the Austrian Army

The Army of Austria-Hungary is made up of so many different races and peoples each of whom have preserved something of their original national dress or uniform in their modern dress uniforms that the varieties in color, design and ornamentation are greater than in any other country.

The field service uniform of all however is nearly the same and is made of light gray cloth.

The officers' service uniform consists of a single breasted sack coat with a standing collar, closed by a row of buttons down the front concealed beneath a flap and having shoulder straps, patch pockets with button flaps, one on each breast and one on each side below the waist; breeches of the same color as the coat; leather puttees and shoes; and a cap of gray cloth, cylindrical in shape with a soft top to the crown and side flaps which are folded up around the band and secured by two buttons in front, and having a sloping visor covered with the gray cloth of the cap. This cap, known as a *tschapka,* is a distinguishing feature of the Austrian uniform.

As variations of the field uniform the Hungarian regiments do not wear leggings but have the trousers tight below the knees; the Alpine troops wear heavy tan colored stockings instead of leggings and the Bosnia troops wear a Turkish fez instead of the gray cap.

The rank of officers is indicated by insignia worn upon each side of the collar. A Field Marshal has gold embroidery on the collar at each side of the neck opening and two wide red stripes down the outer leg seams of the trousers. General officers wear similar gold braid on the collar with the grade of rank indicated by silver stars thereon as follows:—

General .... Three silver stars.
Lieutenant General .... Two silver stars.
Major General .... One silver star.

Field officers have gold or silver braid on the collar according to whether their buttons are of silver or gold. On gold braid they wear silver stars and on silver braid gold stars to indicate the grade of rank, as follows:—

Colonel .... Three stars.
Lieutenant Colonel .... Two stars.
Major .... One star.

Company officers have the collar decorated with cloth on each side of the neck opening, the color being the distinctive color of their arm of the service or regiment. The grade of rank is indicated by stars worn on this colored cloth, the stars being of silver or gold to match the gold or silver buttons worn according to the regiment:

Captain .... Three stars.
First Lieutenant .... Two stars.
Second Lieutenant .... One star.

The arm of the service is indicated by the color of the facings or decorations on the uniform. The infantry have no regimental numbers on their uniforms but a distinctive color for each group of four regiments, each such group of the regular army having two Austrian and two Hungarian regiments, the Austrian regiments wearing silver buttons and the Hungarian regiments gilt buttons.

Chasseur regiments wear green facings or trimming and have the number of the regiment on the buttons.

Dragoon regiments have distinguishing colors worn on the collars for each two regiments, one regiment of each color wearing silver buttons and the other gilt buttons.

Hussar and Uhlan regiments of cavalry have distinctive colors for each two regiments as in the case of dragoon regiments but these colors are also worn on the caps and the number of the regiment also appears on the cap.

Artillery regiments have red facings and the buttons bear a gun and a shell.

In the Austrian Reserves the infantry have green facings and trimmings on their uniforms and the number of the regiment on the buttons and shoulder straps, and the cavalry regiments have the regimental number on the buttons only.

In the Hungarian Reserves the infantry regiments wear the regimental number in dark gray cloth on the sides of the cap and the cavalry regiments wear their number in yellow cloth on the cap.

The rank of noncommissioned officers is indicated by white stars of celluloid worn on the distinctive color patches of the collar, as follows:—

Sergeant Major .... Three white stars.
Sergeant .... Two white stars.
Corporal .... One white star.

With service uniform officers wear tan leather belts with suspender straps across one or both shoulders and the enlisted men wear belts and cartridge boxes of tan leather. General and Staff officers wear the sword slung from a belt beneath the coat and a sash of gold and black silk.

The overcoat for officers is a double breasted ulster with gilt or silver buttons the same as worn on the service coat and collar patches and pipings of the distinctive corps or regimental color; or a long circular cape cloak with a turn-over collar upon which the color patches are worn.

The overcoat of the enlisted man is a double breasted long ulster with standing-falling collar, buttons of silver or gilt to match those worn on the service coat and color patches on the collar.

Enlisted men wear the trousers tucked into the tops of the shoes or in the case of the Alpine troops into the tops of heavy woolen socks of khaki color.

A distinctive feature of the Alpine troops is a small plume of eagle's feathers worn on the left side of the cap.

Various insignia to indicate special duties or assignments are worn by enlisted men upon the left sleeve, some of them being:—

Telegraphist ...... A wreath surrounding a device representing three bolts of lightning crossed with a crown above them.
Medical Corps ..... A circle surrounding a Geneva cross in red.
Gun pointer .... Two cannon crossed surmounted by a crown surrounded by a wreath.

Pioneer ....A medallion bearing a pick and two spades crossed.
Wagon driver .....A wreath surrounding two horses' heads.

In the trenches steel trench helmets of the German pattern are worn by both officers and enlisted men.

In very cold weather fur coats are worn and in the snows of the mountains white coats are worn to make the troops less conspicuous.

Enlisted men wear on the left sleeve a triangle of yellow braid to show long service, one stripe for four years, two stripes for seven years and three stripes for nine years.

Uniforms of the Austrian Navy

The uniforms of the officers and enlisted men of the Austrian Navy are of dark blue cloth for winter wear and of white duck for hot weather and are generally similar to those worn in the British Navy.

Commissioned officers are provided with special full dress, full dress, undress, blue service, white service and white mess uniforms.

The special full dress uniform (gala dress) consists of a cocked hat of the same shape as the one worn in the United States Navy but having more gold braid on it; a short double breasted frock coat with a standing collar; epaulets; dark blue trousers with gold stripes down the outer leg seams; a sash belt of black cloth with interwoven horizontal gilt stripes and a knot and tassels of gold on the right hip; and black shoes. The collar of the coat and the cuffs are trimmed with gold lace braid, the sword is worn suspended by slings from a belt worn beneath the coat, and the rank of the officer is indicated by insignia worn upon the collar and upon the tops of the epaulets.

The full dress consists of the cocked hat; a double breasted frock coat with turn down collar and notched lapels; epaulets; trousers the same as for the special full dress; and black shoes. The sash belt is also worn with this uniform.

The undress uniform consists of a bell-crowned cap of dark blue cloth with a black mohair braid band, sloping visor of black patent leather, gold chin-strap above the visor and the rank indicated by narrow gold stripes around the black band; the frock coat worn without epaulets; plain dark blue trousers and black shoes. White trousers and a cap with the upper portion of the crown white are some times worn with this uniform. The sash belt is not worn with this uniform, the sword being suspended by slings from a belt worn beneath the coat.

The blue service dress consists of the blue or white cap; a square cut double breasted sack coat similar to that worn in the British Navy; plain trousers of dark blue cloth or white duck, and black shoes. When on duty with troops ashore the sword belt is worn outside of this coat.

The white service uniform consists of a white cap or white helmet; a white coat with shoulder straps of the same design as the white service coat worn by the United States naval officer except that there is a patch pocket with flap and button on each side below the waist. When under arms the sword is worn suspended by slings from a belt beneath the coat and the gold and black sash belt is worn outside of the coat.

The mess uniform consists of a white mess jacket upon which the shoulder straps are worn; a white waistcoat; dark blue plain trousers, and black shoes. There is no blue mess jacket and no evening dress coat.

Austrian Navy. Officers' sleeve decorations indicating rank

1. Admiral
2. Vice Admiral
3. Rear Admiral
4. Captain
5. Commander
6. Senior Lieutenant
7. Lieutenant
8. Sub Lieutenant
9. Midshipman
10. Naval Cadet
11. Surgeon General
12. Staff Officer with rank of Rear Admiral

With the frock coat uniforms a plain black silk necktie is worn tied in a flat double-bow knot.

The rank is indicated on the frock coat and upon the blue service coat by stripes of gold lace upon the sleeves above the cuff. In the case of officers of flag rank a gold Austrian Imperial crown is worn above the stripes. These stripes for the different grades of rank are shown in the accompanying illustration.

On the white service coat the rank is indicated by stripes upon the shoulder straps in the same manner as in the United States Navy, these stripes being of the same number, widths and arrangements as upon the sleeves of the frock and service coats.

The corps or branch of the service to which an officer belongs is indicated by the "curl" in the upper stripe of the rank stripes upon the sleeve and shoulder strap, and by stripes of colored silk between the gold rank stripes for the different Staff corps. These distinctive colors for the different corps or branches are:—

Engineers .... Gray.
Medical officers .... Black.
Naval Constructors .... Crimson.
Paymasters .... Light blue.
Professors .... Dark blue.

White gloves are prescribed for all uniforms.

Medical officers of flag rank wear an eight-pointed gold star above the rank stripes on the sleeves, other Staff officers of flag rank wear a four-circle rosette there, and Medical officers wear as a distinctive device on the shoulder strap over the rank stripes the rod of Esculapius entwined with a serpent in silver.

Midshipmen at the Naval Academy wear a dark blue double breasted round-about jacket with a turn down collar and two rows of gilt buttons down the front, a straight visored blue cap, dark blue trousers and black shoes, for dress and a uniform similar to that worn by the seamen, for work and drills.

Chief Warrant officers and Warrant officers wear dress and service uniforms like those of commissioned officers, and Chief Petty officers wear similar uniforms to those of Warrant officers except that the specialty or branch marks are worn on the sleeves between the elbow and the shoulder. The rank of Chief Warrant officers, Warrant officers and Chief Petty officers is indicated by gold stripes upon the sleeves above the cuffs as follows:—

Chief Warrant officer.......Three one-half inch stripes.
Warrant officer ....Two one-half inch stripes.
Chief Petty officer..........One stripe three-sixteenths of an inch wide.

The uniforms of the enlisted men are of the usual sailor cut common to the navies of most naval powers. The blue uniform consists of a dark blue flat cap with the name of the ship in gilt upon a cap-ribbon around the band; a loose jumper worn over a tight jersey, and trousers of the sailor cut with wide spring at the bottoms of the legs. The white uniforms consist of a white flat cap, white duck jumper and white trousers.

The rating is indicated by stars in the corners of the wide collar. These stars are of a material resembling celluloid and first class petty officers wear three such stars in each corner of the collar, second class petty officers two stars and first class seamen one star.

The branch of the service or the special duty detail of an enlisted man is indicated by a specialty mark worn on the left sleeve midway between the elbow and the shoulder, petty officers wearing a crown above the specialty mark, these marks being as follows:—

Deck force	A vertical foul anchor.
Engineroom and Fireroom force	A three bladed propeller.
Quartermasters (Wheelmen)	An anchor with a steering wheel on the shank.
Writers	Two swords crossed.
Torpedomen	An anchor with a bursting bomb on the shank.
Gunnery force	An anchor with two cannon crossed on the shank.
Radio men	An anchor with bars of zig-zag lightning across the shank.
Mining force	A ship's anchor with a mine anchor crossing it.
Band musicians	A lyre.
Hospital attendants	A Geneva cross.
Cooks and stewards	Two blades of wheat crossed.

For Chief Petty officers these specialty marks are in gold embroidery and for others in yellow for blue coats and jumper shirts and for all ratings they are in black for white coats and jumpers.

Aviation pilots, both officers and men, wear the aviation insignia on the right breast. This insignia is of silver and consists of a wreath of leaves surmounted by an Imperial crown with a spread eagle across the wreath.

Uniforms of the German Navy

The uniforms of the officers and men of the German Navy are made of dark blue cloth for winter wear and of white duck for hot weather as in other navies and in general they follow the lines of other navies, but there are several distinctive features. The officers have no special full dress coat with the cutaway skirts or swallow-tail effect, a frock coat taking its place; and the enlisted men have in addition to the ordinary sailor shirts with the wide falling collar a dress jacket reaching to the waist line and roached over the hips like the jackets of the American midshipmen. This jacket has a row of small buttons down each side of the front and also on each cuff and is worn unbuttoned with the falling collar of the shirt outside of it.

The commissioned officers have full dress, dress, blue service and white service uniforms.

The full dress uniform consists of a cocked hat similar to that worn by British naval officers; a long double breasted frock coat; trousers with gold lace stripes down the outer leg seams; black shoes; a sword belt covered with silver and gold lace with a wide red stripe running through it, and epaulets or shoulder knots depending upon the rank and corps of the officer. A distinctive feature of this full dress frock coat is that while it has a standing collar trimmed with gold lace, the front is provided with wide triangular lapels covered with color facing indicating the corps or branch of the service to which the wearer belongs.

The dress uniform consists of a bell-crowned cap of dark blue cloth with a braid of the distinctive corps around the band and a distinctive insignia on the front; a frock coat like that of the British or American naval officer; with which shoulder knots are worn; plain dark blue trousers, and black shoes. With this uniform the same sword belt is worn as with the full dress but instead of the sword a short sword or dirk is worn. As a variation of this uniform the cocked hat is sometimes worn with it for special occasions.

The blue service uniform consists of the blue cap; a

double breasted square cut sack like that worn by British officers; plain dark blue trousers, and black shoes. A plain black double-bow knot tie is worn with this uniform.

The white service uniform consists of a white cap of the same design as the blue cap but with a black band and black visor as in the United States and British navies; a white single breasted sack coat with standing collar, a patch pocket on the left breast and a patch pocket on each side below the waist; white trousers, and black or white shoes depending upon the occasion. The dirk is worn with this uniform suspended from a black leather belt worn beneath the coat. Shoulder straps showing the rank are worn on the white service coat.

The overcoat is a long double breasted coat cut to fit the figure, buttoning to the neck, with a wide falling collar and an outside pocket with flap on each side below the waist. It is closed by gilt buttons, one row down each side.

Following the universal military custom, the rank of German naval officers is indicated on the blue uniforms by stripes worn upon the sleeves of the coat just above the cuff. The number, width and arrangement of these stripes are shown in the accompanying illustration.

On the full dress coat sleeves there is a vertical three-pointed strap on the outside over the rank stripes, its color being the distinctive color for the corps to which the wearer belongs.

The rank is also indicated by insignia upon the tops of the epaulets and shoulder knots. The tops of the epaulets are of the distinctive colors of the corps except those for officers of the Line which are of gold. The lower grade in each branch has no fringe of bullion on the epaulets.

The stripes indicating the rank of officers of the Line are sewn directly upon the cloth of the coat sleeves and have a German Imperial crown above the upper stripe. Officers of the Staff corps do not wear the crown above their rank stripes. The corps or branch of the service to which officers of the Staff corps belong is indicated by stripes of colored cloth worn between the stripes indicating the rank, and the distinctive colors are:—

Engineer officers .... Black.
Gunnery officers ....Dark gray.
Torpedo officers ....Dark gray.
Medical officers ....Dark blue.
Naval Constructors ....Black.
Paymasters ....Light blue.
Legal Department officers..........Red.
Pilot officers ....Light gray.
Dockyard Construction officers......Black.

The insignia worn upon the cap for commissioned officers is a gold wreath surrounding a circular emblem made up of concentric circles of red, white and black (from the center out) and surmounted by the German Imperial crown. This medallion is also worn upon the center of the front of the enlisted men's flat caps.

These distinctive corps colors are also worn as the "facings" on the full dress uniforms, that is on the lapels of the coat and on the three-pointed straps on the cuffs, and around the band of the service cap, blue and white, except that pilots wear a gold band on the cap.

Warrant officers in the German Navy wear a dress uniform and a service uniform both blue and white similar in design to that worn by commissioned officers, with their distinctive rank stripes on the sleeves and on the shoulder straps.

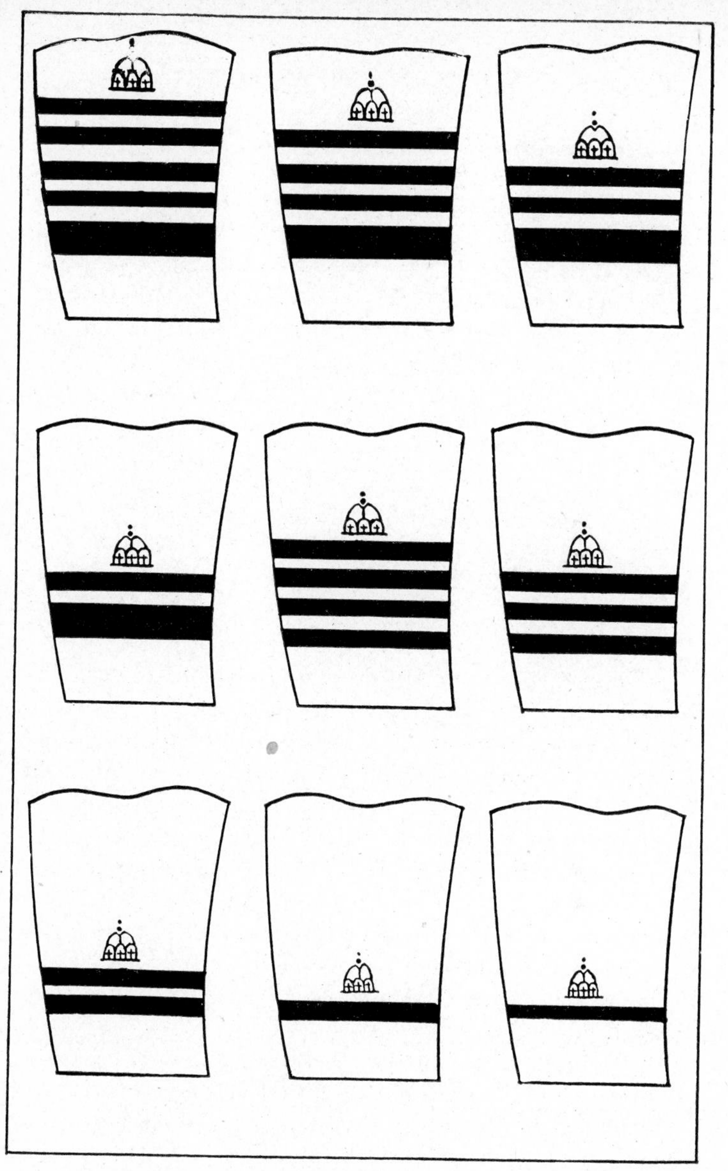

German Navy. Officers' sleeve decorations indicating rank

1. Grand Admiral
2. Admiral
3. Vice Admiral
4. Rear Admiral
5. Captain
6. Commander
7. Senior Lieutenant
8. Junior Lieutenant
9. Sub Lieutenant

In the German Navy there is a rank intermediate between that of Warrant officers and Chief Petty officers which has no counterpart in the American Navy. This is called Feldwebel. His dress uniform is a blue cap; a short dark blue jacket with rolling lapel collar and a row of small gilt buttons down each side of the front; a blue waistcoat with gilt buttons, and plain dark blue trousers; and his service uniforms, both blue and white, are similar to those of other officers. On the cuffs of the dress jacket he has three narrow gold stripes around the sleeve close together and below them three similar stripes around the sleeve and continuing down the outer seam to the bottom edge of the sleeve, with a vertical strap of dark blue cloth across the stripes with six small gilt buttons on it.

The Bandmaster is a Warrant officer and the distinctive mark of his rank is a gold lyre on the center of his shoulder straps.

The uniforms of the enlisted men are the dress or "parade" uniform, the service uniform and the white uniform.

The dress uniform consists of a sailor flat cap; a white sailor shirt with wide dark blue falling collar; the dark blue dress jacket worn with the collar of the shirt outside of it, and dark blue trousers, the trousers being cut without the wide "spring" or flare at the bottom of the legs so common in other navies.

The blue cap is similar to that worn in other navies but the crown is higher in the front than in the back, which tends to give it a military appearance. The name of the ship or station is worn upon a cap-ribbon around the band of the cap, the ends of the ribbon being tied at the back and allowed to fall down the back in streamers. Upon the front of the crown at the center is the red, white and black medallion, the colors of Germany.

The collar of the shirt has three rows of narrow white braid around the edges as in the American and British navies.

The service uniform consists of the blue cap; a dark blue shirt similar to that worn in the American Navy, and dark blue trousers.

The white service uniform is of the same design but of white duck instead of dark blue cloth or flannel.

The rank or rating and the branch of specialty is indicated by distinctive marks worn upon the left sleeve between the elbow and the shoulder. Some of the principal of these marks are:—

Feldwebel ....A vertical gold anchor with a gold crown above it.

Chief Quartermaster ....Two gold anchors crossed with a crown above them. (If certified he wears a red chevron of one stripe below the mark.)

Quartermaster ....Two gold anchors crossed.

Chief Boatswain's Mate.....A vertical gold foul anchor with a crown above it.

Boatswain's Mate ....The same without the crown.

Chief Gunner's Mate.......A vertical foul anchor with two cannon crossed upon it surmounted by a crown, in gold.

Gunner's Mate ....The same without the crown.

Chief Machinist's Mate.....A vertical anchor with a cog wheel on the shank and a crown above it, in silver.

Machinist's Mate ....The same without the crown.

Chief Stoker's Mate........A vertical anchor with two shovels crossed on the shank and a crown above it, in silver.

Stoker's Mate ....The same without the crown.

Chief Torpedoist's Mate....An anchor and a mine crossed with a crown above it, in gold.
Torpedoist's Mate..........The same without the crown.
Chief Radio Operator.......A vertical anchor with a crown above it, in gold, with a zig-zag of lightning in red across the shank of the anchor.
Radio Operator ....The same without the crown.
Telegraphist ....Two bars of forked lightning crossed, in gold.
Chief Signal Mate.........A vertical anchor with a crown above it, in gold, and two signal flags in red crossed on the shank of the anchor.
Signal Mate ....The same without the crown.
Drill Sergeant ....A vertical anchor with two rifles crossed on the shank and a crown above it, in gold.
Drill Corporal ....The same without the crown.
Leading Seaman ....A yellow chevron of one stripe, point down.
Bandsman, first class.......A chevron of two stripes with a curl at the point of the upper stripe and an anchor surcharged by a lyre above it, in gold.
Second Leader of Band.....The same with a crown above it.
Gun Captain, first class.....A flaming shell above a chevron of three stripes, point down, in red.
Gun Captain, second class..The same but with two stripes in the chevron.
Gun Captain, third class....The same but with one stripe in the chevron.
Machine Gun Captain......The same without the chevron.
Range Finder ....A triangle with a flaming shell in the center and a range finding instrument above it, in red.
Submarine Mine Planter....A submarine mine in red.

(The Gun Captains, Range Finders, and Mine Planters of the Marine Artillery, who man the coast defense guns, wear the same rating marks in yellow. In Germany the coast defenses, forts and batteries are manned by the Navy and not by the Army as in the United States.)

The overcoat worn by enlisted men of the German Navy is a short double breasted pilot coat with turn down lapel collar and a double row of gilt service buttons down the front.

For service ashore in landing parties and when on duty at the coast forts in hot weather or tropics, a khaki helmet is worn instead of the white hat with white uniforms and khaki canvas leggings are also worn. For landing parties as infantry or artillery black leather boots are worn with the blue uniforms, the trousers being tucked inside of the boots.

Uniforms of German Marines

The German Marines are a part of the Navy and are divided into Marine Infantry and Marine Field Artillery. They perform duties similar in many respects to the duties of the United States Marine Corps.

The full dress uniform of the officers consists of a black shako with a large red plume which falls over the front down to the visor; a blue single breasted tunic with standing collar; epaulets without bullion fringes; breeches of the same color, and black boots. The front edges of the coat and the tops and bottoms of the collar are piped with white cloth and the cuffs are of white cloth with a vertical strap.

The service uniform is of gray cloth and consists of a bell-crowned cap with a white band and sloping visor of black leather; a single breasted coat with a standing turn-over collar closed by buttons down the front concealed by a fly; breeches, and leggings and shoes of tan leather. The coat has a pocket with flap on each side below the waist. Shoulder straps are worn with the service coat.

The rank of the officer is indicated by insignia worn upon the epaulets and shoulder straps, the insignia being the same as for the German Army officers.

For hot weather a uniform of khaki cotton drill is provided, the general style being the same as for the cloth service uniform except that the head dress is a khaki colored helmet.

The dress uniform of the enlisted men is similar in color and design to that worn by the officers, the epaulets being replaced by shoulder straps of white cloth. The service uniform of the enlisted men is of the same design as that for officers except that the coat is closed by a single row of gilt buttons and the cap has no visor.

Uniforms of the German Army

The peace time uniforms of the various corps and arms of the German Army present a great variety, the traditions of the services of the former separate kingdoms and political divisions that are now united to form the German Empire being preserved in many instances in the color and design of the uniform or in the bright metal decorations and insignia.

Many of these uniforms are gaudy in color and richly decorated with gold, silver and colored cloth and braid ornaments.

The facings colors worn upon the collars and cuffs and as pipings on the coats and trousers often vary with the individual regiments, and the headdress is in many shapes and colors.

The Line Infantry wear a black helmet with brass spike, Prussian eagle and scale chin strap; a blue single breasted tunic with gilt buttons, and dark gray trousers; the facings and piping being red, but the infantry regiments of Saxony, Bavaria, Wurttemburg and some other states have variations from this in both color and design.

The Uhlans wear the Czapka helmet; a blue double breasted tunic with a red plastron front and red facings; and dark gray trousers; the Prussian Hussars wear a black fur busby with heavy gilt decorations and a bag of the distinctive color of the facings, a single breasted blue tunic heavily decorated with white braid, loops and frogs; a blue pelisse with white braid decorations slung from the left shoulder; dark gray tight fitting breeches with white braid decorations, and black Hessian boots with embroidered tops.

The Prussian Cuirassiers wear white uniforms with black hip boots and cuirasses of brass or iron, the iron being black for some regiments and bright for others.

The Saxon Jager regiments wear uniforms of green cloth and a cap with a feather plume.

The Prussian Dragoon regiments wear helmets with drooping white plumes, light blue jackets, dark gray breeches.

The Field Artillery regiments usually wear black helmets with a spike ending in a brass ball; dark blue coats with gilt buttons, dark gray breeches and black boots.

There are many other distinctive uniforms and the varied colors, bright trappings and decorations and waving plumes made a peace time assemblage of German troops of all arms a most imposing sight; but early in the present century the leaders realized that while all this gaudy panoply and pomp added to the attractiveness of the service, kept alive the traditions of the past, and aided in holding the esprit de corps, it would not do for service on the modern battlefield, where the troops must be as inconspicuous as possible to avoid annihilation under the drum fire of artillery and the rapid fire of machine guns.

As a result a field service uniform of a dull gray color was adopted for all arms but it was not generally issued to the troops until just before the opening of the present world war.

The German officer's field service uniform consists of a gray single breasted sack coat with a standing turnover collar; breeches of the same color and black or tan leather boots. With this uniform the old bright helmets are worn with a gray cover to make them less conspicuous, or in many cases a gray cap with sloping visor is worn. The buttons are of gilt allowed to become dull in the field, in some cases of leather or bone, and in other cases the coat is closed by buttons concealed beneath a fly.

The corps and regimental colors are worn in small patches on the collar at each side of the neck opening and also as cuff stripes in some corps. In some corps the distinctive color is also worn around the cap band.

The rank of the German officer is indicated by the braid and insignia on flat shoulder straps covered with braided cord. The shoulder strap for Field Marshal and for General officers is covered with a plaited knot made up of five loops of sets of three cords, the two outer cords being gold and the central cord being silver interwoven with the imperial colors in silk. The shoulder straps for Field officers (Colonels, Lieutenant Colonels and Majors) are of the same design except that the cords are in sets of two, both of silver interwoven with the silk colors. The shoulder straps of the company officers are covered with parallel rows of silver cord interwoven with the silk colors.

The insignia of rank worn upon the shoulder straps on top of the cord decorations are diamond shaped ornaments of gilt metal, and although they do not have the conventional shape of a star they are called stars in the German service.

These insignias are as follows for the various grades of rank:—

Field Marshal	Two gold batons crossed.
Colonel General	Three stars.
General	Two stars.
Lieutenant General	One star.
Major General	No insignia, the shoulder strap knot being plain.
Colonel	Two stars.
Lieutenant Colonel	One star.
Major	No insignia.
Captain	Two stars.
First Lieutenant	One star.
Second Lieutenant	No insignia.

There is no corresponding rank in the armies of other nations for the German rank of Colonel General, and in the German Army there is no rank of Brigadier General.

In the German Army a Feldwebel is an officer between the commissioned officers and the enlisted men, his rank corresponds to that of the Warrant Officers in the United States Navy and Marine Corps. He wears a double cord upon the shoulders and his rank insignia is a circular medallion with a Prussian eagle on each side of the collar.

The German officer's overcoat is a heavy ulster of the same gray color as the field uniform; it is double

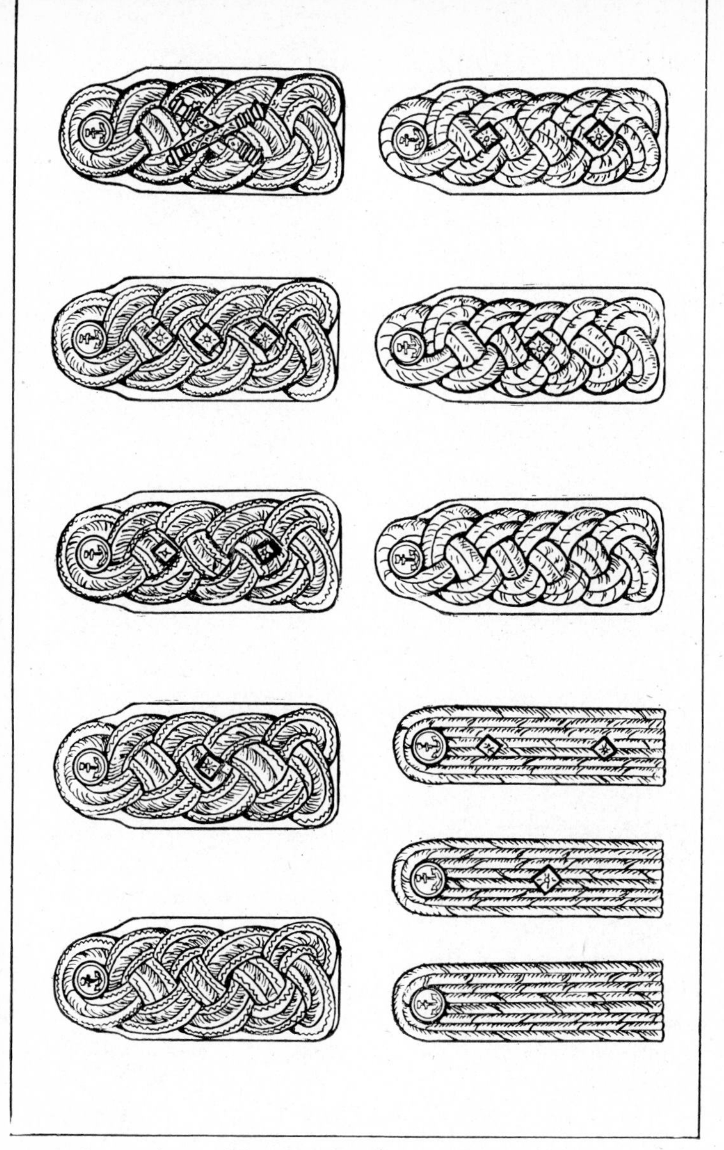

German Army. Officers' shoulder strap insignia indicating rank

1. Field Marshal
2. Colonel General
3. General
4. Lieutenant General
5. Major General
6. Colonel
7. Lieutenant Colonel
8. Major
9. Captain
10. First Lieutenant
11. Second Lieutenant

breasted and the rank of the wearer is indicated by the shoulder straps as in the case of the service coat.

The enlisted men of the German Army wear a service uniform of the same color and general design as that of the officers. The ordinary field cap is a round loose crowned cap without visor, the coat is a single breasted sack with a standing turn-over collar, and the trousers are of the same gray cloth as the coat. Boots of black or tan leather are worn.

Noncommissioned officers wear a stripe of braid around the cuff and the front edges of the collar at the neck opening and for a short distance along the top of the collar back from the neck opening. A Sergeant Major wears a stripe of narrow braid above the noncommissioned officer's sleeve stripe.

The enlisted men's overcoat is a heavy ulster buttoning to the neck with a standing-falling collar, the rank of noncommissioned officers being indicated by the sleeve braid as for the service coat and by patches of color at the front of the collar.

Steel trench helmets are worn in the trenches by both officers and men, this helmet being larger than that worn by the American, British and French troops and having a flaring extension at the rear for the protection of the neck.

CHAPTER XII

HONORS AND DISTINCTIONS

The honors and distinctions shown to the National Flag, to the President and other high Government officials, to the National Anthem and to the officers of the various ranks in the different services composing the Armed Forces of the United States are prescribed in the U. S. Army Regulations and the U. S. Navy Regulations, which are issued by the Secretaries of War and the Navy by authority of the President of the United States.

At Army Posts and Stations the National Flag is hoisted at sunrise and lowered at sunset and on board ships of the Navy the National Flag is hoisted at 8 a. m. and lowered at sunset, these occasions being known as "Morning Colors" and "Evening Colors."

While the National Flag is being hoisted and lowered all officers and enlisted men stand at attention facing the flag, if in uniform and covered they stand at the salute during the hoisting or lowering of the flag and if in civilian dress covered, they uncover and hold the headdress opposite the left shoulder. The latter form of salute is the correct one for all civilians who desire to so honor the flag of their country.

When passing the National Flag flown at an Army post or on board a ship of the Navy, the flag is saluted with the "right hand salute" or if arms are carried in hand, with the prescribed salute for the arm carried.

The same honor is accorded to the flag when it is carried past by any organization of the military or naval forces. The same honor is accorded by members of the military and naval forces of the United States to the flags of other nations under like circumstances.

When a band is present at morning or evening colors the National Anthem is played during the hoisting and lowering of the colors, and when ships of the navies of other nations are in the same port the national anthem of those nations is also played by the bands of ships of the United States Navy.

The National Anthem of the United States of America is the composition consisting of the words and music known as "The Star Spangled Banner," which was officially designated as such by the President of the United States on August 23, 1916.

For many years of its existence as a nation the United States of America had no officially recognized national anthem although various national songs and airs attained widespread popularity. During the Revolution "Yankee Doodle" and "The World Turned Upside Down" were popular military airs and the former still survives to some extent as a national song.

In 1832 the Reverend Samuel Francis Smith, a Baptist minister of Boston, wrote the song entitled "My Country, 'Tis of Thee" and it was set to the music of the British National Anthem, "God Save the King," and widely published in prayer books as the American National Hymn. This has led many people to believe that it was the official National anthem; however this is not the case, as it never received any official recognition as such.

During the Civil War, 1861 to 1865, there were a number of airs that reached great popularity among the soldiers and sailors of both sides, the most stirring of these airs being "The Battle Hymn of the Republic" in the North and "Dixie" in the South.

The Navy Regulations of 1890 prescribed that "The Star Spangled Banner" should be played by the bands at morning colors and "Hail, Columbia" at evening colors, thus giving an official standing to both airs.

In the Navy Regulations of 1893 and the Army Regulations of 1895 "The Star Spangled Banner" was prescribed for use at colors and came to be officially recognized as the National Air, but it was not until the President's order of August 23, 1916, that it became the official National Anthem.

By the order of the President the honors shown to the National Anthem are prescribed in the U. S. Army Regulations as follows:

Whenever the National Anthem is played at any place when persons belonging to the military services are present, all officers and enlisted men not in formation shall stand at attention facing toward the music (except at retreat when they shall face toward the flag). If in uniform, covered or uncovered, or in civilian clothes, uncovered, they shall salute at the first note of the anthem, retaining the position of salute until the last note of the anthem. If not in uniform and covered, they shall uncover at the first note of the anthem, holding the headdress opposite the left shoulder and so remain until its close, except that in inclement weather the headdress may be held slightly raised.

The same rules apply when "To the Color" or "To the Standard" is sounded as when the National Anthem is played.

When played by an Army band, the National Anthem shall be played through without repetition of any part not required to be repeated to make it complete.

The same marks of respect prescribed for observance during the playing of the National Anthem of the United States shall be shown toward the National Anthem of any other country when played upon official occasions.

The U. S. Navy Regulations prescribe the same honors with the exception that when uncovered all persons belonging to the Naval Service stand at attention without saluting.

Civilians wishing to pay the proper honor to the National Anthem should stand at attention whenever present at any place where the National Anthem is played and if covered they should remove the headdress and hold it opposite the left shoulder while standing at attention during the playing of the music.

When the President of the United States visits a Fort or Station of the United States Army he is received with the command formed in line under arms, the national colors and regimental standards being carried by the troops, officers and men saluting with the "Present arms," the band playing the National Anthem followed by four ruffles of the drums and four flourishes of the bugles.

An ex-President and Vice President of the United States are received with the same honors except that the band plays a march instead of the National Anthem.

The President of a foreign republic or the sovereign or a member of the royal family of a foreign country is received with the same honors as the President of the United States except that the National Anthem of his country will be played by the band.

Members of the President's Cabinet, the Chief Justice, the President pro tempore of the Senate, the Speaker of the House of Representatives, American and foreign Ambassadors and Governors (within their respective states or territories) are received with the same honors as the Vice President except that the number of ruffles and flourishes is three.

General Officers of the Army or Marine Corps and Flag Officers of the Navy are received with the national colors and regimental standards, officers and men saluting with the " Present arms," the band playing a march followed by ruffles and flourishes of the drums and bugles, the number of ruffles and flourishes depending upon the rank of the officer being received, as follows:

General or Admiral — four ruffles and flourishes.

Lieutenant General or Vice Admiral — three ruffles and flourishes.

Major General or Rear Admiral — two ruffles and flourishes.

Brigadier General or Commodore — one ruffle and flourish.

In addition to the above honors salutes with cannon are fired upon the arrival and departure of the President of the United States and the president or sovereign or a member of the royal family of a foreign country; and upon the arrival of other officials and military and naval officers in accordance with their rank as follows:

The President of the United States, or the President or sovereign or member of the royal family of a foreign country .... 21 guns

An ex-President of the United States or the Vice President .... 21 guns

Ambassadors, members of the Cabinet and the president pro tempore of the Senate .... 19 guns

The Chief Justice, the Speaker of the House of Representatives, a Committee of Congress, Governors within their respective states or territories, a Governor-General and the Governor of the Philippine Islands .... 17 guns

The Assistant Secretary of War, the Assistant Secre-

tary of the Navy, the Vice-Governor of the Philippine Islands, an Envoy Extraordinary or Minister Plenipotentiary .... 15 guns
A Minister Resident .... 13 guns
A Charge d'Affaires .... 11 guns
A Consul-General to the United States........ 11 guns
Admiral of the Navy .... 19 guns
General or Admiral .... 17 guns
Lieutenant General or Vice Admiral .... 15 guns
Major General or Rear Admiral .... 13 guns
Brigadier General or Commodore .... 11 guns

Officers of foreign armies and navies are received with the same honors as those tendered to officers of like rank in our own services.

At every Army post provided with suitable artillery a cannon salute of twenty-one guns, known as a "National salute," is fired at noon on Washington's Birthday, February 22nd, and on Memorial Day, May 30th, and on Independence Day, July 4th, a salute of one gun for each state in the Union is fired.

The honors and ceremonies to be observed when the President of the United States or the president or sovereign of another country, or a lesser official entitled to such honor visits a ship of the U. S. Navy are given in the following table from the U. S. Navy Regulations.

These honors are decided by international custom and are practically the same in all of the navies of the world and a strict observance of them is necessary to avoid any occasion for international misunderstanding that might arise from an omission of any customary honor or salute.

In addition to the gun salutes described in the above table a National salute, twenty-one guns, is fired by every ship in the Navy at noon on Independence Day,

Rank	Uniform.	Salute Arrival	Salute Departure	Guns.	Ruffles.	Guard.	Music.	Side honors.	Flag.
President	S. F. D.	1	1	21	4	..Full..	National Anthem.	Yards or rail manned and 8 S. boys.	President's, at main, during visit.
President of foreign Republic or a foreign sovereign	...do....	1	1	21	4	..do...	...do..		National, at main, during visit.
Member of royal family	...do....	1	1	21	4	..do...	..do...		National, at main, during salute.
Ex-President	...do....	1	1	21	4	..do...	March.	8 S. boys.	National, at main, during salute in foreign countries.
Vice President	...do....	....	1	19	4	..do...	..do...	....do...	National, at fore, during salute.
Ambassador	...do....	....	1	19	4	..do...	National anthem.	....do...	Do.
Secretary of the Navy	Dress	1	1	19	4	..do...	March.	....do...	Secretary's, at main, during visit.
Assistant Secretary of the Navy	Dress	1	1	17	4	..do...	..do...	....do...	Asst. Secretary's, at main, during visit.
Cabinet officer	...do....	....	1	19	4	..do...	..do...	....do...	National, at fore, during salute.
Chief Justice	...do....	....	1	17	4	..do...	..do...	....do...	Do.
Governor general, United States islands	...do....	....	1	17	4	..do...	..do...	....do...	Do.
Governor of State, Territory, or U. S. islands	...do....	....	1	17	4	..do...	..do...	....do...	Do.
President pro tempore of the Senate	...do....	....	1	19	4	..do...	..do...	....do...	Do.
Speaker of the House of Representatives	...do....	....	1	17	4	..do...	..do...	....do...	Do.
Committee of Congress	...do....	....	1	17	4	..do...	..do...	....do...	Do.

Envoy extraordinary	...do....	....	1	15	3	..do...	..do...	....do...	Do.
Minister resident or "diplomatic representative"	...do....	....	1	13	2	..do...	..do...	6 S. boys.	Do.
Chargé d'affaires	...do....	....	1	11	1	..do...	..do...	....do...	Do.
Consul general	Of the day	....	1	11	...	..Day..	......	....do...	Do.
First secretaries of embassies or legations	...do....	....	....	...	...	......	......	4 S. boys.	Do.
Consul	...do....	....	1	7	...	..Day..	......	....do...	Do.
Vice consul or consular agent (where he is the only representative of the United States)	...do....	....	1	5	...	..do...	......	....do...	Do.
Admiral of the Navy.........	Dress	....	1	19	4	..Full..	March.	8 S. boys.	In case of foreign officers, national, at fore, during salute.
Admiral .... / General	.do....	....	1	17	4	..do...	..do...	....do...	
Vice admiral .... / Lieutenant general	.do....	....	1	15	3	..do...	..do...	....do...	
Rear admiral .... / Major general (Army or Marine Corps)	.do....	....	1	13	2	..do...	..do...	6 S. boys.	
Commodore .... / Brigadier general (Army or Marine Corps)	.do....	....	1	11	1	..do...	..do...	....do...	
Chief of staff, if not a flag or general officer	Of the day	....	....	...	...	..Day..	......	4 S. boys.	
Captain .... / Colonel .... / Commander .... / Lieutenant Colonel .... (If commanding officers.)	Of the day	....	....	...	...	..Day..	......	4 S. boys.	
Lieutenant commander ...... / Major .... (If commanding officers.)	.do....			...	...	..do...	......	2 S. boys.	
All other commissioned officers below lieutenant commander and major	.do....	....	....	...	...	......	......	....do...	

Abbreviations.—S. F. D.—Special Full dress.

S. boys.—Side boys who stand at either side of the head of the gangway or ladder by which the official comes aboard of the ship.

July 4th, Washington's Birthday, February 22nd, and Memorial Day, May 30th.

When a ship of the Navy is in a port of a foreign country upon the National holiday of that country a salute of twenty-one guns is fired at noon on that day.

In accordance with established military courtesy salutes are exchanged between officers and between officers and enlisted men not in a military formation, nor at drills, at work, engaged in playing athletic games or at meals, on every occasion of their meeting or passing or being addressed by a senior, the officer who is junior in rank or the enlisted man saluting first, and the officer senior in rank returning the salute.

When the officer or enlisted man is not bearing arms of any kind in his hands he salutes with the right hand by bringing the hand smartly up to the visor of the cap above the right eye, fingers closed, hand, wrist and forearm straight, palm of the hand to the left and right forearm at an angle of forty-five degrees, and then dropping the arms to the side.

The distance within which salutes are required is that within which recognition is easy, usually considered to be about thirty paces (twenty-five yards).

When troops of the Army, Navy and Marine Corps are reviewed by the President of the United States or by any official or officer entitled to review them, they march past the reviewing officer with the bands playing a suitable march, the colors and standards saluting, officers and enlisted men rendering the marching salute and the drummers and buglers sounding the ruffles and flourishes appropriate to the rank of the reviewing officer.

The salute with the colors and standards is made by drooping them to the front. The marching salute for officers and enlisted men is made by turning the head and eyes toward the person to be saluted and is known as "eyes right" or "eyes left," depending upon whether the position of the reviewing officer is to the right or left of the column as it passes in review, officers also salute with the sword by bringing it up and to the front until the hand grasping the hilt is opposite the chin and then sweeping the hand and sword down and to the right.

Many of the regiments of the Army have distinctive marches which are played when passing in review but no distinctive march has ever been adopted for the Army as a whole.

The march usually played by the bands of the sailor regiments of the Navy when passing in review is "A Life on the Ocean Wave," and that played by the bands of the Marine Corps under the same circumstances is "Semper Fidelis," the title of the march being the motto of the Marine Corps.

THE NATIONAL ANTHEM

"THE STAR SPANGLED BANNER"

Written by Francis Scott Key while a prisoner on board the British Ship *Surprise* during the bombardment of Fort McHenry near Baltimore during the War of 1812.

Oh, say, can you see, by the dawn's early light,
  What so proudly we hailed at the twilight's last gleaming,
Whose broad stripes and bright stars, thro' the perilous fight,
  O'er the ramparts we watched, were so gallantly streaming?
And the rockets' red glare, the bombs bursting in air,
  Gave proof thro' the night that our flag was still there.
Oh, say, does that star-spangled banner yet wave
  O'er the land of the free and the home of the brave?

On the shore dimly seen thro' the mists of the deep,
  Where the foe's haughty host in dread silence reposes,
What is that which the breeze, o'er the towering steep,
  As it fitfully blows, half conceals, half discloses?
Now it catches the gleam of the morning's first beam,
  In full glory reflected now shines on the stream;
'Tis the star-spangled banner; oh, long may it wave
  O'er the land of the free and the home of the brave!

And where is the band who so vauntingly swore
  That the havoc of war and the battle's confusion
A home and a country should leave us no more?
  Their blood has washed out their foul footsteps' pollution.
No refuge could save the hireling and slave
  From the terror of flight or the gloom of the grave:
And the star-spangled banner in triumph doth wave
  O'er the land of the free and the home of the brave.

Oh, thus be it ever when freemen shall stand
  Between their loved home and wild war's desolation;
Blest with vict'ry and peace, may the heaven-rescued land
  Praise the Power that hath made and preserved us a nation.
Then conquer we must when our cause it is just,
  And this be our motto: "In God is our Trust!"
And the star-spangled banner in triumph shall wave
  O'er the land of the free and the home of the brave.

THE END

INDEX